Understanding Hospitals in Changing Health Systems

Antonio Durán • Stephen Wright
Editors

Understanding Hospitals in Changing Health Systems

palgrave
macmillan

Editors
Antonio Durán
ALLDMHEALTH
Seville, Spain

Stephen Wright
Independent Consultant
Ingleton, UK

ISBN 978-3-030-28171-7 ISBN 978-3-030-28172-4 (eBook)
https://doi.org/10.1007/978-3-030-28172-4

This Palgrave Macmillan imprint is published by the registered company Springer Nature Switzerland AG.
The registered company address is: Gewerbestrasse 11, 6330 Cham, Switzerland

Foreword

In this work, the authors have treated the hospital as a concept, an institution and a facility. They plot the irregular path of hospitals from almshouses, where the inhabitants expected (with good reason) to die, to their current status as reliable producers of safe and sophisticated healthcare. The revolutions came about because of scientific and technical advances in, amongst other areas, surgery (anaesthesia and sepsis control), imaging (radiology) and laboratory medicine (biochemistry, haematology and bacteriology). But these advances have not come cheaply, and it sometimes seems as though hospitals as repair shops dominate the public's awareness of the health and healthcare sectors, overshadowing the needs for prevention via public health, and the less glamorous primary care.

The organisation which I lead—the European Observatory on Health Systems and Policies—has published a number of studies and reports on the role of hospitals, as well as the other care settings. The authors of this volume have often been contributors to the Observatory's output across the health sector.

The authors offer an update on the role of hospitals, in a variety of geographic and historical contexts. They therefore capture the path dependency of real-life situations, recognising that this generates a lot of noise and sometimes hides the signal. More important, however, they suggest that the role of modern hospitals can be properly understood by reframing the question. It should not be (just) about how expensive they are, or whether other settings can deliver some or even most of the care—which, evidently, they cannot, or at least not entirely. Instead, they ask how hospitals function within their health and healthcare systems: can we substantiate a rationale for hospitals being the better place to carry out certain things—and correspondingly, of course, the wrong places for other things? This leads them to a three-dimensional characterisation of the role of hospitals. Without adequate governance, hospitals or any other powerful institutions will not deliver happy results to users or payers. In using expensive physical and human resources, hospitals always do operate with a business model, irrespective of whether they are in a public or private-for-profit setting; but their business model may be confused or inefficient. And, finally, any business model necessarily entails a model of care, inside and outside the walls. Throughout all of this, hospitals should be seen as just cogs, albeit large ones, in the wider health system machine.

Evidently, other contingencies come into play, concerning the ownership spectrum—public, private and various colours in-between. And the mechanisms through which hospitals are paid are also important.

This reframing of the discussion about how hospitals function within their contexts is a valuable contribution to policy thinking in health. The authors complement this with an explanation of how to use the framework to make decisions: what sort of hospitals do we want, at what scale, and absorbing what resources?

The issues and analysis addressed in this book do not stop with the above, though my summary of them does! Please read the book to see whether or not the framework sheds some light for you, the reader, on these vital institutions.

Brussels, Belgium

Josep Figueras

Acknowledgements

This work is the result of a collaboration amongst a diverse group of health professionals, from government, academia, finance and consultancy. As editors, we are grateful to our authors individually and collectively for their hard work and motivation—and good humour.

The book was conceived from a collective bemusement. Why are hospitals so popular with some (their users, by and large) and so unpopular with others (health policy experts)? Why do they attract so much resource, in terms of cash and skills, yet are seen professionally as over-sized and wasteful? We hope as authors that we have a better grasp of the issues now. This is largely as a result of wide-ranging discussions with many interlocutors, including attendees at a seminar in London in late 2017, organised by Oxford Policy Management, and with participation from the UK's Department for International Development (DfID) and other organisations and backgrounds. We have also in our various day jobs played out the arguments to many professionals. Thank you to all who have contributed to our thinking, even if you did not realise you were doing so.

We are very grateful to the team at Palgrave Macmillan—particularly Jemima Warren and Oliver Foster—for showing interest in the work, not losing that interest even when we made a regular practice of missing the deadlines, and supporting us through to a conclusion. An anonymous reviewer also helped us with some important pointers. Antonio Moreno of ALLDMHEALTH Consulting provided invaluable assistance in cleaning up the text.

Finally, as editors we would like to express our thanks to our families and friends, who bore the brunt of the stress in producing the book. You didn't deserve the anguish but definitely deserve the credit for helping us over the line. We've retained you in our wills, and perhaps this book is a small testament to you as well.

May 2019 Antonio Duràn and Stephen Wright

Disclaimer

The findings, interpretations and conclusions expressed in this volume do not necessarily reflect the views of the institutions with which the authors are affiliated.

Contents

1 **Introduction: Why This Book?** 1
Antonio Durán, Stephen Wright, Paolo Belli, Tata Chanturidze, Patrick Jeurissen, and Richard B. Saltman

2 **Hospital Governance** 25
Antonio Durán and Richard B. Saltman

3 **Models of Care and Hospitals** 49
Antonio Durán and Stephen Wright

4 **Business Models and Hospitals** 75
Stephen Wright and Antonio Durán

5 **Hospital Care: Private Assets for-a-Profit?** 103
Patrick Jeurissen and Hans Maarse

6 **Hospital Payment Systems** 121
Paolo Belli and Patrick Jeurissen

7 **Hospitals in Different Environments: A Messy Reality** 139
Tata Chanturidze and Richard B. Saltman

8 Why Is Reform of Hospitals So Difficult? 167
Richard B. Saltman and Tata Chanturidze

9 Decision Analysis 193
Stephen Wright and Antonio Durán

10 Conclusions 221
Antonio Durán, Stephen Wright, Paolo Belli, Tata Chanturidze, Patrick Jeurissen, and Richard B. Saltman

Index 239

Notes on Contributors

Paolo Belli is a program leader, Human Development, working in the Africa region of the World Bank. He joined the World Bank in May 2003. Since then, he has led several tasks, including the preparation and supervision of lending operations in India, Sri Lanka, Moldova, Belarus and Ukraine, and analytical tasks in South Asia, Europe and Central Asia and Africa Regions, mainly in the areas of health system reforms, health financing, governance and public private partnerships. He holds PhD in Economics and Public Policy from the London School of Economics. Before joining the World Bank he led several research publications and initiatives, mainly in the areas of improving public sector management, health and education financing, pension reforms, and development of public private partnerships in the social sectors.

Tata Chanturidze is a principal consultant, Health Systems Governance and Financing at Oxford Policy Management, UK. She brings 17 years of experience in supporting Health Systems Strengthening in Former Soviet Union, Central and Eastern Europe, and beyond. She is a former Vice Minister of Health and Social Welfare, Georgia. She is an author of *Health Systems in Transition* (HiT), Georgia, 2002.

Antonio Durán has, through more than 20 years of work, achieved a broad professional record as an international consultant collaborating with many international organizations. He has especially extended working relationships with the World Health Organization and the World Bank, and has also worked for the European Union, and Inter-American Development Bank, the UK Department for International Development, and others.

He has gained particular expertise in working in and leading health system reform projects. His experience in most Eastern European and Former Soviet Union Countries has provided him with particularly deep knowledge of Transition Countries. He has also worked in Africa (South Africa, Ghana, Tanzania and Swaziland), Asia (Bahrain, China, India, Maldives and Nepal) and Latin America (Bahamas, Brazil, Dominican Republic and Panama).

He acts as CEO at ALLDMHEALTH, a private consultancy company in the fields of health policies and systems. He regularly collaborates with and holds an honorary appointment as Technical Adviser for the European Observatory on Health Systems and Policies in Brussels. He is also a visiting lecturer at the Andalusian School of Public Health, in Granada, Spain, where he teaches Health Systems and International Health Policies; a regular lecturer on the same topics for the Management Centre in Innsbruck (until 2018), Austria; as well as a frequent speaker at national and international fora. He has a broad range of publications in the above areas, the latest ones being peer-reviewed articles and a book on governing public hospitals.

Patrick Jeurissen is Full Professor of Fiscal Sustainable Health Care Systems at Radboud University Medical School and the Chief Scientist of the Ministry of Health, Welfare and Sports in the Netherlands. Jeurissen is an expert on the design and implementation of policies that specifically address issues of finance, sustainability and affordability in health care. He has (co)-authored some 75 publications and is a sought-for speaker in (inter)national forums. He is a member of the Steering Committee of OECD's Health Committee and has been a consultant for the EU and WHO on the health care reform and the sustainability of health care system. His major interests are strategic policymaking, health care finance and cost-containment policies, for-profit providers and payers, mental health care, solidarity in health care systems, and comparative health care system research. He holds a PhD in Health Economics, his dissertation covers for-profit hospital ownership in the US, the UK, Germany and the Netherlands, and has an MPA, both from Erasmus University in Rotterdam.

Hans Maarse is professor emeritus of Health Policy and Administration in the Faculty of Health, Medicine and Life Sciences, University of Maastricht, Netherlands. He has a background in political science and public administration. He has written on a broad range of themes including the privatization of healthcare in Europe, the governance of hospitals, public health, solidarity in healthcare, the effects of managed competition in Dutch healthcare and the political and institutional aspects of healthcare policymaking. Currently, he is working on an empirical study on 20 years of healthcare reform in the Netherlands.

Richard B. Saltman is Professor of Health Policy and Management at the Emory University School of Public Health in Atlanta, Georgia. He was a co-founder of the European Observatory on Health Systems and Policies in Brussels in 1998, director of the Spanish research hub from 1999 to 2005, associate director of Research Policy from 2005 to 2017, and an associate advisor (from 2018). During 2002–2008 and 2014–2017 he has been a visiting professor at London School of Economics and Political Science. He was also a co-founder, and from 2011 to 2016 was co-director, of the Swedish Forum for Health Policy in Stockholm, where he continues to serve as a senior advisor (since 2017). He has consulted widely for the WHO, OECD, and the World Bank, as well as a number of European governments. From 1991 to 1994, he was Director of the Department of Health Policy and Management at Emory. He holds a doctorate in political science from Stanford University.

His published work includes 24 books and over 150 articles and book chapters on a wide variety of health policy topics, particularly on the structure and behaviour of European health care systems, and his work has been widely translated. In 1987 and again in 1999, he won the European Healthcare Management Association's annual prize for the best publication in health policy and management in Europe. In 2003, he was the John Fry Fellow at the Nuffield Trust in London. His volumes for the European Observatory book series were short-listed for the Baxter Prize by the European Healthcare Management Association in 2002, 2004, and 2006.

Stephen Wright began his professional career in resource and energy industry issues after a period of university research, with degrees in geography and economics. He joined the European Investment Bank in 1987 to work on energy, and later industrial sectors, transport, mining, economic development in emerging countries, and solid waste. From 1997, he initiated, and then ran until 2007, the Bank's techno-economic and sector development for the health and education sectors, for clients in the public and private sectors, and public-private partnerships.

For a decade from its inception, he was a member of the steering committee of the European Observatory on Health Systems and Policies, and was an editor and co-author of the book *Investing in Hospitals of the Future* (2009), with an accompanying case studies volume *Capital Investment in Health*. He has written many papers on health care policy, capital planning, finance and PPP, and speaks regularly at, and organizes conferences in, Europe and further afield. In 2009, Stephen set up a research and strategic advisory organisation called ECHAA, focused on the interface between the built environment and delivery of health care. In its time, ECHAA supported a number of governments—particularly the Hungarian Ministry of Health (hospital planning, European health policy interface) and the Slovak Ministry (on health policy, health care planning, EU issues, infrastructure development, PPP projects and community health).

Stephen carries out multiple consulting and research assignments annually, for a variety of clients including the European Commission, EIB, World Bank, World Health Organization, and countries including Ireland, Slovakia, Wales and Estonia. Many assignments have been in emerging markets, in Europe or beyond, and cover health policy, finance and PPP, hospital development, energy issues, economic development and trade. In collaboration with others, Stephen also helped establish a new think tank, called Integrate, of which he was the research director (since folded into the research organisation HealthClusterNet, where he is a Research Associate), concerned with fostering long-term investment in social sectors, and use of innovative financial instruments.

Abbreviations

ABS	Agent-Based Simulation
ALoS	Average Length of Stay
CEE	Central and Eastern Europe
CEO	Chief Executive Officer
CGEM	Computerised General Equilibrium Model
COPD	Chronic Obstructive Pulmonary Disease
CPE	Centrally Planned Economy
CT	Computerised Tomography
DALY	Disability-Adjusted Life Year
DEA	Data Envelopment Analysis
DEHW	(US) Department of Health, Education and Welfare
DES	Discrete Event Simulation
DHB	District Health Board
DRG	Diagnosis-Related Group
EBP	Evidence-Based Practice
ED	Emergency Department
FFS	Fee-for-Service
FP	For-Profit
FSU	Former Soviet Union
GBD	Gross Burden of Disease
GBP	United Kingdom Pound
GDP	Gross Domestic Product
GP	General Practice/Practitioner
HaHP	Hospital at Home Programme
ICT	Information and Communication Technologies
ICU	Intensive Care Unit

IMF	International Monetary Fund
ISTC	Independent Sector Treatment Centre
kWh	Kilowatt-Hour
LDC	Less-Developed Country
LMIC	Low- and Middle-Income Countries
LTC	Long-Term Care
MAU	Municipal Acute Unit
MBA	Master of Business Administration
MD	Doctor of Medicine
MOH	Ministry of Health
MRSA	Meticillin-Resistant *Staphylococcus aureus*
NAO	National Audit Office
NFP	Not-for-Profit
NGO	Non-Governmental Organisations
NHS	National Health Service
NPC	Net Present Cost
NPM	New Public Management
NPSV	Net Present Social Value
NPV	Net Present Value
OBPM	Outcome-Based Payment Model
OECD	Organisation for Economic Co-operation and Development
OOP	Out-of-Pocket
OR	Operational Research
P4P	Pay for Performance
P4R	Payment for Results
PC	Personal Computer
PFI	Private Finance Initiative
PH	Public Hospital
PHC	Primary Health Care
PPBS	Planning Programming Budgeting System
PPP	Public-Private Partnership
PS	Payment System
R&D	Research and Development
SCA/SCF	Stochastic Cost Frontier Analysis
SD	System Dynamics
SHI	Social Health Insurance
SUS	Unified Health System (Brazil)
T2A	Tarification à l'Activité
TB	Tuberculosis
UCC	Urgent Care Centre
UHC	Universal Health Care/Coverage

USD	United States Dollar
WB	World Bank
WGI	Worldwide Governance Indicators
WHO	World Health Organization
WHR	World Health Report (2000)

List of Figures

Fig. 1.1	Relations between functions and objectives of a health system (WHO—World Health Organization [2000] *World Health Report 2000. Health System Improving Performance* [Geneva: World Health Organization] 2:25)	4
Fig. 2.1	Hospital governance framework	37
Fig. 4.1	The four components of a business model (Hwang, J., & Christensen, C. M. (2007). Disruptive Innovation in Healthcare Delivery: A Framework for Business-Model Innovation. *Health Affairs, 27*(5), 1329–1335. https://doi.org/10.1377/hlthaff.27.5.1329)	80
Fig. 6.1	Providers and type of reimbursement (Belli 2002)	132
Fig. 8.1	Structure of current health expenditure by financing agent in FSU countries 2000 and 2015 (Adrian Gheorghe (OPM), based on WHO Global Health Expenditure Database. Note: In the first panel (2000), data for Hungary, Poland and Czech Republic are from 2003)	177
Fig. 9.1	Decision-making in (our) context	195
Fig. 9.2	Spider chart of project sensitivities in hospital investment appraisal (NPV, GBP million) (Authors' calculations, based on a PPP "outline business case" for a mid-size English hospital)	207

List of Tables

Table 2.1 Models of increased hospital self-governance 44
Table 5.1 For-profit hospital beds, percentage of total (2000—most recent year) 108
Table 6.1 Comparison of hospital payment methods: from payer (ministries of health, local authorities, national health insurance funds, private health insurance companies) to hospitals 126
Table 7.1 Hospital beds and nurses per 100,000 population, selected countries, 1980 147
Table 7.2 Models of increased hospital self-governance 154
Table 8.1 For-profit hospital beds, some European countries, selected years 170

List of Boxes

Box 1.1	Hospital Expenditure	8
Box 2.1	Hospitals: From a Few Decades Back to Today	28
Box 2.2	A Possible Application of the Framework	38
Box 2.3	Understanding Governance Beyond the Surface: Hospital Reform in Japan	41
Box 4.1	Business Models in Healthcare and Hospitals	82
Box 4.2	Reflecting on Christensen, Critically	93
Box 8.1	Hospital Sector Rationalization in Estonia After Independence	171
Box 8.2	Implications of Hospital Privatization in Georgia	173
Box 8.3	Public Hospital Decision Environment	180
Box 9.1	Public Investment Appraisal in the UK and Its Application to Hospitals	204

CHAPTER 1

Introduction: Why This Book?

Antonio Durán, Stephen Wright, Paolo Belli, Tata Chanturidze, Patrick Jeurissen, and Richard B. Saltman

A. Durán (✉)
ALLDMHEALTH, Seville, Spain
e-mail: aduran@alldmh.com

S. Wright
Independent Consultant, Ingleton, UK
e-mail: steve.wright@echaa.eu

P. Belli
The World Bank, Nairobi, Kenya
e-mail: pbelli1@worldbank.org

T. Chanturidze
Oxford Policy Management, Oxford, UK
e-mail: Tata.Chanturidze@opml.co.uk

P. Jeurissen
Radboud University Medical School, Nijmegen, Netherlands

Ministry of Health, Welfare and Sports, Hague, Netherlands
e-mail: Patrick.Jeurissen@radboudumc.nl

R. B. Saltman
Department of Health Policy and Management, Rollins School of Public Health, Emory University, Atlanta, GA, USA
e-mail: rsaltma@emory.edu

A. Durán, S. Wright (eds.), *Understanding Hospitals in Changing Health Systems*, https://doi.org/10.1007/978-3-030-28172-4_1

Introduction: Hospitals in Health Systems

The authors of this book include health policy, management and finance professionals—mostly European but with different backgrounds and affiliations—across government, academia, international institutions and consultancy. We have been concerned for some time about the presentation of hospitals in public health policy discourse and analysis, and found colleagues sharing our concern and emphasizing the importance of the issue. This chapter represents the group consensus on the main content and on the direction of our effort in the book. We feel that *global health dialogue* has "moved away" from hospitals in recent times in an inappropriate way—yet in most countries hospitals do play today and in the future will continue to play an absolutely critical role (and for good reasons that will be explained in the book!). The point is not to defend the position of hospitals; it is to understand them and therefore be in a position to make judgements about what hospitals should and should not do—within their contexts.

Rather than seeing hospitals always and exclusively as a "problem" ("too costly", "too powerful", etc.), one of the critical issues for this book is that hospitals across low-, middle- and high-income countries can become a true source of hope for people who currently do not have adequate access to quality services. In order to contribute to make hospitals play *such a vital role and develop their future potential*, we address the need to better understand the function that hospitals have now and should have in the health systems of the future, what their core institutional dynamics are, and how they should be governed, structured, owned, paid and so on. We intend these messages principally for the international health policy community and for those involved as decision-makers in health, healthcare and hospital systems.

At first, we wanted merely to warn about the risks of neglecting or misunderstanding hospitals in the global health picture in the face of what we understood as an undeniable evidence (hence the metaphor between us of an "elephant in the room"). It was only when we found resistance even to discussing the core issues that we realized the need to expand and deepen our analysis in the form of this book. A shift in the paradigm of healthcare provision—and within it, of the hospital—based on better understanding of its foundations is required.

Stating the point in these terms immediately raises a first issue regarding the meaning attached to the label of "hospital": is it the same everywhere? Clearly not, and for obvious reasons. The name "hospital" has a known diversity of meanings, affecting aspects such as:

- different things in different places (Western Europe, post-Communist Europe, North America, emerging economies);
- different sizes, functions, shapes, ownerships and so on; and
- different content in different times: past and present.

The main themes which have so far emerged from the discussions go well beyond Europe, into low- and middle-income countries (LMIC)/ and ex-Communist, North American and Asian/Japanese circumstances. In other words, we recognize that there is of course a path dependency in how health systems have developed, but we look for the things that generally distinguish hospitals from other parts of those systems—which are receiving comparatively much more attention.

However, we argue in this volume that there can be significant commonality in the core understanding of the label; and we define it below in ways that we hope will allow the facilities and institutions to be recognized and analysed even if their settings are very different. In Europe alone, the European Observatory on Health Systems and Policies has published in recent years at least four books on hospitals (McKee and Healy 2002; Rechel et al. 2009a, 2009b; Saltman et al. 2011); the intention here is to build on this and related work, but move further in terms both of analysis and of policy significance for confronting the challenges ahead.

Hospitals are conceived in this book as inseparable constituent parts of health systems (Murray and Frenk 2000). Every health system as defined by the World Health Report 2000 (WHO 2000) is supposed to pursue a series of *goals*, the most important ones being health-related (level and equity of health); protecting citizens from the catastrophic financial consequences of fighting disease (i.e. providing "coverage"); and responding efficiently to citizens' expectations/client orientation in the non-medical sphere; this latter goal can be taken to include the provision of information to patients/clients as important collateral. The core end-objective or key outcome target of any health system should be the maintenance, or preferably the increase, of health status (measured at collective and individual levels) in the maximum number of the target population.

The achievement of the above listed objectives of any health system, in this classic World Health Report 2000 view, depends on four central *functions* ("sets of repeated activities and tasks needed to achieve certain distinctive goals and objectives"), namely: (1) service production, (2) finance, (3) regulation/stewardship and (4) inputs creation/development. The graph below addresses such relationship (Fig. 1.1).

In this view of health systems, hospitals are a critical part of service delivery, and essential loci to assemble together specific resources to make modern healthcare possible; they require inputs to be assembled, and they need governance and finance to be made available. The current emphasis on universal coverage is perhaps the most visible application of those ideas and principles (WHO 2011).

There is a genuine and politically crucial concern with respect to the importance of hospitals, often the body of almost ethical confrontations, with some in the health policy community defending a position which essentially challenges their very existence (as though "public health and primary care are all that matter"). Decades of pioneer research have showed that in developed countries, advances in health indicators were historically related to improvements in food, education, housing and so on (Dubos 1959; McKeown 1965). Relatively similar results were obtained when an analysis in developing countries followed suit (Preston 1980). These findings shifted policy attention towards primary healthcare, from around the time of the Alma Ata Conference in the late 1970s, a line of

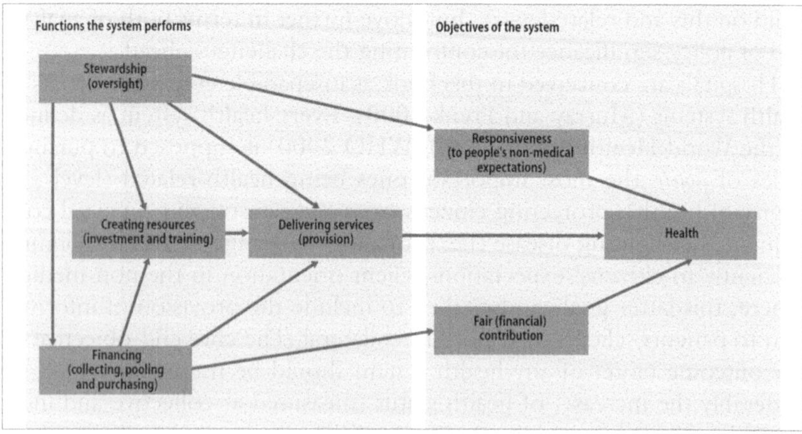

Fig. 1.1 Relations between functions and objectives of a health system (WHO—World Health Organization [2000] *World Health Report 2000. Health System Improving Performance* [Geneva: World Health Organization] 2:25)

argumentation vigorously supported by the policy community ever since (Evans et al. 1994).

Importantly, while the above-mentioned pioneer studies reflected the impact of all healthcare on health outcomes improvement to be around some 20% at its most (with all the rest contributed by environmental and behavioural "social determinants of health"), recent research in OECD countries has put the figure attributable to healthcare higher, at between 44% and 57% (Arah et al. 2006). In Europe, studies like this on "healthcare-amenable mortality" by the London School of Hygiene and Tropical Medicine estimate the influence of medical care on health indicators improvement to be not far from half (Nolte and McKee 2008; Figueras et al. 2008); that is, this proportion of deaths has been avoided in each given country in recent years *because* the healthcare systems were performing well.

These are estimates of "mortality", tightly defined for the purposes of analysis by demographic cohort and disease type. Surprisingly, no comparable work has been carried out on sickness, as distinct from death—"morbidity"—though a first expectation would be of a comparable impact on it from healthcare. Further, a substantial part of progress in both avoidable mortality and avoidable morbidity will undoubtedly be due to hospitals. It is, however, a rather surprising issue that the topic has scarcely been studied, which explains that not even approximate figures are available. Such a research void needs to be filled as urgently as possible.

Confusion About What a Hospital Is

One major problem is that definitions of a hospital are invariably superficial. For example:

- *Oxford English Dictionary* (n.d.): "*An institution providing medical and surgical treatment and nursing care for sick or injured people*" (… but there are many institutions which do that but which are not hospitals);
- WHO (www.searo/who/int/topics/hospitals/en, accessed 17/11/2017): "*Health care institutions that have an organized medical and other professional staff, and inpatient facilities, and deliver services 24 hours per day, 7 days per week*" (… but not all hospitals have inpatient facilities, as emergency care hospitals and selected facilities show, or work continuously on 24 × 7 bases);

- Center for Global Development (2015): "*A healthcare facility that provides inpatient health services with at least 10 beds and operates with continuous supervision of patients and delivery of medical care, 24 hours a day, 7 days a week*" (… but the definition adds on to the previous problem the arbitrary threshold of ten beds);
- Miller (1997): "*An institution which provides beds, meals, and constant nursing care for its patients while they undergo medical therapy at the hands of professional physicians. In carrying out these services, the hospital is striving to restore its patients to health*" (… most of the applicable criticisms have already been explained).

Such definitions do not have embedded within them any explanatory concept (i.e. they are ad hoc). It will be shown below as a critical issue that hospitals need to be categorized not by *attributes* (arguments from correlation, not causality—for example, "places where sick people go", or "where the most severely sick people go", or "where many doctors work") but rather by *functions* (as indicated, "sets of repeated activities and tasks needed to achieve certain distinctive goals and objectives"—such as diagnosing, treating, etc.).

The existence or number of beds (mentioned in two of the four definitions above) as a key criterion has seen its validity drastically reduced over time. Although it is still the most common parlance, even by hospital directors and health ministers, to express hospital size in terms of beds, it is evident that many hospitals have learned to develop their operational capacities rather separated from such a single input (Rechel et al. 2010).

In the current state of knowledge, it is not possible to state or even calculate what the capacity of a hospital actually is. And without an ability to assess capacity, how could we rigorously know how much of it to build or maintain? The real capacity of a hospital is its ability to do work, and this cannot be determined on the basis of just one or other parameter. Hospitals are complex dynamic systems, and cannot/should not be characterized by one static feature; it poses a system modelling problem, which we return to particularly in Chap. 9 below.

The word "hospital" currently covers a wide range of institutions, from small rural facilities to large university clinics, small community centres to giant complexes with several headquarters and huge numbers of staff. The mix between inpatient and outpatient hospital services can vary drastically, both between and within countries. Hospital owners can extend from the public authority (national, regional or municipal) to various types of private enterprise, both without profit objectives (religious and/ or voluntary hospitals) or for profit (commercial hospitals and public-private partnership structures—PPP). Publicly operated companies can also vary from units directly managed by government to quasi-independent entities. As their nature and scope vary on country-by-country bases, so the way each hospital is governed, organized, and financed may differ (Ettelt et al. 2008).

Country comparisons in the 1990s, partly linked to both the first massive availability of computers and the changes due to the fall of the Berlin Wall, revealed enormous differences in health systems' (and within them, hospitals') inputs. The polygons used to illustrate input mixes in the World Health Report 2000 made the differences fully visible (WHO 2000). Institutional as well as functional characteristics were indirectly included in the comparisons mentioned later on in this book (Joumard et al. 2010).

Perhaps all the above reasons together explain why it is often not easy to clarify what exactly the now-standard messages on hospital reform deal with. In many texts, contents get blurred between issues pertaining to (1) all hospitals in all health systems (e.g. US as well as Europe, developed as well as developing countries, etc.), (2) public hospitals in publicly funded health systems, for example, mostly in Northern/Southern European tax-funded health systems, (3) modified/re-structured/semi-autonomous publicly owned hospitals in tax-funded health systems—but also in Central European hybrid/state-attached social health—insurance models, (4) privately owned not-for-profit (e.g. the Netherlands) and (5) for-profit (Germany, France, the US) hospitals.

Awareness of Inefficiency and Inequity Problems

While there can be significant commonality in the core understanding of the label "hospital" in different geographic contexts, it is evident that in many senses, hospitals in low- and middle-income countries, including China, India and others, ***aren't quite the same*** as those in the developed world. Significantly, in many low- and middle-income countries, hospitals consume enormous fractions of available health resources (see Box 1.1), with, for example, Turkey spending 53% of healthcare in hospital settings, often with uncertain incremental returns, especially in terms of efficiency. With nuances linked to income levels, modalities of care, types of health system and so on, the potential for change is daunting.

Box 1.1 Hospital Expenditure

Analysing published data on hospital expenditure requires some care:

- Data for European countries data show a range of 29–47% as a current hospital share of total current health expenditure (Hospital Healthcare Europe 2018). Specifically, for Eastern Europe, where the systems have been changing fast, the shares of hospital expenditure are CZ 41%, SK 34%, Hungary 36%, Estonia 47% and Latvia 32% (see also Romaniuk and Szromek 2015, which reports an average for the region of 35%).
- OECD data for member countries show a range between 26% (Mexico) and 53% (Turkey) for hospital expenditure within the total for all providers (OECD 2017).

Two main concerns have to be highlighted to use such data properly:

- Figures usually refer to *current* expenditure, so will slightly underestimate the total expenditure when allowing as well for *capital* expenditure for a comparison against total system-wide expenditure (capital expenditure will be disproportionately in hospitals rather than elsewhere in the system).
- Frequently, data come from "inpatient care" statistics that are taken as equivalent to "hospital care" (but some proportion of "outpatient care" is in hospitals as well, with the rest being in community or GP settings).

Hospital Healthcare Europe (2018) *Hospitals in Europe: Healthcare data* [Accessed March 29, 2019] Available online at: http://www.hospitalhealthcare.com/hope/hospitals-europe-healthcare-data-0

Romariuk, P. and A. R. Szromek (2015) "The evolution of the health system outcomes in Central and Eastern Europe and their association with social, economic and political factors: an analysis of 25 years of transition" *BMC Health Services Research* 2016 16:95 [Accessed March 29, 2019]. Available online at: https://doi.org/10.1186/s12913-016-1344-3

OECD (2017) *Health at a Glance 2017. OECD Indicators* (Paris: OECD Publishing): 143 [Accessed March 29, 2019]. Available at: https://doi.org/10.1787/health_glance-2017-en)

Hospitals are the biggest point resource users in every health system, but they obtain unclear returns and are the source of inequities linked to access and continuity of care issues. Notably, many around the world deliver, at high cost, services of insufficient quality which in addition are scarcely accessible especially to vulnerable populations (Aiken et al. 2012). Such a resource and human wastage in hospitals is unacceptable both economically and ethically, in view of widespread resource scarcity problems.

That being said, the truth is that some inefficiencies are transitory consequence of the sector's own evolution rather than evil attributes of hospitals only. In any event, the health sector often accepts intellectually its own costs and inefficiencies in whichever of its sub-sectors, but is singularly unable to describe on the other side of the ledger the benefits it creates. This makes a true assessment of net value added difficult. The whole assessment of health systems remains work in progress in many senses, with rather different theoretical frameworks making comparisons rather complex—while the population de facto worships hospitals whenever disease hits.

Another indication of the complex challenges faced by the hospital industry is that its developments are related to broader technological advances that occurred over the last few decades. Remarkably, and contrary to what has happened with other sectors (e.g. electronics, telecommunications, computers, cars, travel, etc.), the health industry has failed to articulate let alone capture the widespread productivity benefits of new technologies, for a number of reasons, especially in terms of affordability permitted by disruptive innovations (Christensen 2009). As indicated, the societal response, however, hardly includes any rejection of such behaviour, probably reflecting the high esteem in which health services in general and hospitals in particular are held.

Pioneering work had shown in developed countries early concern about unwarranted variations in care (including hospitals), which were interpreted as a response to complexities in the way medicine is practised as well as insufficient performance of employed resources (Cochrane 1971). Variations in health system/hospitals' products and outcomes are traditionally ascribed to variations in inputs plus previously designed "quality" processes (Donabedian 1980). This issue of unwarranted variations of products, results and costs is addressed further in this book.

Healthcare as a Production Industry in a New Context; Models of Business Requiring Governance

Inputs to Create Outputs: "Two Models"

The above-mentioned discussion around the influence of healthcare in its attempt to fight disease produced different analytical frameworks for the position and role of hospitals (Starfield 1974). In this book, we structure our understanding principally around a "Tale of Two Models": models of governance and models of business. As a first guiding methodology for the book, we lean—in our study of hospitals as a service industry—on the thinking approaches used to analyse other sectors of economic importance. In addition to many other frequently explained things, healthcare is *also* an industry which creates outputs by consuming inputs ("factors of production").

This "economic sector" approach underpins the idea of business models (see below and Chap. 4). It has been accepted in studying the health sector since the seminal paper in health economics by Arrow (1963).[1] The pattern of use of factors of production in healthcare varies by time and place—in some cases such as in primary care (which provides the first level of care), the predominant element is labour (often but not always highly skilled). At the other end of the spectrum, the mix is much more technology- and physical capital-intensive while still retaining human capital—intensity. The attribution of the secondary and tertiary care hospital as part of the health system is, we will argue in this book, this latter domain, and in the context of this book, it constitutes *the true definition of what we currently characterize as "the hospital"*.

The above attributes then give rise to the hospital's role in increasing the achievement of the end-objectives of improved health status and so on. Critically, we are arguing that the valuation of those end-objectives should be seen in the light of the resource cost incurred as well; there is a trade-off. Other healthcare settings have less capital stock than hospitals, and usually less human capital and technological intensity, supporting their processes.

Hospitals were somehow created as a result of a serendipitous combination of factors (patients available, professionals interested, technology

[1] Arrow refers to "…the operation of the medical-care industry and the efficacy with which it satisfies the needs of society…" (op. cit., p. 141) whilst emphasizing the pervasive uncertainty which implies this can never be a classically competitive market.

being developed, and willingness to pay for it all) over which economies of scope and scale would play. As innovation in equipment or process occurs, the technological frontier—what the system at the limit *can* create as output in order to apply specialized care (especially at diagnosis and treatment level) to certain group(s) of patients in different ways (indeed not the same as what it *should* create)—is always expanding. As institutions and facilities, hospitals concentrate combinations of qualified staff and asset-specific investments as well as technology. It is this specific grouping of factors of production that enables the hospital, as an institution and a facility, to produce care *in a way that other arrangements cannot do, or at least not as efficiently* (as a result of clinical or resource economies of scale and/or scope).

Trying to shed further light into the role of hospitals as institutions, hospitals and the expenditure on them should be seen as the product of a few contrasting and/or complementary drivers. Using economic parlance, in each given societal and economic environment, some factors are demand-driven and others supply-driven. The demand for health status is continually shifting, with changes in demography, epidemiology, income and lifestyle. In practice, the expectations of the population for health status tend to rise inexorably (specifically, in all societies where access appears to be granted universally), and experience shows that these demands can virtually never be satisfied. Given this unstoppable tendency for demand to rise in any circumstances, the system will always show a supply response to produce more, moving out towards its (expanding) technology frontier, inevitably trying to adopt new and more capable technologies as and when they become available. There can be no expectation that this will occur at lower cost, and certainly not when meeting new or previously unarticulated demands: not surprisingly, healthcare and hospitals become increasingly expensive.

The OECD has attempted to quantify the effects in terms of healthcare costs. Key expenditure drivers (de la Maisonneuve and Martins 2015) can be split between demographic (age-related), non-demographic (principally income) and "residual" (particularly a technology supply issue, but also relative prices and policies). The results indicate that for OECD countries and for the period 1995–2009, of the real health spending growth per capita and per annum of 4.3%, the age effect is 0.5%, the income growth effect contributes 1.8% and the residual is 2.0%. Perhaps surprisingly, the OECD's projections for the long-term future show that demographic pressures do not as such become much more prominent.[2] Depending on the scenario chosen, healthcare expenditure inflation will, however, rather certainly continue. What is happening here is effectively that national and personal income growth permits health spending growth—unless there are very strict cost-containment policies (in the case of just one of the scenarios, driving down the "residual" eventually to zero—but only by 2060).

In the short term, there is a certain amount of flexibility a real-world healthcare system can apply to supply/production in response to any shift in demand. However, most real-world healthcare systems run hot most of the time, with restricted buffers, and this limits their responsiveness. The reason for the cost inflation is that technology and innovation never run in a vacuum. They develop as long-term mechanisms attempting to improve health services in order to satisfy patients' demands, all the while fulfilling the "reasonable" health policy of the country instead (this "systems thinking" runs alongside cultural issues which will often determine what a system is asked to do and how it responds, what is "affordable", acceptable, what is not, etc.).

The empirical results of the twin trends in demand and supply drivers are therefore that cost of practically all health systems rises inexorably. Further, much of this cost is inevitably incurred in the hospital, precisely *because* that is where the expensive technology and knowledgeable staff are. It is easy to criticize hospitals for sucking patients and resources from the rest of the system—but in fact this is mainly the result of the collision between rising expectations (demand) and technological capability (which rests more in the hospital than elsewhere), in the "hope" that society will somehow be able to pay for it. So far, with struggles, it has.

Governance

As explained in Chap. 2 below, no social system can function physically or economically without a means of steering the effort. "Governance" is a much-misused new term—in general, and in the context of health system and

[2] "The fact that the share of older people in the population is growing faster than that of any other age group, both as a result of longer lives and a lower birth rate, should generate an automatic increase in the average. However, this intuition finds little support in the data and assessing the effect of population ageing on health and health care has proved to be far from straightforward," op. cit. p. 68.

hospitals in particular. It tries to capture changes in both the number and types of stakeholders involved, as well in the mechanisms through which influences are exerted in contemporary society (an obviously decisive element in light of the many pressures in favour of new "models of care"—with uncertain costs, even if there are claimed benefits).

Why invent "governance" as a new word? By the end of the twentieth century, society was already fundamentally different in key technical, organizational and financial aspects compared to when hospitals (and other institutions) became prestigious in their communities:

- A global context of major geopolitical change had slowly but firmly become self-evident in previous decades (e.g. the fall of the Soviet Union, displacement of the economic centre of gravity to emerging countries for the benefit of China, India, Brazil, etc.).
- In parallel, and facilitated by technologies that ensure the availability of multiple sources of information and distance-reducing transport improvement, the perception of power in society had changed to rest less exclusively on formal structures.
- The actors in the political arena had been multiplied and the boundaries between the private and the public sector had become blurred, while the central government's claim of legitimacy had diminished and requests for its accountability became much more frequent (Peters 2004).

In this new context, revisiting the concepts and the nature of "governance" as distinct from "management" and "politics" is key to understanding institutional responsibility in its own right now that hospitals have become immensely more complex institutions, inserted in more complex health systems and in turn in more complex societies. In short, the necessary hospital governance is *more than* government policies and *more than* management alone, and is becoming a cornerstone in the institutional building of the "new" hospitals. Political theory has advised the use of the word "governance", which as a new term could be interpreted as efforts in:

1. ensuring results within units and inside the wider system through different ways, once the traditional ones have shown basic limitations;
2. balancing autonomy and responsibility (effective incentives, transparency and accountability) in a more fluid context; and

3. putting the focus on processes and instruments in relation to corporatization/more autonomy, or hospital privatization if responsibility over the centres is transferred to the private sector—for profit or not).

The definition of governance proposed in 2011 by some members of this group of authors (Saltman et al. 2011) already noted the insufficiency of many approaches in the context of contemporary societies, and proposed the definition of *governance* as "*processes and tools related to decision making in steering* ***all*** *institutional activity, influencing most aspects of organizational behaviour and recognizing the complex relationships between multiple stakeholders—with a scope of normative values (equity, ethics), results (access, quality, responsiveness and patient safety) plus political, financial, managerial as well as daily operational issues*" (Duran et al. 2011).

In summary, the theory of governance will fully affect hospitals, especially public ones, even if at the moment some aspects of how resources should be allocated, and conflict-solving in applying the "hospital governance" concept, remain at a rather embryonic stage.

Models of Care

A *model of care* is a theoretical construct prescribing physically how healthcare *is to be* delivered, and is a core component of a business model. Within healthcare, very often a given output can be achieved with very different combinations of factors of production (i.e. in very different settings)—for example, many diagnoses can be done in both primary and secondary level facilities (the current involvement of primary care staff in controlling hypertension is an obvious example). It was already said above that, across any health system, all delivery settings use a variety of factors of production—capital stock in terms of infrastructure and equipment, human capital in terms of skilled or crude labour, materials, utilities and energy and so on. What distinguishes one setting (e.g. a hospital) from another (for example, a primary care facility) is the varying combinations of those factors of production, which are mixed together via appropriate process routes (the hypertension in the first case, the hospital, will be diagnosed and treated with a substantially bigger amount of technological endowment and qualified staff than in the second).

That a given output can be achieved with very different combinations of factors of production (i.e. in very different settings) does not mean that the results in terms of quality at any given cost would be equivalent.

Although it might not be desirable to do heart surgery in a primary care setting, in theory it could be done; but merely to contemplate it is to reveal its inappropriateness. Correspondingly, hospitals do a very great deal of things that could easily be carried out at “lower” levels—and this is just as inappropriate. Therefore, a hospital from that point of view is the setting with the highest levels, compared with others, of physical capital, human capital and technological intensity supporting certain healthcare processes, articulated in particular ways. In other words, it is just a place with a set of factors of production used to deliver certain process routes. Notably, it is not necessarily associated in this sense with any specific input item as such (for example, beds), though at high levels of abstraction, some types of capital stock can be probably regarded as fairly intrinsic to what a hospital is (e.g. the “hot floor”, where all capital-intensive functions—operating rooms, diagnostic imaging and intensive care facilities—are jointly located).[3]

This feature is crucial in terms of the endless discussions about inappropriate health services delivery, excessive power residing in hospitals, and bloated expenditure. Those in favour of shifting care out of the hospital usually say that, for all sorts of good reasons, care should be delivered elsewhere (Kringos et al. 2015) (as well as hoping that suitable changes to the social determinants of health would boost health status such that repair of degraded status is less needed, or in fact not at all [Donkin et al. 2017]). A key result of this book should be progress in the way of determining what should be in the hospital and what should be elsewhere, or even—in extreme cases—be left aside, and why.

Models of care as introduced thus concern the physical processes used to meet the demand for care. However, decisions on this will always involve opportunity cost—that is, if resources are used for one end, they cannot usually be used for another. For that reason, such a ‘model of care’ framework cannot be used on its own to make serious decisions on the running of the system (certainly not in the medium-to-long term). In this situation, policy (and management)—that is, governance—decisions are only possible by moving into questions twinning the cost of resource

[3] The Netherlands Board for Health Care Institutions published in 2006 a document explaining that each hospital has four different functional areas: a “hot floor”, with all capital-intensive functions—operating rooms, diagnostic imaging and intensive care facilities; a hotel-like area for residential low-care nursing function; some offices for administration, staff departments and outpatient care; and utility facilities housing energy services, kitchens and not primary production line functions)—see also Chap. 10.

use and the value of the benefits created. Only then is it possible to choose between differing desired potential states of the system, that is, between the various alternative models of care.

Models of Business

Groupings of factors of production constituting a model of care therefore carry no implication whatsoever as to whether a given hospital facility is on the production frontier to improve health status or, more directly, create healthcare outputs, relative to other hospitals or to other ways of delivery (e.g. all countries set up "specially endowed hospitals" for the sole reason that they want to have at least one "top" institution, irrespective of costs, etc.). Substantial variations between sites within any one country, let alone between different countries, are undeniable and, what is worse in terms of lost opportunities, merely removing that variation would have the gain of reducing resource use in the system as a whole. That is, any one hospital—and certainly its departments—could well be some way inside the frontier, and therefore inefficient (as mentioned above, hospitals as a whole are not always the optimum way of gathering together factors of production to deliver many types of healthcare; the quality issues involved within a given setting, or between them, will be addressed later in the book).

In other words, associated with the notion of models of care, the way resources are used to create economic and financial value is critical (Magretta 2002). This notion is captured by the concept of *models of business*. If there were valid market prices for outputs and for the costs for all the relevant factors of production (opportunity cost-reflective), healthcare would be very much more like other industries; at any given income distribution and ownership of the factors of production, and for an endowment of technology, the system would "settle".

But healthcare is very far away from the required conditions, such that markets can in reality never clear at all, in the economic sense of reaching a stable state under the influence of internal parameters. This is contrary to most markets for goods and services, which do clear reasonably well (*never* "optimally" in economic terms because in the real world, the criteria for competitive market functioning are almost never completely met—although the alternatives can be substantially worse; for a more complete discussion about market issues in health and hospitals, see the chapters in this volume on payment mechanisms and ownership structures).

For healthcare, then, in the absence of many of the needed price signals guiding the system, surrogates have to be invoked. In healthcare or any other sector, this issue of "valuing" both the output generated and the resources used goes a long way to characterize a "business model" for the activity concerned. It is *still a "business" model*, even were the output to be managed 100% by the state and all the resources concerned were public (a beehive is like this, but no human society comes anywhere close).

Each model of care then will have a physical input and a pattern of outputs which necessarily carry resource costs and benefits, and always have values attached in a specific governance context. Therefore, in order to arrange the factors of production and set the outputs, in healthcare, a model of care will necessarily be attached to a business model (and vice versa, a business model will necessarily incorporate within it a model of care, both of them highly dependent on how society perceives the value of things).

The intellectual distinction between the model of care and the business model is important because it enables policymakers to consider change in the physical processes separately from the institutional economic arrangements between stakeholders. Choosing a desired model of care (from among the alternatives available) requires thinking through their compatibility with the possible business models, with the respective cost, benefits, values and so on, in a precise governance (and government!) context.

Other Critical Issues in the Shaping of Hospitals

Public and Private

Intimately involved in the concepts above is the ownership of the resources consumed: public or private. As mentioned, all societies use a blend of both, which in recent times has generated a massive amount of heat, and sometimes some light, together with pleas for more research (Herrera et al. 2014). In substance, it is not the role of the private sector in its totality which is sensitive in (some) modern healthcare and hospital systems, but some aspects undoubtedly are.

Ancillary services (construction services, utility and drug supply, retail pharmacy, most of dentistry etc.) are invariably dominated by private companies all over the world. It is the role of the private sector close to the main secondary healthcare delivery processes (but often not primary healthcare in the form of general practice!) which is the most controversial, in many countries. This means that much of the political heat around the performance of the "private sector" concerns the role of private hospitals, or perhaps public-private partnerships. Still, it is clear to the authors of this book that the solution to the challenges faced by hospitals in developed and in middle-income countries (and in selected low-income countries as well, under specific circumstances) will require a solution to the conundrum of private sector involvement. The core question is thus: what should be the balance, in its given governance context?

Payment Mechanisms

Allied to this point about the private sector are considerations of the structure and type of payment mechanisms. There has often been much hope embedded in the notion that system leaders can determine outcomes by setting a price, probably in an overambitious way (Waters and Hussey 2004). This is at best a pious hope, given how poorly markets work in healthcare (because of asymmetric information and principal-agent problems and so on; see Arrow 1963, op. cit.). Decades of experience indicate that endless tinkering with output price structures produces some positive short-term results (e.g. typically with introduction of a diagnosis-related group [DRG] scheme), but then there is gaming by players in the system and the long-term effectiveness can be jeopardized. In this context, see the EU research project EURODRG: "Despite the fact that diagnosis-related groups (DRGs) have been adopted in an increasingly large number of countries around the world, knowledge about the effects of DRG systems and DRG-based hospital payment systems, as well as about optimal design features of these systems, remains surprisingly limited" and "the incentives of DRG-based payment systems have the potential to contribute to achieving the intended consequences, as long as the unintended ones can be adequately controlled through the mechanisms described" (http://www.eurodrg.eua and Busse et al. 2011).

More specifically, with the limited current information systems, payment methods are blunt tools to achieve desired results at granular scale—they are *necessary but not sufficient conditions* to make hospitals or other parts of the health system work significantly better. The net lesson here from this book is emphasizing is that design of payment mechanisms likely must be better worked upon, but with the ambition of making them consistent with wider reforms rather than expected to drive them in their own right.

Decision-Making About "Hospitals-in-Healthcare Systems"

As will be seen, hospitals are attempting to move forward, incorporating the best features and lessons from all over the world, with uneven outcomes. Being the most complex and resource-consuming single units within healthcare, hospitals offer an enormous potential for wastage, but also the perspective of an enormous step forward in effectiveness and productivity if some of the identified bottlenecks are resolved. This book will pay attention to this dilemma by suggesting the kind of decision-making needed. When speaking about governance and about models of care and of business, it will be seen that, most likely, the solutions will need to go beyond the boundaries of the hospital proper and, additionally, involve physical parameters as well as economic ones. Should hospitals simply be reconfigured, and if so, how should that be done? Should resources be pushed into primary care? And if so, how much—and for what exactly? How would such system modelling even be done?

Healthcare almost everywhere involves complex flow processes. Patients pass along what are often ill-defined paths which operate at different speeds, reverse themselves periodically and—certainly for co-morbid patients—use several processes at the same time. The elements to deliver the processes, as will be seen, are made of human and physical capital, of varying vintages and efficiency: primary care facilities and hospitals somehow need to be coordinated in that perspective.

Any complex flow system like this can be modelled as *stocks* (e.g. but not only, of beds) and *flows* (of patients, staff, visitors, materials, drugs, utilities). All real-world complex systems exhibit bottlenecks to changes of flow, and these bottlenecks can only be discovered in the real world or, better in advance, by simulation modelling: they will not be intuitive. A characteristic feature of such systems includes "latency" and, classically, that could be the average length of stay of a patient. Other things being equal, it is better to drive down that latency—though clearly not at the cost of welfare if patients are discharged before the rest of the system, including home, can safely receive them. In this modelling, if "beds" are one part of the system stock (a long-term concept), one of the confusions about their importance to hospital functioning is that they are also an example of a short-term "buffer" that the system uses in order to handle the inevitable variability of flow; merely increasing the buffer to allow the system to function in the short term is *not a satisfactory solution* in the long term.

It is a major problem that our ability to understand hospitals as flow systems is so poor. A central part of this book will therefore be the argument that the key to understanding "capacity" of the hospital system is the ability to model it as a complex flow system (see Chap. 9 below).

One of our intentions here is to get away from the syndrome that wishes for certain ends (e.g. "a primary care-led health system") but fails to will the means to achieve them. We therefore attempt to give recommendations which are actionable, based on concepts of how the health system as a whole works, and with ways of testing policies before applying them.

The Structure of This Book

What problems is this book addressing? The book will try to contribute to hospital analysis by suggesting disciplined, pragmatic dimensions of the debate on core issues that frame today's private and mostly public health systems and hospitals. The focus is on options and alternatives for key parameters, outlining particular areas of work in response to the challenges, and suggesting partial solutions under diverse lenses.

A true "elephant in the room" which some seem to refuse to see when addressing solutions to the health challenges, the hospital holds multiple assets, human resources including knowledge, which society needs and which other healthcare providers simply do not have. The core message and our main contribution is an optimistic analysis and statement that the hospital isn't going—and shouldn't go—away, and for very good reasons. In our opinion, hospitals are crucial to health system functioning now; and many elements determine that the delivery of specialized care will remain critically important for the foreseeable future. Clarifying the core issues related to this "elephant" (the current position hospitals find themselves in, and why it is the case) is more important than ever.

At the same time, in order to flourish, (all) hospitals need to change in their contexts in many respects; they cannot simply count on their traditional powerbases and they probably will not be the natural centre of the future action that they themselves sometimes seem to think they are today. Our thesis, again, is that for hospitals to stay a vibrant part of the future healthcare landscape, a much better job is needed of deciding what role hospitals have to play and thus what should happen within their walls and how; in what way resources are applied to generate value; how we govern this part of the health system; and the balance of public and private resources and guidance tools used in this sub-system.

This book is arranged as follows:

- After this introduction,
- Chapter 2 is devoted to governance—both in institutional units and systems, balancing autonomy and responsibility, with specific attention to governance processes and instruments;
- Chapter 3 deals with mapping physical service delivery via processes—the emergence of primary care and modern hospitals, models of care, with personal and population services and healthcare practice culture;
- Chapter 4 addresses the issue of creating value from resources—models of business, drivers of supply and demand, human and physical capital, process flow versus craft, economies of scale and scope;
- Chapter 5 is devoted to the public-private spectrum with emphasis on when to use the private sector in medical service delivery, as well as on the public/not-for-profit-private/PPP/for-profit-private hospitals domains;
- Chapter 6 deals with payment systems—block grants/payment by activities/capitation/P4R; emphasis is put on the need to achieve consistency with models of care and, especially, models of business;
- Chapter 7 addresses the complexity of hospitals in several contexts. First, in developed countries—the origin in historic systems; current low growth/tax-constrained futures of hospitals in ageing developed societies. Hospitals in LMIC as well as in post-Communist countries will also be analysed—with emphasis on service production in low-resource environments, and the efficiency and other challenges which this brings;
- Chapter 8 discusses some reasons why the complexity has appeared in the various geographic areas—why this is a wicked problem;
- Chapter 9 reviews the necessary decision-making challenge emerging from our analysis—defining and measuring hospital capacity, the meaning of flexibility, simulation and economic modelling; and
- Chapter 10 will finally bring us to our conclusions—in the light of the above discussions, what hospitals need to be, where to go from here, and how.

References

Aiken, L., et al. (2012). Patient Safety, Satisfaction, and Quality of Hospital Care: Cross Sectional Surveys of Nurses and Patients in 12 Countries in Europe and the United States. *British Medical Journal, 344*. https://doi.org/10.1136/bmj.e1717.

Arah, O. A., et al. (2006). Conceptual Framework for the OECD Health Care Quality Indicators Project. *International Journal of Quality Health Care, 18*(Suppl. 1), 5–13.

Arrow, K. J. (1963). Uncertainty and the Welfare Economics of Medical Care. *The American Economic Review, 53*(5), 941–973.

Busse, R., Geissler, A., Quentin, W., & Wiley, W. (2011). *Diagnosis-Related Groups in Europe: Moving Towards Transparency, Efficiency and Quality in Hospitals*. Maidenhead: Open University Press. World Health Organization on Behalf of the European Observatory on Health Systems and Policies.

Center for Global Development Hospitals for Health Working Group. (2015). *Better Hospitals, Better Health Systems, Better Health, a Proposal for a Global Hospital Collaborative for Emerging Economies*. (Washington) Box 1. What Is a Hospital? Retrieved from http://www.cgdev.org/sites/default/files/Hospitals%20for%20Health,%20Consultation%20Draft.%209.22.14.pdf.

Christensen, C. (2009). *The Innovator's Prescription a Disruptive Solution for Healthcare* (p. 101). New York: McGraw Hill.

Cochrane, A. (1971). *Effectiveness and Efficiency. Random Reflections on Health Services*. London: The Nuffield Provincial Hospital Trust. Retrieved from http://www.nuffieldtrust.org.uk/sites/files/nuffield/publication/Effectiveness_and_Efficiency.pdf.

de la Maisonneuve, C., & Martins, J. O. (2015). The Future of Health and Long-Term Care Spending. *OECD Journal: Economic Studies, 2014*(1), 61–96.

Donabedian, A. (1980). *Explorations in Quality Assessment and Monitoring, Vol. 1. The Definition of Quality and Approaches to Its Assessment*. Ann Arbor: Health Administration Press.

Donkin, A., Goldblatt, P., Allen, J., et al. (2017). Global Action on the Social Determinants of Health. *British Medical Journal Global Health, 3*, e000603. https://doi.org/10.1136/bmjgh-2017-000603.

Dubos, R. (1959). *Mirage of Health: Utopias, Progress, and Biological Change*. New York: Harper & Row.

Duran, A., Saltman, R. B., & Dubois, H. F. W. (2011). A Framework for Assessing Hospital Governance. In R. B. Saltman, A. Duran, & H. F. W. Dubois (Eds.), *Governing Public Hospitals, Reform Strategies and the Movement Towards Institutional Autonomy*. Brussels: European Observatory on Health Systems and Policies. Observatory Studies Series No. 25, 38.

Ettelt, S., Nolte, E., Thomson, S., & Mays, N. (2008). *Capacity Planning in Health Care: A Review of the International Experience*. International Healthcare Comparisons Network. Copenhagen: European Observatory on Health Systems and Policies. Policy Brief.

Evans, R., Barer, M., & Marmor, T. (1994). *Why Are Some People Healthy and Others Not?* New York: Aldine de Gruiter.

Figueras, J., McKee, M., Lessof, S., Duran, A., & Menabde, N. (2008). *Health Systems, Health and Wealth: Assessing the Case for Investing in Health Systems?* Tallin Conference. Background Document. Copenhagen: World Health Organization – EURO.

Herrera, C. A., Rada, G., Kuhn-Barrientos, L., & Barrios, X. (2014). Does Ownership Matter? An Overview of Systematic Reviews of the Performance of Private For-Profit, Private Not-for-Profit and Public Healthcare Providers. *PLoS One, 9*(12), e93456. https://doi.org/10.1371/journal.pone.0093456.

Joumard, I., André, C., & Nicq, C. H. (2010). *Health Care Systems: Efficiency and Institutions*. Paris: OECD, Economics Department Working Papers, No. 769, ECO/WKP (2010)25.

Kringos, D. S., Boerma, W. G. W., Hutchinson, A., & Saltman, R. B. (2015). *Building Primary Care in a Changing Europe*. Copenhagen: European Observatory on Health Systems and Policies, Observatory Studies Series No. 38. Retrieved from https://www.ncbi.nlm.nih.gov/books/NBK458728/.

Magretta, J. (2002). Why Business Models Matter. *Harvard Business Review, 80*(5), 86–92, 133.

McKee, M., & Healy, J. (Eds.). (2002). *Hospitals in a Changing Europe*. Buckingham: Open University Press. European Observatory on Health Systems and Policies.

McKeown, T. (1965). *The Modern Rise of the Population*. London: Blackwell Scientific Publications.

Miller, T. S. (1997). *The Birth of the Hospital in the Byzantine Empire*. Baltimore, MD: Johns Hopkins University Press, quoted in M. McKee and J. Healy (Eds.), *Hospitals in a Changing Europe*. Buckingham: Open University Press, 2002, European Observatory on Health Systems and Policie.

Murray, C. J., & Frenk, J. (2000). A Framework for Assessing the Performance of Health Systems. *Bulletin of the World Health Organization, 78*(6), 717. Geneva: World Health Organization.

Nolte, E., & McKee, M. (2008). Measuring the Health of Nations: Updating an Earlier Analysis. *Health Affairs, 27*(1), 58–71.

Oxford English Dictionary. (n.d.). Retrieved July 18, 2018, from https://en.oxforddictionaries.com/definition/hospital.

Peters, B. G. (2004). Back to the Centre? Rebuilding the State. In A. Gamble & T. Wright (Eds.), *Restarting the State* (pp. 130–140). London: Blackwell Publishing.

Preston, S. H. (1980). Causes and Consequences of Mortality Declines in Less Developed Countries in the Twentieth Century. In R. A. Easterlin (Ed.), *Population and Economic Change in Developing Countries* (p. 315). Chicago: University of Chicago Press.

Rechel, B., Erskine, J., Dowdeswell, B., Wright, S., & Mckee, M. (2009a). *Capital Investment for Health. Case Studies from Europe.* European Observatory on Health Systems and Policies. Observatory Studies Series No. 18.

Rechel, B., Wright, S., Edwards, N., Dowdeswell, B., & Mckee, M. (2009b). *Investing in Hospitals of the Future.* European Observatory on Health Systems and Policies. Observatory Studies Series No. 16.

Rechel, B., Wright, S., Barlow, J., & McKee, M. (2010). Hospital Capacity Planning: From Measuring Stocks to Modeling Flows. *Bulletin of the World Health Organization, 88*, 632–636. Geneva: World Health Organization. https://doi.org/10.2471/BLT.09.07336.

Saltman, R. B., Duran, A., & Dubois, H. F. W. (Eds.). (2011). *Governing Public Hospitals, Reform Strategies and the Movement Towards Institutional Autonomy.* Brussels: European Observatory on Health Systems and Policies, Observatory Studies Series No. 25, 38.

Starfield, B. (1974). Measurement of Outcome: A Proposed Scheme. *Milbank Memorial Fund Quarterly, Health Society, 52*(1), 39–50.

Waters, H., & Hussey, P. (2004). *Pricing Health Services for Purchasers: A Review of Methods and Experiences.* Washington, DC: The World Bank. HNP Discussion Paper.

WHO – World Health Organization. (2000). *World Health Report 2000. Health System Improving Performance.* Geneva: World Health Organization.

WHO – World Health Organization. (2011). *World Health Report 2010. Health System Financing; The Path to Universal Health Coverage.* Geneva: World Health Organization.

WHO – World Health Organization. (n.d.). Retrieved July 18, 2018, from http://www.who.int/hospitals/en/.

CHAPTER 2

Hospital Governance

Antonio Durán and Richard B. Saltman

Introduction

The previous chapter has explored (and the following ones will come back to the topic) the challenges and intrinsic need for strategic leadership that contemporary health systems now confront. Special emphasis will be put on the notions of business models (and associated models of care). This need affects hospitals' intra-institutional relationships at "micro" level (typically expressed through the word "management"). The importance of those relationships was noted previously by lead authors, pointing out the difficulties of existing management doctrine to capture the growing number of stakeholders involved. They suggested, among other things, the need for broadening the scope of the definitions traditionally used to analyse contemporary institutions (Mintzberg 1996).

A. Durán (✉)
ALLDMHEALTH, Seville, Spain
e-mail: aduran@alldmh.com

R. B. Saltman
Department of Health Policy and Management, Rollins School of Public Health, Emory University, Atlanta, GA, USA
e-mail: rsaltma@emory.edu

A. Durán, S. Wright (eds.), *Understanding Hospitals in Changing Health Systems*, https://doi.org/10.1007/978-3-030-28172-4_2

The need to re-think hospitals can also be anchored in the importance of attaining better health impacts—for example, improved personal well-being, social stability, higher productivity, contribution to equitable social policies and so on (Deaton 2003)—an area from which hospitals have been kept substantially separated, as indicated in the introduction to this book. Hospitals therefore need everywhere to re-articulate also their broader relationships with the "political" dimension—the ownership and regulatory spheres in the external world at "meso" and "macro" levels; see below.

These viewpoints emphasize that society is now fundamentally different compared to when hospitals first became prestigious in the eyes of their communities, in key technical, organizational and financial aspects. Concerning affordability, at the same time technological developments in the health industry have not triggered patterns comparable to those of computers, cars, travel, telecommunications and so on—that is, health technologies have often failed to generate the widespread cost reduction from production improvements seen in other economic sectors in recent decades (Christensen 2009). Some of this could be the difficulty of increasing productivity in many service (as distinct from manufacturing) industries, but part of this productivity failure could be related to the way the health sector *governs* hospitals as a key depositary of high-level technology and medical specialization.

This chapter reviews the multiple issues that impact this complex picture. It focuses on three key dimensions of the impact of governance dimensions on the hospital renewal debate:

- Concepts, definitions and historical origins of governance, in the context of the so-called globalization.
- Operationalization of governance processes and instruments for ensuring results in units and systems.
- The process of balancing hospital autonomy and responsibility, with the need for an update, including the case of (semi) autonomous hospitals.

Why "Governance", Why Now?

The New Context: Geopolitical Changes, Globalization and Hospitals

A former mayor of New York famously exclaimed: "*This world of today simply moves too fast; improvements, politics, reform, religion, all fly!*" His observation would aptly express the current puzzlement with technologies and change... if it is noted that Philip Hone was actually reacting in 1844 to Samuel Morse's telegraph (Gordon 2004). Major technological and geopolitical changes make the world appear again today as "too different" in key aspects compared with the way it was in the mid-twentieth century.

Parallel social and political phenomena need to be noted as well. Technological changes increase competition and re-location of industries. Demographic changes linked to decades-long success in prolonging life expectancy and an increase in both the absolute number and relative proportion of pensioners affect the ratio between active workers and dependents. Access to goods and services that decades ago seemed a luxury become customary in many parts of the world. A transformation of the relative power of the state, on the one hand, and markets, civil society, social networks and individuals, on the other, has been underway since at least the end of World War II.

Simultaneously, the number, type and character of actors in the political arena have multiplied, with more complex forms of both public and private sector involvement. The boundaries between public and private actors have become more diffused, and central government control over a complex political process has had to change in both content and process. "Governments retain the power to steer and regulate, but it is now difficult to imagine significant progress on issues of global importance (e.g. health, food security, sustainable energy and climate change mitigation) without the private sector playing an important role" (WHO 2013).

Hospitals in developed countries personify these processes rather vividly. The "Weberian"/bureaucratic model of public administration in modern states formally separated policymaking (ministers) from the public administration civil servants responsible for advising them for almost two centuries (Richards and Smith 2002). In many countries, hospitals developed complex links to various levels of government—national, regional or local. While professionals in other sectors were typically private practitioners, the majority of doctors and nurses in a number of European and developing world countries either were or became public employees (although in other countries, like The Netherlands, the United States, Japan and Taiwan, the preponderance of hospital physicians have retained their independence). Strategic decision-making in many European countries was formally placed in the hands of sector officials, generally within the Ministry of Health. For public hospitals, the scenario remained prevalent in many countries until well after World War II, when the need for skilful *management* became increasingly visible (in the Netherlands, for example, doctors were mostly private practitioners and hospitals were and are private non-profits, but the oversight function still rested with the state, if only through licencing).

Although they had become socially successful institutions in large parts of the developed world by the mid-twentieth century,[1] the monolithic way of running both public and non-profit private hospitals started to confront major *pressures for change* in the 1970s and 1980s. Many of these pressures were related to the technological, epidemiological and sociological foundations of those institutions, whilst others were linked to their specific political forms of organization and the results thereof. In developed and in some middle-income countries, the difference in many dimensions between the hospital a few decades back and the present reality was sharply perceived (see Box 2.1):

Box 2.1 Hospitals: From a Few Decades Back to Today

	30–40 years ago	*Today*
Epidemiology-related workload	Single-cause disease, mostly infectious. Patients generally "young" because most major diseases (even NCDs—brain haemorrhage, cardiac arrest, renal failure, metabolic coma, etc.) would have killed the affected persons in their first episode	Most cases with multiple causes, predominantly non-infectious diseases. Many co-morbid cases, essentially with non-curable but amenable to stabilization at the hands of skilled professionals diseases.
Attitude of the affected	Literally "patients" (people ready to bear the pain and anxiety caused by a "highly skilled person doing his/her best for me"). Attitude usually reinforced by information asymmetry	Better trained/medically informed customers/citizens, aware of their rights, indeed able to check on the Web how to address their diseases. More having "a health professional relative"...

[1] From being "almshouses"/"poor old people's homes" without antisepsis, laboratory, radiology nor pharmacology and mostly structured as associations of senior physicians in the nineteenth century.

	30–40 years ago	*Today*
Facilities, equipment and technology available	Standardized building layouts. Limited technical specificity and sophistication in the equipment, rather circumscribed to their diagnostic, therapeutic, surgical and medical, etc. spheres. In a significant number of areas, only a limited review of facility options could be carried out	Greater range in functionality and architectural building design. Ultra-sophisticated equipment at top level, and a plethora of broadly supporting equipment plus many precise devices below to determine what could be done, etc.; concern about "not being comprehensive, etc…"
Staff involved	(A limited number of) patriarchal unchallenged figures leading groups of faithful members in their department, mostly dependent on them professionally. New recruits' selection often involved co-option mechanisms. Bosses able to "negotiate with directors the annual budget"…	Much more competitive selection methods. Many more professional leaders (from four to dozens of specialties) would find work elsewhere if needed. Staff members often know "as much" as their bosses and would push for "more money to do more things in more areas", etc…
Potential expenditures	By definition, especially in public hospitals, money to be spent in strictly predictable ways ("this money we have/this is the available amount per patient") and not challenged	Every department could conceivably "spend the totality of the hospital resources". The running cost is very often more expensive than the capital needed to acquire machines
Options for the hospital	Military model used as organizational reference for post-World War II hospitals in many countries. Directors had a long professional life, with very limited episodes of distress. Almost any "medical director" could do their work in alliance with heads of units. Ideally, only some "management" is explicitly necessary (in the sense of maximizing outputs and outcomes)	Good management only is not enough since: (a) everybody claims to deal with important issues, (b) decisions by one manager affect many others, and (c) need to share in a transparent way incentives and controls. Performance appraisal is vital "because always many potential courses of action" exist. Managers/board members are directly at risk if things go wrong…
Options for the government	Government "can do the job" maintaining responsibilities (and influence)". No private alternative in practice (often "too distant and complex" to be taken into account)	Often evidence that "better relinquish some control in order to avoid conflict". Private sector growth will increasingly offer alternatives (from sharing and outsourcing to selling) in case of need

In many areas of industry and services, centre-stage has been now occupied by "new" concepts such as efficient leadership, pluralism, accountability, transparency, participation, communication, fair regulation and so on. Overall—it is argued—while "government used to consist of a 'one-way traffic from governors to governed' it now rests less exclusively on formal structures" (Peters 2004).

Definitions: A New Word in Addition to Administration and Management

This chapter adopts an historical perspective on the birth of "governance", as explained. At the end of the twentieth century, many public institutions sought better outcomes through the mechanism of what was termed "new public management", by getting *closer to the mode of functioning of private companies without changing their existing model of ownership* (Hood 1991; Osborne and Gaebler 1992), or, in a few cases, were *privatized* (for example some non- and for-profit hospitals were acquired by commercial hospital groups in Central and Eastern Europe). The term *governance* was applied to the healthcare sector overall around this time to describe the changed decision-making requirements under the new twenty-first century circumstances.

That a new concept had to be applied to designate these changes underscores the extent of the organizational challenge. Political scientists started proposing the inclusion of qualitatively new aspects of policymaking within the name governance, linking regulation (*institutional governance*) to management (*operational governance*) and giving importance to the dimension of "*governing without government*" (Rhodes 1996).

Experts offered various *definitions of governance*:

- The processes and institutions, both formal and informal, that guide and restrain the collective activities of a group (Nye and Donahue 2000).
- Rules, enforcement mechanisms and organizations (World Bank 2002).
- The International Monetary Fund (IMF) defines it slightly differently from the WB, though both institutions agree that good governance should include "promoting transparency, accountability, efficiency, fairness, participation and ownership" (Woods 2000).

In the field of health, the definitions of governance put forward rapidly became highly expansive, if not all-encompassing:

- "The notion of governance is linked to health policies, strategies, and plans as "expressions of a country's vision, priorities, budgetary decisions and courses of action for improving and maintaining the health of people". [...] "Accountability is an intrinsic aspect of governance that concerns the management of relationships between various stakeholders in health, including individuals, households, communities, firms, governments, nongovernmental organizations, private firms and other entities with the responsibility to finance, monitor, deliver and use health services" (Baghdadi-Sabeti and Serhan 2010).
- Governance capacity is "the ability of a nation's institutions to implement health policies, provide medical services, allocate resources efficiently and help countries respond to global health crises" (West et al. 2017, Brookings Institution).

As illustrated above, the later, more expansive definitions placed predominant emphasis on existing formal tools of *government* authority and control as compared to the initial theoretical focus on *new processes and tools* to be utilized (e.g. Rhodes' 1996 argument that contemporary governance requires a different tool box and processes than those associated with traditional government). For example, writing in 2010, Kaufmann et al. concluded that "Although the concept is widely discussed among policymakers and scholars, there is as yet no strong consensus around a single definition of governance or institutional quality"—nonetheless, they produce "Worldwide Governance Indicators (WGI)" with statistics that they contend "capture perceptions of the extent to which agents have confidence in and abide by the rules of society, and in particular the quality of contract enforcement, property rights, the police, and the courts, as well as the likelihood of crime and violence". More precisely, the WGI started in 1996 and cover over 200 countries and territories, measuring six dimensions of governance, namely (1) voice and accountability, (2) political stability and absence of violence/terrorism, (3) government effectiveness, (4) regulatory quality, (5) rule of law, and (6) control of corruption. The indicators are based on several hundred individual underlying variables, taken from a wide variety of data sources, reflecting the views on the topic of survey respondents and public, private, and NGO sector experts worldwide. It is understood that even after taking into account margins of error accompanying each country estimate, the WGI permit meaningful cross-country and over-time comparisons[2] (Kaufmann et al. 2010).

In 2011, the authors of this chapter proposed a pragmatic working definition of hospital governance (Saltman et al. 2011) as the set of

> *processes and tools related to decision making in steering* ***all*** *institutional activity, influencing most aspects of organizational behaviour and recognizing the complex relationships between multiple stakeholders—with a scope of normative values (equity, ethics), results (access, quality, responsiveness and patient safety) plus political, financial, managerial as well as daily operational issues.*

In this view, the scope of the term needs to take into account three inter-connected dimensions—macro, meso and micro (Duran et al. 2011):

- The "micro" governance level of a hospital focuses on the day-to-day operations, staff and services inside the organization, incorporating subsets such as personnel management, clinical quality assurance, clinic-level financial management, patient services and hotel services (cleaning services, catering, etc.) and so on. It is, in fact, similar to what has traditionally been known as "hospital management".
- The "meso" level looks at the "senior decision-making" for each hospital—in a growing number of countries, separate as a subsector. Key organizational policy decisions that a hospital is allowed to take have been lodged in a structure resembling that of private companies, with its own rules and a separate institutional Board (of Trustees or Supervisors) plus the hospital's Chief Executive Officer (CEO), and so on;
- "Macro" level is where the analysis of government decisions are located—for example, about the health system and hospital structural, organizational and operational profiles, maintaining it or not publicly operated, tax-funded hospitals and so on. The range and specificity of the requirements and regulations vary considerably between countries, with important distinctions, given their specific objectives, referring to the difference between public and private hospitals.

[2] The aggregate indicators and the disaggregated underlying source data are available at www.govindicators.org.

As the above suggests, the fact that the term "governance" often refers in current parlance about health systems and hospitals almost exclusively to "the action of government" misses the essence of the phenomena that the newly created concept seeks to capture. Meeting attendees in present-day organizations often seem to focus their reasoning around the idealized coming of "a powerful manager who would put the things straight"—as if "good management" alone was the solution. In turn, policy formulations of what governments "should do" with hospitals (often citing the word *stewardship* as defined by WHO's World Health Report 2000) are not infrequent in many texts either (although the true content of those prescriptions extends well beyond the capacity or responsibility of most Ministries of Health).

In practice, traditional government-dominated models of governance are now insufficient, if not plainly wrong. Public-private partnerships (PPPs), for one example, require *more, but different, governance* than direct public sector provision, particularly in areas with a large service component and social sensitivity—that is, compared to PPPs in sectors such as transport with potentially marketable outputs (Barlow et al. 2013). Robust results are the "justification" for good governance, yet the capacities of Ministries of Health in that sphere are inherently limited—see also Chaps. 5 and 6).

Operationalizing "Governance" in the Health Sphere

One of the key theses of this book is that contemporary health facilities in many countries have been transformed by technology, demography, epidemiology and political economy into different types of institutions from their antecedents, with changed structure, functions, decision-making, service patterns and so on. Now that hospitals are immensely more complex institutions, embedded in more complex societies, hospital governance needs to be applied as "*more than government policies and more than management alone*". Thus, revisiting the nature of "governance" in practice is vital to implement institutional responsibility in its own right.

The operational definition of "governance" in the health sphere in general and in hospitals in particular should be interpreted to entail:

- Ensuring results inside units and within the wider system through different mechanisms, since traditional approaches have shown important limitations; the processes and tools whose combined action generates better results need to be identified.
- Focusing on processes and instruments and not only on the text of the norms in order to assess performance as against objectives—for example, explicit contracts. This affects corporatization/more autonomy, but also hospital privatization issues, if responsibility over the centres is transferred to the private sector—for profit or not.
- Balancing autonomy and responsibility (effective incentives, transparency and accountability) in a fluid context, with changes in both the number and types of stakeholders involved as well as in the mechanisms through which their influences are exerted.

In a very aggregate manner, the results achieved by public or private hospital(s) in the framework of its health system (namely, in the categories of access to and effective utilization of services, quality and safety, efficiency and responsiveness) can be essentially related to the following:

1. The potential/*technical capacity* of the hospital, measured by its physical inputs/technology endowment, knowledge and competence endowment, and clinical/operational potential. This technical capacity defines its competence/potential in providing quality services (that is, in dealing with "medical" problems in practice), including the type(s)/profile of services that better defines the facility, be it (1) complex services of low (epidemiological) frequency, high variation and cost/case, (2) value-adding treatments to diseases of high (epidemiological) frequency, relatively low complexity and variation and rather low cost/case performed according to a relatively standard steps sequence, or (3) the care of mostly chronic cases in a close network with other hospitals, elderly nursing homes, and/or primary healthcare delivery. The *planned* technical capacity of the hospital is directly correlated with the prevalent type of staff and with the infrastructure—especially equipment and sophisticated technology.

2. The *managerial capacity* of a hospital refers to the skills, tools, approaches and schemes with which the hospital operates—that is, how it sets the strategic goals and general as well as particular objectives, plus the expected outputs of units and the necessary clinical and general activities/tasks to develop them. All are obviously related in a rather direct way with the prevailing values in the context, as it happens also with the decision-making capacity allowed to the hospital (see below). In that context, managers determine the inputs and resources needed, be they financial, staff and so on (they, among other things, mobilize funds, invest capital, purchase equipment, adjust operational expenses and allocate budgets, hire and fire different categories of personnel, set up salary levels within an agreed range, outsource support services and prepare contracts as necessary). While the issue of whether MDs or MBAs would better serve the purpose[3] remains rather unresolved, managers do assign the corresponding responsibilities and workloads, and determine the chronograms for action and the information system to keep the entire organization together while providing the methods for control and evaluation—that is, organize the architecture and operations of the hospital units.
3. The status given to the hospital as measured by its legal form, decision-making capacity, accountability and incentives. The *autonomy* of the hospital (some prefer the expression "semi-autonomy", since no hospital can be fully autonomous; even for-profit private hospitals have to adjust to the behaviour marked by state regulation at central and regional levels) incorporates the institutional arrangements and legal form of the hospital. The notion also sets its decision-making capacity in relation to social and political objectives without undue political interference, as well as in determining relationships with professional organizations, unions and stakeholders,

[3] The London School of Economics and McKinsey conducted over 40 interviews and studied almost 1200 hospitals in Canada, France, Germany, Italy, Sweden, the United Kingdom and the United States with rather inconclusive results. It seems that hospitals with the best management practices (analysed as if they made things happen rather than curing people per se) also ranked best on a standardized measure of medical success: death rates among emergency patients who had experienced heart attacks. The score works across countries and cultures, and has unambiguous results—see Dorgan S., D. Layton, et al., (2010), Management in healthcare: why good practice really matters, McKinsey and Comp and LSE.

power sharing with clinicians and so on. The incentives offered to individuals and units (including expressions of their individual and collective professional ethics) as well as the checks and balances in line with the formally allocated responsibilities are additional elements. Also, the way service providers are held answerable for processes and outcomes (monitoring, follow-up and evaluation, etc.), and the possibility to impose sanctions in case of failure to deliver are included.

In this chapter, in summary, it is thus proposed that properly balanced hospital governance, understood as "*the relationship between the organization and its owner(s)* including the right to any remaining income after fixed obligations are met, as adequate" (Preker and Harding 2003), should include the technical capacity of the hospital, plus the clinical and general management capacity, plus the space to make decisions and the status of hospital in that regard.

Through the above composite variables and categories, a valid and reliable account of the right to make decisions on each hospital assets' use and results thereof plus the framework for doing so is presented. Other frameworks have grouped those variables into a bigger number of headings; for example, La Forgia et al. (2000) used five categories: (a) *decision rights*, (b) *technical capacity*, (c) *incentives in operation*, (d) *managerial capacity* and (e) *accountability mechanisms*. Duran et al. (2011, op. cit.) used four categories, namely (a) *institutional arrangements*, (b) *financial arrangements*, (c) *accountability arrangements* and (d) *decision-making capacity* versus *responsibility*. However, the general picture being described is rather common across these authors.

Figure 2.1 presents in a diagrammatic form this chapter's framework of hospital governance. The diagram spins around an (*intermediate*, as opposed to *final*[4]) results-based, patient-centred approach, with a broad perspective of the facility context. Robust results are linked to robust governance—in other words, governance can only be rather good if the consequential hospital outcomes are also rather good.

[4] According to most theoretical frameworks, including the World Health Report 2000, the *final* outcomes produced by health systems are expected to be "improving health status of the population", "protecting the population against the financial risk of health care costs" and "improving citizens' satisfaction". There is more debate about what *intermediate* results hospitals and other service providers should pursue towards achieving the final ones, but most frameworks coincide on the above-mentioned four objectives that we are using here).

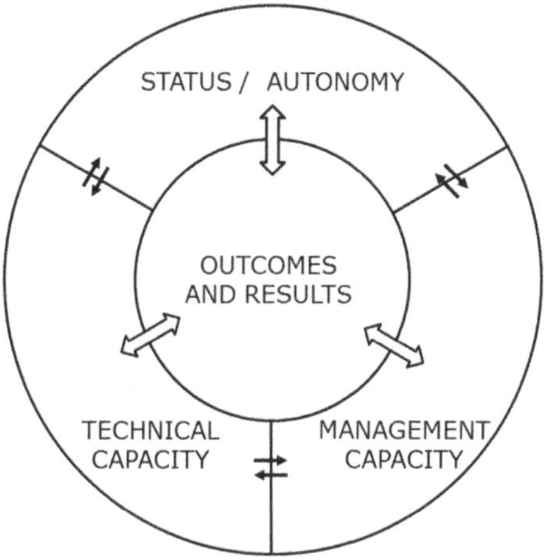

Fig. 2.1 Hospital governance framework

The arrows in between the composite variables are also critical, as follows:

1. It is clear that, for a start, many facilities are not given the legal and operational capacity to adapt under their own responsibility to the risk-involving decisions currently needed to cope with uncertainty in daily operations, within a strategic institutional perspective.
2. Equally frequent is the problem of not providing sufficiently qualified staff, skills and instruments necessary for proper managerial activity to the hospital. Combined with intrinsic limitations of information systems, payment methods and organizational arrangements to involve professionals, such absences together drive management to become just a much more pedestrian administrative-level duty.
3. Often also, the inability to stick to a given service profile further reduces the outcome in terms of quality. By over-equipping and/or overstepping the boundaries of its mandate in the context of a hospital's particular health system, evaluation becomes invalidated in practice.
4. Finally, many hospitals do not achieve the expected results because of poor planning and the inability to determine feasible, quantifiable goals and objectives in the clinical and financial spheres; hospitals *have to really be* more than buildings plus some complex machines plus specialized doctors, which was often what they were before (Box 2.2).

Box 2.2 A Possible Application of the Framework

The proposed three groups of variables in Fig. 2.1 are a convenient structure, *because* the three together determine the results of the hospital. A possible application of this framework would include, for example, the following variables:

I. Hospital outcomes and results

I.1. Access and effective utilization of hospital services

1.1. Admissions and hospitalization refusals
1.2. Healthcare skipped due to costs
1.3. Planned and unplanned admissions
1.4. Elective and unplanned surgeries
1.5. Provision of care after admission/completion of treatments
1.6. Waiting times for receiving care
1.7. Patients waiting more than three months for selected surgeries

I.2. Quality and safety

2.1. Hospital-acquired infections
2.2. Birth trauma
2.3. Health services for patients with cancer
2.4. Adverse events
2.5. Unplanned returns to operating theatre
2.6. Emergency patient readmissions within 30 days of hospital discharge
2.7. Selected causes of intra-hospital mortality
2.8. TIA patients evaluated and treated within 24 hours of admission

I.3. Efficiency

3.1. Bed occupancy rates
3.2. Inpatient length of stay
3.3. Operating room and other facilities productivity
3.4. Costs per activity
3.5. Drugs stock-outs
3.6. Staff absenteeism

I.4. Responsiveness

4.1. Information received by patients upon discharge
4.2. Patients' and relatives' global satisfaction at discharge
4.3. Patient specific satisfaction with medical and non-medical consumable and equipment availability
4.4. Patients and relatives' complaints
4.5. Staff satisfaction

II. Determinants of the outcomes

II.1. Technical capacity

1.1. Physical inputs and technology endowment

a. Infrastructure
b. Analytical and diagnostic equipment
c. Therapeutic equipment
d. Office and industrial equipment

1.2. Knowledge and competence endowment

a. Staff numbers and profiles
b. Clinical protocols and guidelines
c. Standard operating procedures
d. Training and research capacity

1.3. Clinical and operational potential

a. Hospital service catalogue/portfolio
b. Clinical specialties and general services organization
c. Service profile in practice
d. Business model(s) in the facility

II.2. Management capacity

2.1. *Clinical* management

a. Care standardization
b. Patient-related operations
c. Activity management
d. Quality management/continuous improvement

2.2. General management

a. Customer services
b. Staff management
c. Supplies management
d. Financial management
e. Infrastructure management

II.3. Status/Autonomy for decision-making

3.1. *Legal* form

a. Hospital identity
b. Catchment population
c. Hospital legal category
d. Hospital ownership

3.2. *Decision*-making capacity

a. Corporate purpose as per legal documents
b. Specific decision-making authority
c. Hospital leadership processes
d. Hospital leadership structures

3.3. *Accountability*

a. Institutional accountability
b. Areas of accountability
c. Accountability arrangements
d. Accountability consequences

3.4. *Incentives*

a. Nature of the incentives
b. Incentives by recipient target groups
c. Types of incentives

(Duran, A. (2017). World Bank Support to the Health Sector in Swaziland, Health Financing and Hospital Governance & Management Project)

While "result variables" are amenable to quantitative treatment, it is very likely that "technical capacity", "managerial capacity" and "hospital status/autonomy" variables will only be subject (at least at the beginning) to qualitative assessments. Needless to say, progress towards the use of comparable quanti-qualitative scores will require a very trial-and-error process of successive drafts and the associated debate. Notably, here, *the role of international agencies will be indispensable (mostly but not only) for low and middle-income countries.*

There is a clear need to produce elements of a new overall framework for analysing hospitals in different locations and societies (e.g. developed countries, post-communist countries, low- and middle-income countries, etc.) in a reasonably comparable and productive way. Further disaggregation(s) offer(s) the possibility to analyse each hospital as the product of discrete, specific decisions in each society by means of governance-oriented hospital performance assessment. This book emphasizes the importance of doing so in the context of the particular health system (for a reference to wider geographic socioeconomic context groups, see Chaps. 7 and 8) (Box 2.3).

Box 2.3 Understanding Governance Beyond the Surface: Hospital Reform in Japan

At first sight, the notion of hospital governance could be understood to include a sort of unfettered claim for quick decentralization. As per the framework proposed in this book, things are more complex. Naoki Ikegami presents an extremely interesting (and only superficially counter-intuitive) evidence from recent Japanese hospital reform (Ikegami 2014) of the importance of assessing governance of combining the potential/technical capacity measured by many attributes relevant to this chapter.

The amount of management skills and the momentum for change in each public hospital in Japan was found in previous work to be limited (Ikegami et al. 2011). The idea of *first* including those public hospitals into one organization in order to make them compete with each other was originally feared to lead possibly to an equally rigid and bureaucratic solution. However, the initiative to form one organization and provide dynamic leadership plus adequate training made reform possible rather smoothly.

The author finishes by saying: "In retrospect, the decision to transfer all hospitals to one National Hospital Organization, NHO, and not to make each hospital an Independent Administrative Agency allowed management resources to be concentrated and facilitated healthy competition and cooperation among hospitals, within regional blocks and throughout the NHO. These reforms may be relevant for low- and middle-income countries—if payment regulations to protect equity can be enforced."

Japan's reform raises obvious questions about how centralization worked in this case: in particular, how did a more centralized public administration result in more competition as well as more cooperation between hospitals? Potentially the outcome reflects structural (pay arrangements, role of unions, etc.) as well as cultural expectations (deference to constituted authority) that were inherent in a specifically Japanese governmental organization. However, municipality-owned hospitals have been less successful, precisely through lacking those factors (while cultural issues such as conformity to norms etc. are held in common). It is possible that the expectations and behaviour of Japanese physicians and also citizens differ from those observed elsewhere, but there are key elements to the new design that many countries can potentially learn through paying serious comparative attention.

Need for an Update in the Process of Balancing Hospital Autonomy and Responsibility

In parallel with the developments above, a process of change to *reform the legal status of hospitals* giving them decision-making capacity and tools to behave like business units and entities able to defend *their own* interests became widespread in the mid-1990s in many countries. This was at *meso* level, where most innovations were made in publicly operated hospitals across the world—for example, through labels such as *self-governing trusts, foundation trusts, joint stock companies, state enterprises, public stock corporations, administrative concessions*, etc.). The term "hospital autonomy" was often used (especially in Europe) to designate the changes introduced in order to allow better *oversight and more flexibility* in response to the above reality.

For years and under diverse labels and cultural prisms, countries became laboratories of change in legal status and functional arsenal. Many public hospitals started the incorporation of higher accountability elements, such as supervisory boards and management boards, in order to facilitate more structured and participatory decision-making. Hospitals became funded through explicit contracts, both within the public sphere and between public and private sectors. The boundaries between public and private sector *status* were blurred in some countries—mostly with the exception of university clinics—and the distinction between the political, managerial and administrative spheres was further diluted.

Arguably, in general, transparency in the political debate was limited, but whatever happened inside and outside hospital walls was better explained than before. Incentives were addressed in a rather opened way. Physicians, nurses and other professionals received more space as managers of a substantial amount of resources in their clinical practice (over which traditional management still has limited say due to professional self-responsibility). Boards were often capable of signing (short-term) personnel contracts under private law, to encourage (up to a ceiling) staff financially according to performance, to keep operating surpluses for the following year, and/or to borrow capital (with a limit); many hospitals massively outsourced support services when organizing the operations of the units and so on; some others finally opened (or even closed) clinical services on their own authority (Duran and Saltman 2013).

The names and regimes of affected (European) public hospitals differed between countries, and often had somewhat different mixes of incentives and constraints (see Table 2.1):

The economic crisis starting in 2008 created a much less favourable political climate for these initiatives. Risk transfer to hospitals, in theory a core feature of the ongoing experience, became in practice reduced for obvious fear of the danger of public budgets being affected. Direct political interference also weakened hospitals' flexibility and the ability to introduce explicit incentives, or staff selection. The pressure from labour unions to make the new working environment converge with traditional schemes (in contrast with what was initially agreed) further lessened the success of the innovations. Scandals of contracts behind closed doors and/or opaquely explained obscured the degree of involvement of the private sector, bringing—perhaps disproportionately—privatization and corruption to the front page as the controversial drivers of reform.

Table 2.1 Models of increased hospital self-governance

Country	*Forms of incorporation*
Czech Republic	Limited Listed Companies
Estonia	Corporations
	Foundations
Israel	Private non-profit
	Governmental
	Private Insurance Principal shareholder
Italy	Azienda Ospedaliera
	Azienda Socio—Sanitaria Territoriale (ASST)
Netherlands	Private non-profit foundations
England	NHS Trust
	Foundation Trust
Norway	Regional Healthcare Companies
Portugal	Public Business Entities EPE
Spain	Public Health Company
	Foundation
	Consortium
	Administrative Concession
Sweden	Public Stock Corporations

Source: Saltman et al. (2011)

Many of the governments involved have not assessed their experiences in public yet. In some countries, the slowdown or stoppage of a process towards autonomy virtually affected all initiatives—for example Spain, where since the beginning of the 1990s a range of different alternatives such as *public health companies, foundations, consortiums and administrative concessions* had been explored with implicit agreement of future cross-fertilization, which in fact never occurred. The recent wiping out of the experience with concessions, especially in Valencia, has been truly remarkable.

Seen in perspective, it was probably intellectually arrogant that pro-autonomy management models with limited private involvement were introduced mostly in already-operating hospitals (*reforming hospitals from a previous status*). It now seems clear that a number of those arrangements should have only been introduced *in new, purpose-built hospitals* (Duran and LaForgia 2016), as follows:

- Political leadership—ideally, a broad agreement on the desirability of the changes;

- Agreement with at least a number of key stakeholders to increase resilience against almost unavoidable resistances that would emerge; and, crucially
- An explicitly formulated change management strategy with higher transparency throughout the process, in order to help everybody understand "what should come next".

That governance theory will continue affecting hospitals is beyond doubt. Some symptomatic issues remain at a rather embryonic stage for now—for example, conflict-solving approaches to how resources should be allocated according to performance. However, the changing modalities of acute and scheduled clinical care involving all the health system, adapting the demands for comprehensive care to chronically ill and elderly patients, the insistence upon voice and choice by the patient, all mean already a thorough challenge to the way hospitals are currently run and governed. For the reasons explained, also, the voice of professional groups (doctors, nurses, etc.) will be heard in more specific ways. The notion of governance will also call for better applications of the cooperation between public and private sectors. Increasingly, hospitals—especially those publicly operated—will have to adapt to the new circumstances.

The expectation can safely be that many hospitals will "search for" sufficient resources to develop their activities as solvent corporate entities, *even while remaining within the public sector*. The political processes will incorporate "new governance elements" (Ezzamel and Reed 2008). National governments are indispensable in addressing governance properly, but non-governmental contributions are also vital, with emphasis on social communication. Addressing the above issues upfront will be a precondition for taking the indispensable next steps in hospital development. In that regard, shifting towards explicit new governance rules will be both a symptom and a tool for moving in the right direction. The identification of models of care and business, plus the review of hospital ownership and payment methods will be crucial steps.

References

Baghdadi-Sabeti, G., & Serhan, F. (2010). *WHO Good Governance for Medicines Programme: An Innovative Approach to Prevent Corruption in the Pharmaceutical Sector*. Geneva: World Health Organization. World Health Report, Background Paper, 25.

Barlow, J., Roehrich, J., & Wright, S. (2013). Europe Sees Mixed Results from Public-Private Partnerships for Building and Managing Health Care Facilities and Services. *Health Affairs, 32*(1). https://doi.org/10.1377/hlthaff.2011.1223.

Christensen, C. (2009). *The Innovator's Prescription a Disruptive Solution for Healthcare*. New York: McGraw Hill.

Deaton, A. (2003). Health, Inequality, and Economic Development. *Journal of Economic Literature, 41*(1), 113–158.

Duran, A., & La Forgia, J. (2016). Challenges and Lessons in Public Hospital Governance and Management in China. In China Joint Study Partnership: World Bank Group, World Health Organization, Ministry of Finance, National Health and Family Planning Commission, Ministry of Human Resources and Social Security. *Deepening Health Reform in China: Building High Quality and Value-Based Service Delivery*, Policy Summary. Retrieved from https://openknowledge.worldbank.org/bitstream/handle/10986/24720/HealthReformInChina.pdf?sequence=6.

Duran, A., & Saltman, R. B. (2013). Innovative Strategies in Governing Public Hospitals. *Eurohealth, 19*(1), 3–7. Retrieved March 5, 2019, from http://www.euro.who.int/__data/assets/pdf_file/0018/186021/EuroHealth-v19-n1.pdf.

Duran, A., Saltman, R. B., & Dubois, H. F. W. (2011). A Framework for Assessing Hospital Governance. In R. B. Saltman, A. Duran, & H. F. W. Dubois (Eds.), *Governing Public Hospitals, Reform Strategies and the Movement Towards Institutional Autonomy* (Observatory Studies Series No. 25) (p. 38). Brussels: European Observatory on Health Systems and Policies.

Ezzamel, M., & Reed, M. (2008). Governance: A Code of Multiple Colours. *Human Relations, 61*(5), 597–615.

Gordon, J. S. (2004). *An Empire of Wealth: The Epic History of American Economic Power*. New York: HarperCollins.

Hood, C. (1991). A Public Management for All Seasons? *Public Administration, 69*(1), 3–19.

Ikegami, N. (2014). *Universal Health Coverage for Inclusive and Sustainable Development – Lessons from Japan*. Washington, DC: The World Bank. Chapter 9. Retrieved August 18, 2017, from http://documents.worldbank.org/curated/en/2014/09/20278271/universal-health-coverage-inclusive-sustainable-development-lessons-japan.

Ikegami, N., Yoo, B. K., Hashimoto, H., Matsumoto, M., Ogata, H., et al. (2011). Japanese Universal Health Coverage: Evolution, Achievements, and Challenges. *Lancet, 378*(9796), 1106–1115. Retrieved August 18, 2017, from https://www.thelancet.com/journals/lancet/article/PIIS0140-6736(11)60828-3/fulltext.

Kaufmann, D., Kray, A., & Mastruzzi, M. (2010). *The Worldwide Governance Indicators: Methodology and Analytical Issues.* Washington, DC: The Brookings Institution.

La Forgia, J., Harding, A., & Hawkins, L. (2000). *Organizational Reform of Hospitals: Overview of Cross Country Experience.* Washington, DC: The World Bank. World Bank Flagship Program in Health Sector Reform and Sustainable Financing.

Mintzberg, H. (1996). Managing Government, Governing Management. *Harvard Business Review, 74*(3), 75–83.

Nye, J., & Donahue, J. (2000). *Governance in a Globalizing World.* Washington, DC: Brookings Institution.

Osborne, D., & Gaebler, T. (1992). *Re-inventing Government.* New York: Addison-Wesley.

Peters, B. G. (2004). Back to the Centre? Rebuilding the State. In A. Gamble & T. Wright (Eds.), *Restarting the State* (pp. 130–140). London: Blackwell Publishing.

Preker, A., & Harding, A. (Eds.). (2003). *Innovations in Health Service Delivery, The Corporatization of Public Hospitals* (p. 25). Washington, DC: The World Bank.

Rhodes, R. A. W. (1996). The New Governance; Governing without Government. *Political Studies, XLIV*, 652–667.

Richards, D., & Smith, M. (2002). *Governance and Public Policy in the UK.* Oxford: Oxford University Press.

Saltman, R. B., Duran, A., & Dubois, H. F. W. (Eds.). (2011). *Governing Public Hospitals, Reform Strategies and the Movement Towards Institutional Autonomy.* Brussels: European Observatory on Health Systems and Policies, Observatory Studies Series No. 25, 38.

West, D., Villasenor, J., & Schneider, J. (2017, January 5). *Spurring Private Investment in Global Health Research and Development.* Washington, DC: The Brookings Institution TechTank.

WHO – World Health Organization. (2000). *World Health Report 2000. Health System Improving Performance.* Geneva: World Health Organization.

WHO – World Health Organization. (2013, April 19). *Sixty-Sixth World Health Assembly Draft Twelfth General Programme of Work.* Geneva: World Health Organization, A66/6, Provisional Agenda Item 12.2.

Woods, N. (2000). The Challenge of Good Governance for the IMF and the World Bank Themselves. *World Development, 28*(5), 823–841.

World Bank. (2002). *World Development Report 2002. Building Institutions for Markets.* Washington, DC: Oxford University Press.

CHAPTER 3

Models of Care and Hospitals

Antonio Durán and Stephen Wright

Introduction

Omnipresent pain and death since the beginning of human existence explain the universal need in all societies to develop *health* services, that is, including healthcare services. Historically, as outlined in Chap. 1, advances in health status were mostly due to operating on the "determinants of health" amenable to inter-sectoral actions (more balanced nutrition, better housing and environment, between individual and social habits, improvements in availability of information and education, higher income etc.), but were almost not at all directly related to healthcare proper (Dubos 1959; McKeown 1965, 1979). This pattern was confirmed virtually everywhere, both in what would then become developed countries and in developing countries (Preston 1980; Evans et al. 1994).

In different cultures, a myriad of *visions* have dealt with how to stay healthy but also with how to get cured when sick and so on. In addition

A. Durán (✉)
ALLDMHEALTH, Seville, Spain
e-mail: aduran@alldmh.com

S. Wright
Independent Consultant, Ingleton, UK
e-mail: steve.wright@echaa.eu

A. Durán, S. Wright (eds.), *Understanding Hospitals in Changing Health Systems*, https://doi.org/10.1007/978-3-030-28172-4_3

to "factors not directly related to health care", therefore, the social response to health needs has also involved various healthcare proposals, typically structured in care "levels" including community, primary, secondary and so on. A range of personal and population health *services*,[1] some of them of private and others of public and semi-public economic nature[2] (Moon et al. 2017) have been variously established to cater for health problems. Such diverse forms of healthcare applied the knowledge, technology, innovation, equipment, skills and so on of the day, and have been organized in variable ways (Duran and Kutzin 2010).

Specific formulations of all the above using symbolic figures (e.g. the figures of Hygieia and Asklepios in ancient Greece) remain a source of inspiration against the challenges of the twenty-first century regarding the need for a balance between health-enhancing activities on the one hand and caring for the sick on the other, between preventative versus curative approaches and so on (Frenk and Gomez Dantés 2016). That is how the contemporary concept of health system emerged, as defined by the World Health Report 2000 (WHO 2000)—namely, "the ensemble of *All organizations, institutions and resources devoted to producing 'health actions'—any effort, whether in personal healthcare, public health services or through inter-sectoral initiatives, whose primary purpose is to improve (promote, restore or maintain) health*".

It is accepted that the core end-objective or key outcome target of each health system is/should be the maintenance, or preferably increase, of health status (measured at collective and individual levels) in the maximum number of the target population.[3] The WHO 2000 report predicates

[1] Depending on whether the services are delivered to individuals (personal health services, like in an appendicitis operation) or to entire populations (like in sanitation and sewage).

[2] Depending on whether the benefits from the delivered services accrue just to the person receiving them (private goods, in the parlance of economics), or extend beyond to others (services with externalities) or the entire population (public goods). As a function of whether the good is excludable (i.e. can a party be stopped from consuming it?) or rivalrous (i.e. does its consumption reduce its availability for others or not?), economists often speak about four kinds of entities—namely, private goods (e.g. pills and syringes), club goods (e.g. knowledge protected by patent), common goods (e.g. universal healthcare), and public goods (e.g. public information or pandemic preparedness).

[3] One way of caricaturizing this is to posit that each individual has maximum health status at birth and it goes downhill from there to reach zero at the point of death. The formulation does beg all sorts of questions about the impact of health systems on distribution across the population and the equity of this, as there are evidently sick babies—these issues are best avoided for the purpose of this note.

that every health system is supposed to pursue some *goals*, the most important ones of which are health-related (level and equity of health), but protecting citizens from the catastrophic financial consequences of fighting disease (i.e. providing "coverage") and responding efficiently to citizens' expectations/client orientation in the non-medical sphere are also included.

The proposition linking goals with what in the industrial world are called "functions" (sets of repeated activities and tasks to achieve the former) can be formulated in simple words by saying: "Access to and coverage for effective services plus better individual and population health will be achieved *if* the necessary inputs and resources are adequately created, *if* the system is properly financed so that people are protected and *if* services are provided in sufficient quantity and quality *while* regulation and stewardship mechanisms respond to people's expectations and preferences". Thus the achievement of health system objectives, in the World Health Report 2000, depends on four central *functions*, namely: (1) service production, (2) finance, (3) regulation/stewardship and (4) input creation/development (see diagrammatic picture in Fig. 1.1 in Chap. 1).

The way in which service production facilities are articulated at territorial level, the split between the public and the private sectors, what services are produced and to whom they are offered, but also where are they located and so on, are some of the (various) keys to a good system *performance* (Murray and Evans 2003).[4] This chapter will address the physical way in which healthcare and hospitals support/develop the changing health status in modern societies, and the policy issues this raises in terms of combination of inputs.

Throughout this book, the distinction between *outcomes* ("end-objectives", as used above) and *outputs* is worth emphasizing; outcomes are more important, but outputs are usually easier to determine and the more direct element of our interest. A significant contribution which this book makes is to elaborate the link between creating (perhaps more properly said, mobilizing) resources and the delivery/provision of services by hospitals in particular, as a key part of the system (though the idea works across all elements of healthcare delivery too). The book will lay out

[4] The measurement of how a health system performs requires (1) ascertaining what goals are achieved; (2) determining what resources have been used to obtain them; (3) estimating the efficiency with which resources were used to achieve those results; (4) assessing the extent to which functions influence the achievement and efficiency observed and (5) designing and implementing policies to improve those achievements and their efficiency.

a way to categorize how *resources* are used to produce *health services*. As explained in Chap. 1, there is a physical dimension to this (the actual processes of care applied to patients—the *model(s) of care*)—and a socioeconomic dimension to it as well (which includes the cost of the resources used and the perceived value created—the *business model(s)*).

This chapter is structured as follows:

- After this introduction, the notion of *model(s) of care* will be explained.
- The next section will address how modern *healthcare models* took shape.
- The (rather frequent) misunderstanding of these issues will be expressed through the misleading labels often applied to "hospitals".
- The chapter will close, identifying how the above notions have affected *models of care in hospitals* and the decision-making challenges it still raises today.

A Guiding Thread for the Book: Models of Care (and Their Input to Models of Business)

As discussed in Chap. 1, in our study of hospitals as a service industry, we lean on the analysis, models and thinking approaches used to study other sectors of economic importance; modern healthcare is *also* an industry which creates outputs by consuming a variety of *factors of production* (capital stock in terms of infrastructure and equipment, human capital in terms of skilled or crude labour, materials, utilities and energy). Notably, the pattern of use of factors of production in healthcare varies. In some cases such as in primary care, it is predominantly labour—often but not always highly skilled); at the other end of the spectrum, a more technology- and capital-intensive domain is what we currently characterize as "the hospital".

A *model of care* is a theoretical construct describing or prescribing how healthcare is expected physically to be delivered. This can have a number of subtly different interpretations—the patient's pathway to and through services; clinical decision rules about what treatments to offer to whom and when, and by whom; conceptualization and organization of services; and procedures to allocate service resources at system level (University of Otago 2010). In any event, a model of care—or at least, a good one—will necessarily incorporate elements such as evidence-based practice, quality improvement and project management, and it will take on board issues of health promotion and disease management (see the literature survey in Davidson et al. 2006).

One setting is distinguished from another in the combinations of factors of production, which are mixed together via the respective appropriate *process routes* in each of them. For our purposes, then, a hospital is thus a place with a set of factors of production used to deliver certain process routes—that is, the setting, compared with others, with the highest levels of physical capital, human capital and technological intensity supporting certain healthcare processes, articulated in particular ways. The hospital's model of care exists in the wider, system-wide model of care. Indeed, setting a model of care for one part of a health system necessarily impacts on, and may decide, the feasible model of care for other parts; see also the discussion in Chap. 9 on decision analysis for what this may mean on the ground.

No grouping of factors of production constituting a *model of care* (no *healthcare processes*, as per the parlance of this chapter) carries any implication as to whether a given hospital facility is *on the production frontier* to help deliver health status or, more directly, healthcare outputs, better relative to other hospitals or to other ways of delivery.[5] In classic economic descriptions, there might be two inputs (e.g. "labour" and "capital")—this is easy to show graphically, but in principle large numbers of inputs can be accommodated in the analysis. Varying ratios of these inputs will produce varying amounts of outputs. When the system is working efficiently, the feasible levels of output will typically be convex to the origin. Less efficient results are inside the frontier: the system could unambiguously do better. Health system and hospital efficiency can be tested with a number of statistical techniques, of which the best known is data envelopment analysis (Fragkiadakis et al. 2016; Barros et al. 2007; Peacock et al. 2001; Jacobs 2000). Such analyses normally show that, within any one country, large proportions of the hospitals will be in some sense "inefficient". Again, Chap. 9 deals with the topic of comparative efficiency analysis in more depth.

A key result of this book should hopefully be progress in determining what should be in the hospital and what should be elsewhere. Thus, any one hospital and certainly departments within it could well be some way *inside the frontier* and therefore by definition inefficient. Should they

[5] The production frontier is what the system at the limit *can* create as output from a given set of inputs.

remain in that state? As it will be seen in more detail in Chaps. 7 and 8, the point is that cultural issues will often determine what a system is asked to do and how it responds, what is acceptable and what is not, and so on. Changes in demography, epidemiology, income and lifestyle "invite" the expectations of the population for health status (and the associated processes of care) to grow unrestrictedly. Technology and innovation are developed to establish long-term mechanisms in order to improve health services to satisfy patients' demands while fulfilling the health policy of the country.

For those reasons, the health system will tend to incorporate new technologies and in general more inputs in the prescriptions of how healthcare is expected to be physically delivered, with the obvious correlate of increasing costs. The usual next step is that those inflationary trends will usually find ways to twin the policy and political expectations of decision-makers. As hospitals are at the "technological end of the scale" regarding what the country's health facilities and institutions could achieve, rising expectations—including patients' demands and the technological capability of hospitals—will get aligned in the "hope" that society will be able to pay for it.

Healthcare would be rather more like many other industries if there were valid prices for outputs and for the costs for all the relevant factors of production (reflecting opportunity cost, among other things). But healthcare is different from (most) other service activities; it is almost a truism that healthcare cannot satisfactorily operate as a true market, and certainly not one which is "perfectly competitive" (Arrow 1963). Health and healthcare are permeated with *uncertainty*, and there is *asymmetry* between patients as *principals* and medical professionals acting as the *agents* simultaneously providing necessary advice but with a financial stake in the outcome. Healthcare rights also complicate the bargaining between the parties, as does the fact that patients rarely (in the West; less so in many developing markets) pay the full cost of healthcare, which indeed shades their sensitivity to prices.[6]

[6] A series of protocols attempts to manage the conflicts which emerge from this institutional framework—professionalism, not-for-profit status, prohibition of advertising, prohibition of price competition, imperfect or no obligation for any guarantee of outcomes. In practice, about the only things observable to patients as consumers are, on the one hand, the quality of the amenities and, on the other, the professionals' interpersonal skills (not surprisingly, whilst public hospitals often cannot afford to pay great attention to these aspects within their ruling tariff, many private hospitals do so).

In practice, about the only things which are readily observable to patients as consumers are, on the one hand, the quality of the amenities and, on the other, the interpersonal skills of the professionals. Not surprisingly, many private hospitals pay great attention to these aspects, whilst public hospitals often cannot afford to do so within their ruling tariff. The role of the medical professional as an agent to a necessarily less-informed principal creates a solution-oriented, supply mindset, and allows significant—apparently unexplained—variability in performance. This is unlike most consumer-facing industries/markets, where there is drive from consumer needs creating information-enriched expectations which providers have to face (Castano 2014), and this typically evens out variation in delivery.

In the absence of many of the needed prices guiding the system, surrogates need to be invoked. In healthcare or any other sector, this issue of "valuing" both the output generated and the resources used just says that the resources used need to be accounted for, and then compared with the value created. These (implicit) prices are of course part of the social arrangements between stakeholders (consumers of the services and owners of the factors of production)—see Chap. 2 on governance. Also, in complementarity to the notion of "model of care", *business models* analyse how resources *are used to create economic and financial value*. The above introduced models of care framework concerns the physical processes used to meet the demand for care, but cannot be used on their own to make sustainable decisions in the running of the system—especially in the medium-to-long term. In this situation, policy (and management) decisions are only possible by moving into questions of cost of resource use and value of the benefits created; only then will it be possible to choose between differing desired potential states, that is, the various *alternative* models of care in the system. Sustainability considerations make this more than a simple cost-benefit analysis, and that is where the notion of business model will come into play (see Chap. 4).

Payment mechanisms have been extensively studied, sometimes considered almost as magic solutions in the hope that hospital professionals would *mostly* react to economic incentives. OECD studies (OECD 2016) on payment mechanisms, among others, show some good results, but with caveats that there are no magic bullets (see Chap. 6 of this volume).

A Chronological Account of How Specialized Health Needs Servicing Was Developed

Honouring the famous reference that "The further back you look, the better you will be able to see the future" (Morris 2010), a good way to *understand* the above issues in service provision is by analysing its modalities and its "changing societal goals/functions" through history.

The resources meant to be combined (labour/intellectual power and capital *as factors of production*) have determined models of personal care since the early ages. Primary care (which provides the first level of care) has lived for centuries within the model of individual clinics and similar institutions, paradigmatically visible in the figure of Hippocrates as a wandering physician, an extreme representation of the predominant dominance of the labour element in his job.

For hospitals, it is remarkable that their initial objective as institutions (before gaining professional/clinical and socio-political prestige) was essentially "hosting" (hence the name *hospedale* from the Latin *hospitium*) poor patients—especially in their waiting for death. Hospitals had two objectives above providing healthcare—one ethical (showing mercy) and another social (cleaning out the streets of the dying poor).

In Italy, "ospedali" were frequently annexed to monasteries as they also carried out social functions (raising orphans, distributing food to the poor, and practicing herbal medicine). The Florentine "Ospedale di Santa Maria Nuova" was first founded in 1288 mainly to service pilgrims. "*Magna Domus Hospitalis* (*Ca' Granda*—the 'great house')" is one of the first "modern age" hospitals—a legacy of the Renaissance. Created in Milan in 1456, it had three wards for men and one for women, with individual rooms, water and sanitary facilities (Cosmacini 1999). One of the signature buildings for Milan that still exists today, it had the classical cross-shaped architectural design ("*crociera*") of ancient basilicas, with a central altar and crucifix which all patients could see; people received confession and forgiveness for their sins before being admitted, and were treated by doctors as well as surgeons (Albini and Gazzini 2011). When after 1495 a dark period ensued with wars of religion and epidemics devastating the Italian peninsula, several cities built "*lazzaretti*" to confine lepers and pestilence victims outside the city walls. Only after the 1800s did hospitals begin to admit communicable diseases patients, earlier confined in the *lazzaretti*, and built wards to keep these patients in isolation.

In Spain, resources were also dedicated during several centuries to "social/charitable—as opposed to strictly medical—purposes". The efforts often involved remarkable proportions visible, for example, in the 400+ bedded Hospital of the Five Wounds or "*de la Sangre*" in Seville, founded in 1559 and now the building of the Andalusian Parliament. As health institutions proper, however, hospitals at the beginning of the nineteenth century were still far from exemplary, as noted by the Minister of Finance of the day: "Anyone who has a home, a family, a friend, does not need a hospital at all—he will be better taken care of in his home" (López Alonso 1990).

The description of the first hospital in Pennsylvania, United States, co-founded in 1752 by Benjamin Franklin, offers a similar picture: "a cramped, chaotic place, the last place where any respectable person would want to be in (…) where medical experiments are carried out with people who had nowhere else to go to die" (Rosenberg 1987).

More specifically in terms of "models of care", in those institutions:

- doctors and medical science had a very limited technical arsenal. The microscope had been invented by van Leeuwenhoek in 1668, but when in 1854 an outbreak of cholera took place in Broad Street, London, John Snow, who eventually would control the outbreak, still did not accept microbes as a cause of illness (Snow 1855);
- Surgeons were little more than barbers who in their extra hours pulled teeth and performed amputations—without anaesthesia, as inhaled anaesthesia was first used in England in 1846 (the above-mentioned John Snow used it in 1852 with Queen Victoria during the births of her eighth and ninth children) (Caton 2000);
- Those who actually ran the hospital (the "nurses") were literally Sisters of Mercy; Florence Nightingale set up the first non-religious nursing school in London's Saint Thomas Hospital only in 1860, establishing the foundations of a solid nursing profession (Funnell et al. 2008);
- After Semmelweis' pioneer work in Vienna, Pasteur's discoveries took years to have impact on hospital practice; only in 1865 did Joseph Lister start applying his discoveries to remove living organisms from wounds and surgical incisions; Pasteur himself recommended military hospitals to boil instruments, bandages and laboratory equipment in a so-called "Pasteur furnace" only in 1871;

- Roentgen discovered X-rays in 1895 and Hoffman synthesized aspirin in 1899 (though the white willow bark was a medicinal product against fever and pain since Hippocrates, and impure acetylsalicylic acid was used for decades);
- The serendipitous discovery of penicillin by Fleming only took place in the 1930s.

Beyond strong anecdotes, some relevant facts are valuable here. Patients almost only depended on doctors' "knowledge" rather than evidence-based practice or scientifically established protocols at the beginning of the twentieth century, as few hospitals had any antisepsis, laboratory, radiology or pharmacology. Having patients deposited in galleries full of beds was the only difference between the *models of care within hospital buildings* and in *single clinics*. This "alms houses phase" of hospitals only moved to a "curative care with emphasis on diagnostics and surgery phase" *with the birth of modern hospital medicine*.

In London, the Westminster and Guy's hospitals developed in the nineteenth century into complex organizations that combined care and treatment of the patient with research, teaching and education of the corresponding staff, opening the way to becoming modern university centres. This change of the model of care critically *depended on the introduction of four capital-intensive components* (McKee and Healy 2002):

1. Operating rooms for safe surgery, feasible because of the combination of anaesthesia and antisepsis;
2. Laboratories of biochemistry, haematology and bacteriology;
3. Departments of imaging/radiology (x-ray and other devices);
4. Emergency departments, increasingly introduced over the years with a profile running up to trauma management (ambulances were first experimented with by Union troops during the US Civil War, based on the idea that it might be a good thing to go quickly to a hospital in case of emergency).

Putting together in the same building resources and specialized professionals to handle these four capital-intensive "functionalities" made sense because:

- Once an operating room is installed, more working hours distribute costs among more cases (with lower unit costs and better use of resources—so-called "economies of scale"). Also, a hospital with specialties such as cardiology, pneumology and so on and good emergency services can treat, for example, serious childhood pathologies immediately after childbirth (leveraging infrastructures allows for better quality outcomes in several departments—these are "economies of scope/reach");

- Internal economies of scale and scope (as well as external economies of scale and network effects—*economies of agglomeration* in more recent literature) provided the fertile ground for the birth of new institutions. Doing so facilitated the dissemination of best practices and technological know-how, shifting from osmotic education of professionals to providing *structured training* in teaching hospitals—"see one, do one, teach one" (Duran 2009);
- Doctors understood from the beginning the significance of these propositions. Physicians gave high importance to accessing hospitals—much less direct in Europe than one might imagine, with continuous professional conflicts (Abel-Smith 1964). In the first half of the twentieth century, it was also common for (groups of) physicians jointly to create private clinics if they did not have access to other types of hospital property in which to practice (Jeurissen 2010).

For decades, how to handle the four particularly capital-intensive components (operating theatres, laboratories, imaging, ED) remained a nuclear issue in configuring/arranging hospitals functionally. Modern institutions with *changed model(s) of care* were created as a result of a rather serendipitous combination of factors over which economies of scope and scale would play (patients available, professionals interested, technology being developed, and willingness to pay for it all). Economies of scope in particular were crucial because they (help to) explain why activities cluster in the hospital rather than separately, or anywhere else.

Hospitals became set up by a process where (voluntary) capital merged gradually with the human capital of the academically-trained physicians of the day. In each country, hospitals entailed specific combinations of the public and private sectors, the medical and nursing professions and so on. Qualified staff and asset-specific investments and technology were core elements of the "service delivery response model". The fact that the response was eminently private in the US and more public in Europe did not alter the fact that *specific* groupings of *factors of production* enabled the hospital, as an institution, to produce care *in a way that other arrangements could not do, or not do as efficiently*.

At first, then, physician clinics and hospitals lived immersed in what is now called ***intuitive medicine***, with highly qualified physicians using their analytical skills to recommend solutions through trial and error after diagnosing the likely cause of problems. As equipment and process innovation developed, the technological or production frontier (defined earlier) progressively shifted outwards. Compared to the physician clinic, the hospital always had more technology available, and usually the patient was separated from his/her normal environment. Both locations moved first to *empirical* and then to *precision* medicine (Christensen et al. 2009), as science and technology started providing new operating frameworks during the twentieth century. Models of care differences—derived from being at opposite ends of the labour versus capital continuum—increased, and this irrespective of ownership (i.e. comparable trends occurred in state-controlled Europe and private health USA—see Chap. 8).

Misleading Labels for Hospitals

The first wave of battles in search of social legitimacy for hospitals was against the plagues that affected humanity in the early twentieth century: high infant mortality due to poor maternal and childbirth conditions, infectious diseases, work-related trauma to middle-aged adults due to accidents and violence, and so on. The development of antibiotics further contributed to make the first hospitals successful in the face of their communities. As hospitals silently demonstrated the solvency of their updated model(s) of care, they increasingly became the *site of reference* where birth would face less risk, infections could be cured, serious injuries would best resolve and so on. Their social prestige grew exponentially after World War II, when heavy capital investment by government in buildings, technology and qualified personnel improved their financial and functional strength (Duran 2005).

In barely a few decades, the first kidney transplant, beta-blockers, laser treatment, coronary by-pass and heart transplant showed the increasing competence of science-based medicine. From just four specialties, the general hospital became home to more than a dozen, for a correspondingly growing catchment population. After a trip with different departure points, speeds and itineraries, the old "alms houses"/"poor old people's homes" which had been structured essentially as associations of senior physicians *consolidated their key assets*: intermediate-care and outpatient consultation units around central emergency departments, operating rooms and specialized equipment—soon increased with intensive (ICU) and critical care (UCC) units. Nobody else could do what they did, while their model of care was glossed with admiration in films and television series:

- In rich countries, such developments came indeed with significant costs. By the early 1970s, hospitals had jumped from absorbing a marginal part of the wider economy to costing 2–4% of GDP. Despite the call in the late 1970s in the Alma Ata Conference to redirect attention to primary healthcare, hospitals reached the centre of the medical scene across the globe through a myriad of mechanisms (World Health Organization 2008);
- In developing countries (many formal or informal colonies), hospitals were established through combined initiatives by the colonial/master power and charity institutions, often in favour of particular groups (mother and children, people affected by specific infectious diseases etc.). Political economy logic made them part of the public sector in districts or similar territories, overseen by various government levels. Hospitals were usually surrounded by a multitude of solo practices, or nurse-run primary care centres, mostly poorly-operated and not interacting much with each other. Some vertical programmes (mainly mother and child, but also TB, etc.) completed the picture (Atun et al. 2008). Substantial out-of-pocket (OOP) financing favoured an emerging private sector which dwelled on the profitable market segment(s) in urban areas, but private sector hospitals were at first smaller and worse equipped than public ones (only rarely—until recently—would owners have the capital for major investments).

Some governments complicated things by allowing duplications, overlaps and substantial imbalances in periods of expansion—for example, a never-ending race to over-equip them, sometimes by stealth, irrespective of their planned role, oversupply in certain areas, mono-thematic centres of questionable effectiveness for certain diseases and so on. In one post-Soviet Union country, official statistics still record 34 hospital categories, depending on the service they provide, the population they serve and so on (OECD 2018).

Needless to say, in the last few decades, the situation has evolved but—perhaps as a consequence of their fast emergence—the name "hospital" now covers a broad wide range of institutions with different technological endowments and models of care. Someone who applied engineering principles to hospital analysis described them as "very complex systems scarcely understood, extremely expensive and filled with inefficiencies" (Kopach-Konrad et al. 2007). A significant problem in this regard is that most definitions of what a hospital is are superficial: a multiplicity of meanings limit comparability and often give operations within the walls of so-called hospital a confusing overtone (referred to in Chap. 1).

In this context—as also explained in Chap. 1—perhaps the most frequent problem in defining hospitals is the mistaken use of *attributes*. As indicated, one of the typical examples is measuring inputs as the number of beds—still a common parlance to express hospital size despite the fact that beds as a defining criterion have seen their validity drastically reduced as hospitals have developed their capacities separated from such an input (Rechel et al., op. cit.). Also, saying that a hospital is "a healthcare facility that provides inpatient health services *with at least 10 beds* and operates with continuous supervision of patients and delivery of medical care, 24 hours a day, 7 days a week" (Center for Global Development 2015) is very arbitrary.

Arguments from correlation and not causality are also frequent, with ad hoc definitions without any explanatory concept. Note that there are other parts of the healthcare system (e.g. imaging centres), which are also highly capital-intensive, but are not sensibly "hospitals" because their production is constrained to certain care components (capital intensity again is an attribute here, not a function). In a wider sense, the technology of a primary or secondary/tertiary healthcare setting has two different elements:

1. that which is embedded in its *capital equipment*, and
2. that which is embedded in the nature of the used *process routes.*

They are closely related, but not the same (knowledge can suggest new ways of doing things with or without the need for new equipment or materials). At either the system or the facility/institution level, the two manifestations of healthcare technologies are synonymous with *model(s) of care*.

In our view, hospitals need to be categorized by what they do—that is, by *functions* ("sets of repeated activities and tasks needed to achieve certain distinctive goals and objectives", such as diagnosing, treating, etc.) which they intend to *achieve their goal(s),* and by *processes.* The real **capacity of a hospital is its ability to do work**, and this cannot be determined based on just one or other parameter; it is a system modelling problem; focusing on the model(s) of care hospitals delivers and the goals they pursue should help clarify the necessary *decision-making process* they pose, which we will return to in Chap. 9.

In brief, again, hospitals are complex dynamic systems and cannot be characterized by one static feature. In the current state of knowledge, the truth is that it is impossible to state or even calculate what the capacity of a hospital actually is (and without a *real* ability to assess capacity, how could one possibly know how much of it to build or maintain?).

Supply and Demand at Play, and Recently Affecting Hospital Models of Care

It has already been explained that in each given environment (societal and economic), hospitals respond to *demand-driven* (for health status and more directly for better healthcare outputs) as well as by *supply-driven* factors. Since most healthcare systems have limited responsiveness, the flexibility of the supply/production response to a shift in demand is smaller in the short than in the medium-to-long term. In the latter, investments in new physical and human capital and other resources might change the effective deployable quantities of factors of production and their combinations (the *process* routes) trying to adopt new and more capable technologies as and when they become available. All this is even more true in an era dominated by chronic multi-morbidity, shifting from "industrial" processes to "digitalization and ICT technologies", genome sequencing, personalized medicine and so on, opening up the issue of the unresolved position which this book is trying to address.

Hospitals emerged messily out of historical accident, but a discussion of what they can/should contribute should also include the re-drafting of hospital boundaries, sculpted by epidemiological and demographic changes. Hospitals began to experience intense *pressures for change* barely a few decades after their transition to centre stage in the healthcare scene, with many of those pressures having technological, epidemiological and sociological foundations in the context of their respective health system, while others were related to their general organization, running of facilities and models of care. As a consequence, the complexity of hospitals has increased exponentially, with whole parts of the organization responding to divergent incentives and operating schemes, requiring assets, procedures and human capacities aligned with different demands. Each unit often tends to offer as many services as possible, in a permanent expansionary strategy.

Experience in many sectors (and theory by very different authors!) demonstrates the arguable economic viability when almost all facilities try to produce virtually all and any types of services, thus failing to exploit economies of scale and scope—be it in "search for any possible source of income" that should be funded through price and volume increases (US cliché) or by generating chronic deficits that "in the end will be financed by the public purse, hopefully" (Europe cliché). The *planned* technical capacity of the hospital is supposed to be directly correlated with the prevalent type of staff and with the infrastructure—especially equipment and sophisticated technology.

As archetypal models, one could orient the hospital towards (1) complex services of low (epidemiological) frequency, high variation and cost/case, (2) high (epidemiological) frequency, relatively low complexity and variation and rather low cost/case performed according to a standard steps sequence, or (3) mostly chronic cases where care rather than cure is the objective, in close network with other hospitals, elderly nursing homes, and primary healthcare delivery.

In developed countries (and increasingly in middle-income countries), improvements in life expectancy have deeply changed disease patterns and service needs in recent decades (WHO 2016). Some decades back, in addition to suffering higher infant mortality, people died at younger ages (Newey et al. 2004; Levi et al. 2007; Parker and Thorslund 2007). Many countries are also confronting at the moment higher volumes of cancer, senile dementia and poly-medications, hip fractures, cerebrovascular accidents, and other so-called chronic diseases. Few service delivery institutions have been more ready to *adapt to their changing social and economic contexts* than hospitals—they have undergone since their modern incarnation many dynamic changes, contingent on the circumstances of each country, rather than being static and rigidly prescriptive. Given both the prestige and direct economic benefits that modern hospitals carry with them, such adaptations have been accompanied/supplemented by internal and external political pressures.

Linking hospitals to the rest of the system gave shape to the *proto*-response in all this process of change; the idea of substituting traditional models of care with other forms of care, advocated, for example, in the Dutch Dekker Report (Ministry of Welfare, Health and Cultural Affairs 1988; Warner 1996): the objective was to move as many processes as possible out of the core building, linking the outpatient and day-care sectors to patient needs, and meanwhile looking for "savings". There have been proposals to set up "hospital process re-engineering" via clinical protocols, multidisciplinary care teams, cross-training, integrated registries and grouping of homogeneous patients, emphasis in decentralized decision-making within the hospital, and even a certain design/redesign of the physical environment (Walston and Kimberly 1997).

A similar purpose led to the idea to establish closer links between "inside and outside the hospital", called *transmural care* in the Netherlands (van der Linden et al. 2001). In England, the closing from 1982 to 1998 of 154,479 hospital beds coincided with the creation of 153,119 other beds in privately owned but (partly) publicly funded "nursing homes" (Hensher and Edwards 1999). Between 1973 and 2003, the total number of beds in England (acute, chronic, psychiatric, etc.) was reduced by approximately one half (Macfarlane et al. 2005), but 90% of all "nursing home" beds' residents in 2007 were already accommodated in independent housing, compared with 88% in 2003 and only 20% in 1993 (NHS Digital 2008). Many hospitals reduced the number of acute beds even while increasing the intensity of care, and treated more people with the same resources (OECD 2015).

Epidemiological and demographic changes have also had an impact. With pathologies amenable to behavioural change, the criticism is that "the *service modalities* available to many people with long-term conditions are characterized by their high dependency on acute care, their singularly clinical focus, their reactive character, their fragmented and sporadic nature, their lack of emphasis on personal experience and the residual character of community services and secondary prevention" (sic) (Wilson et al. 2005).

The response by hospitals to the pressures by educated and informed consumers has often involved *new service provision models.* Some countries decided to shift the power of decision over part or the entire hospital budget to primary care actors: municipal healthcare and social agencies in Finland, district/sub-district boards in Sweden, primary care trusts and GPs in England (Dowling and Glendinning 2003). The Adel Reform in Sweden decentralized the coordination of hospitals to the municipal community and reduced acute beds, increasing treatment of chronic care in nursing homes (Twaddle 1999). There even was a proposal to "put primary care in the driver's seat" (Saltman et al. 2003). Since the early 1990s, geographically defined alliances of district health boards (DHBs) in New Zealand own and run cooperating public hospitals. This model has had direct influence on Canada, and countries like Holland and Denmark in Europe—with renovated PHC lines of work in support of certain primary care patients—for example, frequent users of hospital emergencies, self-referred and so on (Letford and Ashton 2010).

Participating in "non-traditional" healthcare networks and changing the location of care are also significant. (Almost) the same medical intervention can be provided or, more important, the same healthcare outcome can be achieved in settings which differ considerably in their (physical and human) capital and technology intensity (although there are not yet fully settled "protocols").

Better anaesthetic, laparoscopic procedures and less invasive surgical techniques as well as more efficient organizational schemes are very often provided in day centres and even in the patient's home, outside the hospital walls, so the ratio of scheduled *inpatient* surgeries in American hospitals has continued declining (American Hospital Association 2014). In Europe, some elective/programmed surgeries and, most of all, dialysis and so on are also no longer only inpatient-based hospital treatments by hyper-specialized professionals (National Kidney Foundation 2017). Managing some cancers now requires less expensive hospital support services, such as oral chemotherapy. Pharmaceutical and biochemical advances operate in the fight against diabetes—for example, insulin pump, devices for continuous measurement of blood glucose (Nolte et al. 2006) and against mental illness, like major tranquilizers (Heath 2005).

The fight against incompetent operations has also emerged in some cases as a priority; the core issue now is not necessarily doing new things but rather "doing the same things more efficiently" (Gawande 2009), with less frequent medical errors and shorter recovery times linked to quicker and less invasive treatments and standardized procedures. High added-value activities are designed to optimize results, especially in high frequency, low cost and low variation processes (e.g. arthroscopies, cholecystectomies, herniorrhaphies, etc.). Cataract surgery and many other scheduled ("elective") surgeries in particular have already been operating with minimal hospital stay in most OECD countries for years (Lafortune et al. 2012). Also, specific centres have become highly specialized in the management of some conditions—for example, prostate cancer treatment at the Martini Clinic in Hamburg (Porter and Guth 2012).

Dutch "Independent Treatment Centers" have grown in numbers (from 31 in 2000 to 280 at the end of 2010, with prices 15–20% lower than those of hospitals) after the law covering funding in this area was changed, allowing them to sell their services massively (Maarse et al. 2015). The phenomenon is nurtured by innovations in middle-income countries such as India—for example, cataract treatment (Bhandari et al. 2008) and even in paediatric cardiac surgery (Anand 2009).

There have, finally, been movements looking for economies of scale and scope, less duplication of resources, more effective training, greater market influence and more efficient service provision. The new models of care merge, integrate, or functionally converge several hospitals, creating multi-hospital groups or chains. In the USA and Europe (especially Germany and France), more than 60% of hospitals are now part of some form of partnership, system or network, as defined in the country, with back-office unification and normalization (especially when done by the private sector). In England, a similar phenomenon took place without privatization by means of fusions of neighbouring public centres; between 1997 and 2006, some 112 of 223 short-term general hospitals were "merged" (Angeli and Maarse 2012).

The expansionary process described may well involve other fractions of the health system through various formulations in new models of care, in principle without major economic restrictions. A growing range of "new" comprehensive care services, for example, is thus being suggested/requested across sectoral borders, with emphasis on "continuity of care", "networks and chains with various service providers", "better coordinated (*integrated*) services inside and outside the hospital", "interconnected external consultation models", "good E-health support" and "patient involvement", "emphasis on collective population-based social determinants of health linked to individual illness experience for addressing the global health challenges", "patient-centred care" to "change the paradigm and achieve greater efficiency as well as interventions in an optimal environment, in hospitals, at home or in communities" (sic) (ESG 2014), and so on.

Interestingly, many of these much-trumpeted organizational models seem to have been carried out and presented on ideological bases, while their evaluation only takes place afterwards. A review of 18 randomized controlled trials studied whether "primary care based patient-centred interventions" actually improve outcomes for patients living with multimorbidity; the results were negative (Salisbury et al. 2018).

Have new *models of care* at large improved health? And were the expenditures worth it? In the next chapter, *business models* will be presented, trying to explain in more depth how they shape what healthcare institutions such as hospitals do, or at least should do. The intellectual distinction between the *model of care* and the *business model* is important in enabling us to think about changes in the physical processes separately from the institutional economic arrangements between stakeholders. As it will be seen in the next chapter, each model of care has a physical input "factors of production structure" and a pattern of outputs, but these necessarily carry resource costs and benefits, which always have values (and sometimes prices of some kind) attached. In healthcare, therefore, a model of care will necessarily be associated with a business model to arrange the factors of production and set the outputs (and vice versa, a business model will necessarily does incorporate a model of care).

As it happens, adopting a new model of care often does imply a new business model—but not always, since health services regularly adopt new process routes and kit while keeping the social arrangements intact. Equally, adopting a new business model will often involve a new model of care—but not always immediately.[7] What can definitely be said from this chapter and the next is that to choose a desired model of care (from among the alternatives available) requires thinking through, simultaneously, the desirable business models—and all this without losing sight of the need for adequate *governance*.

[7] For example, the uneven pace of adoption of cataract surgery without hospital admission in OECD countries in the past decade (OECD 2017) shows that, above technical viability per se, some incentive—in this case, in the form of payment modalities—might be needed in order for an improvement to be fully adopted. Similarly, transferring asset ownership by means of a private finance initiative, PFI (see Chap. 5) did not identifiably change most NHS models of care at all—even if perhaps it should have done!

References

Abel-Smith, B. (1964). *The Hospitals, 1800–1948: A Study in Social Administration in England and Wales*. Cambridge: Harvard University Press.

AHA – American Hospital Association. (2014). Chartbook 2014, Trends Affecting Hospitals and Health Systems. Retrieved from www.aha.org/aha/research-and-trends/chartbook/index.html.

Albini, G., & Gazzini, M. (2011). Materiali per la storia dell'Ospedale Maggiore di Milano: le Ordinazioni capitolari degli anni 1456–1498. *Rivista Reti Medievali, 12*(1).

Anand, G. (2009, November 25). The Henry Ford of Heart Surgery. *The Wall Street Journal*. Retrieved March 9, 2019, from http://online.wsj.com/article/SB125875892887958111.html#articleTabs%3Darticle.

Angeli, F., & Maarse, H. (2012, May). Mergers and Acquisitions in Western European Health Care: Exploring the Role of Financial Services Organizations. *Health Policy, 105*(2–3), 265–272. https://doi.org/10.1016/j.healthpol.2012.02.012. Epub March 21.

Arrow, K. J. (1963). Uncertainty and the Welfare Economics of Medical Care. *The American Economic Review, 53*(5), 941–973.

Atun, R., Bennet, S., & Duran, A. (2008). *When Do Vertical (Stand-Alone) Programs Have a Place in Health Systems?* Brussels: European Observatory on Health Systems and Policies. Policy Brief, Health Systems and Policy Analysis. Retrieved from http://www.who.int/management/district/services/WhenDoVerticalProgramsPlaceHealthSystems.pdf.

Barros, C. P., Gomes de Menezes, A., Vieira, J. C., Peypoch, N., & Solonandrasana, B. (2007, March). *An Analysis of Hospital Efficiency and Productivity Growth Using the Luenberger Productivity Indicator*. Bonn: The Institute for the Study of Labor, IZA. Discussion Paper No. 2689. Retrieved from http://repec.iza.org/dp2689.pdf.

Bhandari, A., Dratler, S., Raube, K., & Thulasiraj, R. D. (2008). Specialty Care Systems: A Pioneering Vision for Global Health. *Health Affairs, 27*(4), 964–976.

Castano, R. (2014). Towards a Framework for Business Model Innovation in Health Care Delivery in Developing Countries. *BMC Medicine, 12*, 233. Retrieved from https://bmcmedicine.biomedcentral.com/articles/10.1186/s12916-014-0233-z.

Caton, D. (2000). John Snow's Practice of Obstetric Anaesthesia. *Anaesthesiology, 92*(1), 247–252.

Center for Global Development Hospitals for Health Working Group. (2015). Better Hospitals, Better Health Systems, Better Health, A Proposal for a Global Hospital Collaborative for Emerging Economies. Washington. (Box 1. What Is a Hospital?) Retrieved from http://www.cgdev.org/sites/default/files/Hospitals%20for%20Health,%20Consultation%20Draft.%209.22.14.pdf.

Christensen, C. R., Grossman, J., & Hwang, J. (2009). *The Innovator's Prescription a Disruptive Solution for Healthcare* (pp. 44–68). New York: McGraw Hill.
Cosmacini, G. (1999). *La Ca' Granda de i milanesi. Storia dell'Ospedale Maggiore.* Roma: Laterza.
Davidson, P., Halcomb, E., Hickman, L., Phillips, J., & Graham, B. (2006). Beyond the Rhetoric: What Do We Mean by a 'Model of Care'? *The Australian Journal of Advanced Nursing, 23*(3): 47–55. Retrieved from http://www.ajan.com.au/Vol23/Vol23.3-7.pdf.
Dowling, B., & Glendinning, C. (Eds.). (2003). *The New Primary Care: Modern, Dependable, Successful?* Berkshire: Open University Press.
Dubos, R. (1959). *Mirage of Health: Utopias, Progress, and Biological Change.* New York: Harper & Row.
Duran, A. (2005). *Política y Sistemas Sanitarios* (in Spanish, Health Policies and Systems). Granada: Publicaciones de la Escuela Andaluza de Salud Pública.
Duran, A. (2009). Los hospitales del futuro. *Eidon, 29*, 62–67 (in Spanish).
Duran, A., & Kutzin, J. (2010). Financing of Public Health Services and Programs: Time to Look into the Black Box. In J. jutzin, C. Cashin, & M. Jakab (Eds.), *Implementing Health Financing Reform. Lessons from Countries in Transition* (Observatory Studies Series No. 21) (pp. 245–268). Brussels: European Observatory on Health Systems and Policies. Retrieved from http://www.euro.who.int/__data/assets/pdf_file/0014/120164/E94240.pdf.
ESG – European Steering Group on Sustainable Healthcare. (2014). *Acting Together: A Roadmap for Sustainable Healthcare.* Retrieved from https://www.sustainable-healthcare.com/content-assets/uploads/2016/11/2_Sustainable-Healthcare_EU-White-Paper-short-version-FINAL.pdf.
Evans, R., Barer, M., & Marmor, T. (1994). *Why Are Some People Healthy and Others Not?* New York: Aldine de Gruiter.
Fragkiadakis, G., Doumpos, M., Zopounidis, C., & Germain, C. (2016). Operational and Economic Efficiency Analysis of Public Hospitals in Greece. *Annals of Operations Research, 247*, 787–806. https://doi.org/10.1007/s10479-014-1710-7.
Frenk, J., & Dantés, O. G. (2016). Healthcare or Sickcare: Reestablishing the Balance. *Salud Publica Mex, 58*(1), 84–88. Retrieved from http://president.miami.edu/_assets/pdf/publications/Healthcare-or-sickcare.pdf.
Funnell, R., Koutoukidis, G., & Lawrence, K. (2008). *Tabbner's Nursing Care: Theory and Practice.* Chatswood: Churchill Livingston.
Gawande, A. (2009, June 1). *The Cost Conundrum: What a Texas Town Can Teach Us About Health Care.* New York: The New Yorker Magazine. Annals of Medicine. Retrieved from http://www.newyorker.com/magazine/2009/06/01/the-cost-conundrum.
Heath, D. (2005). *Home Treatment for Acute Mental Disorders: An Alternative to Hospitalization.* New York: Routledge, Taylor & Francis Group.

Hensher, M., & Edwards, N. (1999). Hospital Provision, Activity, and Productivity in England Since the 1980s. *British Medical Journal, 319*. https://doi.org/10.1136/bmj.319.7214.911.
Jacobs, R. (2000, February). *Alternative Methods to Examine Hospital Efficiency: Data Envelopment Analysis and Stochastic Frontier Analysis*. York: University of York. Centre for Health Economics, Discussion Paper CHE DP177. Retrieved from https://www.york.ac.uk/che/pdf/DP177.pdf.
Jeurissen, P. P. T. (2010). *For-Profit Hospitals. A Comparative and Longitudinal Study of the For-Profit Hospital Sector in Four Western Countries*. Rotterdam: Erasmus University. Dissertation.
Kopach-Konrad, R., Lawley, M., Imran Hasan, C., Chakraborty, S., Pekny, J., & Doebbeling, B. N. (2007). Applying Systems Engineering Principles in Improving Health Care Delivery. *Journal of General Internal Medicine, 22*(Suppl. 3), 431–437.
Lafortune, G., Balestat, G., & Durand, A. (2012). *Comparing Activities and Performance of the Hospital Sector in Europe: How Many Surgical Procedures Performed as Inpatient and Day Cases?* Final Report on Work Package II. Paris: OECD Publishing. Retrieved from https://www.oecd.org/health/Comparing-activities-and-performance-of-the-hospital-sector-in-Europe_Inpatient-and-day-cases-surgical-procedures.pdf.
Letford, K., & Ashton, T. (2010, April). Integrated Family Health Centres. *Health Policy Monitor*.
Levi, F., et al. (2007). Continuing Declines in Cancer Mortality in the European Union. *Annals of Oncology, 18*(3), 593–595. https://doi.org/10.1093/annonc/mdl437.
López Alonso, C. (1990). La acción pública no estatal. In Solana (Ed.), *Historia de la Acción Social Pública en España. Beneficencia y Previsión*. Madrid: Ministerio de Trabajo y Seguridad Social, in Spanish.
Maarse, H., Jeurissen, P. P. T., & Ruwaard, D. (2015). Results of the Market-Oriented Reform in the Netherlands: A Review. *Health Economics Policy and Law 2016, 11*(2), 161–178. https://doi.org/10.1017/S1744133115000353. Epub 2015 Aug 17.
Macfarlane, A. J., Goden, S., & Pollock, A. (2005). Are We on Track – Can We Monitor Bed Targets in the NHS Plan for England? *Journal of Public Health, 27*(3), 263–269. https://doi.org/10.1093/pubmed/fdi035.
McKee, M., & Healy, J. (Eds.). (2002). *Hospitals in a Changing Europe*. Buckingham: Open University Press, European Observatory on Health Systems and Policies.
McKeown, T. (1965). *The Modern Rise of the Population*. London: Blackwell Scientific Publications.
McKeown, T. (1979). *The Role of Medicine, Dream, Mirage or Nemesis* (p. 138). Princeton: Princeton University Press.

Ministry of Welfare, Health and Cultural Affairs, The Netherlands. (1988). *Dekker Committee on Changing Health Care in the Netherlands*. Rijswijk: The Netherlands.

Moon, S., Røttingen, J.-A., & Frenk, J. (2017). Global Public Goods for Health: Weaknesses and Opportunities in the Global Health System. *Health Econ Policy Law, 12*, 195–205. https://doi.org/10.1017/S1744133116000451.

Morris, I. (2010). *Quoting Winston Churchill in Morris I. Why the West Rules – For Now* (p. 30). London: Profile Books.

Murray, C. J., & Evans, D. (2003). *Health Systems Performance Assessment: Debates, Methods and Empiricism*. Geneva: World Health Organization.

National Kidney Foundation. (2017, August 25). *A to Z Health Guide: Hemodialysis*. Retrieved from https://www.kidney.org/atoz/content/hemodialysis.

Newey, C., Nolte, E., et al. (2004). *Avoidable Mortality in the Enlarged European Union* (p. 44). London: London School of Hygiene and Tropical Medicine.

NHS Digital. (2008). *Community Care Statistics, Home Help and Care Services for Adults: England, 2007*. Retrieved July 18, 2018, from https://digital.nhs.uk/data-and-information/publications/statistical/community-care-statistics-social-services-activity/community-care-statistics-home-help-and-care-services-for-adults-england-2007.

Nolte, E., Bain, C., & McKee, M. (2006). Diabetes as a Tracer Condition in International Benchmarking of Health Systems. *Diabetes Care, 29*(5), 1007–1011. https://doi.org/10.2337/dc05-1550.

OECD. (2015). *Health at a Glance 2015: OECD Indicators*. Paris: OECD Publishing. https://doi.org/10.1787/health_glance-2015-en.

OECD. (2016). *Focus on Better Ways to Pay for Health Care*. Retrieved July 18, 2018, from https://www.oecd.org/els/health-systems/Better-ways-to-pay-for-health-care-FOCUS.pdf.

OECD. (2017). *Health at a Glance 2017: OECD Indicators*. Paris: OECD Publishing. http://dx.doi.org/10.1787/health_glance-2017-en.

OECD. (2018). Improving the performance of hospital care in Kazakhstan. *OECD Reviews of Health Systems: Kazakhstan 2018* (p. 152). Paris: OECD Publishing. http://dx.doi.org/10.1787/9789264289062-7-en.

Parker, M. G., & Thorslund, M. (2007). Health Trends in the Elderly Population: Getting Better and Getting Worse. *Gerontologist, 47*, 150–158. https://doi.org/10.1093/geront/47.2.150.

Peacock, S., Chan, C., Mangolini, M., & Johansen, D. (2001, July). *Techniques for Measuring Efficiency in Health Services*. Productivity Commission Staff Working Paper. Retrieved from https://www.pc.gov.au/research/supporting/measuring-health-services/tmeihs.pdf.

Porter, M. E., & Guth, C. (2012). *Redefining German Health Care: Moving to a Value-Based System*. Berlin: Springer-Verlag.

Preston, S. H. (1980). Causes and Consequences of Mortality Declines in Less Developed Countries in the Twentieth Century. In R. A. Easterlin (Ed.), *Population and Economic Change in Developing Countries* (p. 315). Chicago: University of Chicago Press.

Rosenberg, C. E. (1987). *The Care of Strangers: The Rise of America's Hospital System*. New York: Basic Books.

Salisbury, C., Man, M. S., Bower, P., Guthrie, B., Chaplin, K., Gaunt, D. M., et al. (2018). Management of Multimorbidity Using a Patient-Centred Care Model: A Pragmatic Cluster-Randomised Trial of the 3D Approach. *Lancet, 392*, 41–50. Published Online June 28, 2018. https://doi.org/10.1016/S0140-6736(18)31308-4.

Saltman, R. B., Rico, A., & Boerma, W. G. W. (eds.) (2003). *Primary Care in the Driver's Seat?* Berkshire: Open University Press, European Observatory on Health Policies Series.

Snow, J. (1855). *On the Mode of Communication of Cholera*. London: John Churchill, New Burlington Street, England. Retrieved from http://www.ph.ucla.edu/EPI/snow/snowbook.html.

Twaddle, A. C. (1999). *Health Care Reform in Sweden 1980–1994*. London: Auburn House.

University of Otago. (2010). *Reference Guides (Guides to Specific Issues/Models of Care)*. Retrieved February 8, 2019, from https://www.otago.ac.nz/wellington/otago023714.pdf.

Van der Linden, B. A., et al. (2001). Integration of Care in the Netherlands: The Development of Transmural Care Since 1994. *Health Policy, 55*(2), 111–120.

Walston, S. L., & Kimberly, J. R. (1997). Reengineering Hospitals: Evidence from the Field. *Hospital & Health Services Administration, 42*(2), 143–163.

Warner, M. (1996). *Implementing Health Care Reforms Through Substitution*. Cardiff: Welsh Institute for Health and Social Care.

WHO – World Health Organization. (2000). *World Health Report 2000. Health System Improving Performance*. Geneva: World Health Organization.

WHO – World Health Organization. (2008). *World Health Report 2008. PHC Now More Than Ever*. Geneva: World Health Organization.

WHO – World Health Organization. (2016). *World Health Statistics 2016: Monitoring Health for the SDGs, Sustainable Development Goals*. Geneva: World Health Organization. Retrieved from https://www.who.int/gho/publications/world_health_statistics/2016/en/.

Wilson, T., et al. (2005). Rising to the Challenge: Will the NHS Support People with Long Term Conditions? *British Medical Journal, 330*. https://doi.org/10.1136/bmj.330.7492.657.

CHAPTER 4

Business Models and Hospitals

Stephen Wright and Antonio Durán

Variance in the Use of Resources in Healthcare Production

Hospital care is a *huge economic subsector within healthcare, ranging within the OECD from 26% in Mexico to 53% of the total healthcare expenses in Turkey* (OECD 2017). However, as explained in Chap. 1, "unclear issues" related to hospitals remain widespread (see Box 1.1). Further, as discussed in Chap. 3, hospitals de facto constitute in many places a *poorly defined* hodgepodge of institutions between—and even within—countries, pretending to do similar things but in fact performing rather different functions. They are supposed to be at the top of a pyramid of institutions, yet the *boundaries* between them and with other institutions are unclear and the *resource/patient flows* involved are often arbitrary. In all of high-, middle- and low-income countries, epidemiological and technological changes are now making the picture *even more complex.* Traditional economic analyses are clearly not enough, as also shown in Chap. 2.

S. Wright (✉)
Independent Consultant, Ingleton, UK
e-mail: steve.wright@echaa.eu

A. Durán
ALLDMHEALTH, Seville, Spain
e-mail: aduran@alldmh.com

A. Durán, S. Wright (eds.), *Understanding Hospitals in Changing Health Systems*, https://doi.org/10.1007/978-3-030-28172-4_4

Unwarranted variation and the related problems between and within hospitals, compounded by the lack of effective responses to much of the new and previously existing variability, are most remarkable symptoms of these problems. Unplanned over-equipment and so on leads to the frequently observed abandonment of original planning mandates and the equalization of hospital profiles, with abundant inefficiencies. In England, six months of work with 136 acute hospitals during the second half of 2015 indicated—from procurement and logistics to nosocomial infections—where the relative variation of each hospital should be reduced in order to achieve savings, compared to the NHS' or similar hospitals' average ("unnecessary" spending in the hospital sample was estimated to be not less than £5 billion—10% of the annual £55.6 billion acute hospitals spend in the country) (Department of Health 2016):

- Adjusted by severity, the average cost per inpatient in the sample was £3500, with a 20% variation between the most (£3850) and the least expensive (£3150).
- The average purchase price for a hip prosthesis ranged from £788 to £1590 (and the hospitals paying the lowest prices were not the ones that bought *most* prostheses).
- The range of deep infection rates in primary hip and knee replacements ranged from 0.5% to 4% (just 1% reduction in all would transform the life of 6000 patients, and would save the NHS £300 million a year).
- In situ drug stocks covered from 11 to 36 days (15 days for all would save £50 million).
- For hospital trusts, operating costs per facility building area are considered to be at a good level when below £320/m^2, but the variation was from £105 to £970—if every site were at the median value, it would save £1 billion a year).
- The hospital's non-clinical surface area proportion is considered optimum somewhere below 35%, yet with current variations from 12% to 69%.
- And so on.

Many authors suggest that the current concentration of resources and personnel in a single institution is a central cause. Hospital systems often seem messy and full of paradoxes, uncertainties and performance variations—hence the claims, for example, that hospitals are a "problem" simply due to their size, high cost and relative poor access, often a core element in the claim that "hospitals should be downsized".

Frequent concerns are also expressed about the best location for many services, how inadequately service delivery institutions are coping with the challenges they face, and what services should be produced for whom, where and with what organizational patterns and so on (O'Connell et al. 2008). A study in the field of logistic activities, for example, analysed the room for efficiency improvement derived from applying particular decisions in Singapore hospitals (such as developing efficiency activities, internally concentrated in clusters of services or not; outsourcing them between specific local providers, or also with other providers, etc.). The study suggested that the use of information and communication technologies is becoming a serious competitive factor for service improvement and operational costs reduction (Pan and Pokharel 2007).

Many aspects of health service production, however, continue, to a substantial extent surrounded by dogma and myth (Nolte and McKee 2008; Engström et al. 2001; Starfield 1994) rather than elucidated by an "evidence-based analysis". Operational research remains insufficient (Maarse and Normand 2009), despite the abundant information on the comparative performance—for example, capacity, efficiency, waiting times, patient safety and quality and so on—of hospitals and other institutions (Ham and Dixon 2012). A variety of organizational configurations is emerging in different places—with different status, financing schemes, accountability arrangements and decision capacities—all in response to the incentives under which individual hospitals operate (Nolte et al. 2014). Nevertheless, it seems that in many parts of health systems, there is resistance to launch deep evaluation processes. Hospitals are probably reluctant because of their very corporate interests as institutions (in the case of private hospitals) or because of politicians (for public hospitals).

Truth be told, in reality, problems are hardly unique to hospitals, as medicine itself is still practiced "partly as an art, partly as a science" (Cochrane 1971), and thus in primary care/outpatient specialized services similar if not greater variation would undoubtedly be found—per patient treated, hospitals are much more expensive than GP centres, but the latter handle many more patient contacts! In fact, similar levels of dramatic divergence would certainly be repeated in health and hospital administrations outside the UK examples, obviously synonymous with very resource-stressed health systems. So there is clearly a need for a deep evaluation, although signs of concern outweigh effective responses. This is discussed at length below.

One issue also developed in this chapter is: what are the reasonable boundaries in mixing together different sorts of activities? Modern business schools try to unravel commercial or industrial conglomerates with their functional complexities into more coherent groups of assets, and thus in the case of healthcare to redesign the hospital (Herzlinger 2004). Many aim at collecting information on comparative performance (capacity, efficiency, waiting times, patient safety and quality, etc.). These tasks are usually carried out by government agencies, but in places like England they are also run by private organizations such as "Dr. Foster",[1] which annually scores individual hospitals performance (Dixon et al. 2010).

The introduction of new models of care involving hospitals and beyond (often underlined by almost-ideological considerations) is expressed in an intention using the slogan to provide *the right care, at the right time, in the right place, by the right team*; but these have frequently been implemented without testing their implications. In the end, a failure to think through adequately the nature of the connections between the resources used and the services delivered has precluded a proper understanding of the repercussions on the hospital fundamental organization as an economic entity; that is, the impact of altering the existing *business model.*

The Missing Element: Business Models for Hospitals Within Health Systems

What Is *a Business Model?*

The argument made in this book is that hospitals as social organizations are not just medical institutions. In abstract terms, they transmute enormous volumes of economic resources into medical care, and the intersection between the two can be described as their business model.

In relation to the topic of our book, while in many sectors of the economy—for example, airlines, computers, (container) shipping, and so on—any progress linked to changes in the business model is immediately tested, sometimes but not always within a market (and, if adequate, accepted), the health sector is extremely resilient to such an examination. Business models in health are just as critical to structure and activity as in the above-mentioned sectors. Why then are business models (in health and in hospitals) not properly developed—or even discussed and analysed?

[1] https://www.drfoster.com/.

Sometimes it seems that the above relationships are not well known and/or, as already suggested, nobody seems to want the economic aspects of alternative models of care to be properly studied.[2] The complexity of hospitals as institutions and facilities has grown significantly, but debate remains partial and anecdotal, rather than systematic. At this stage, enough evidence hints that improvements in results are feasible by changing or adapting business models. This is not about privatization per se, a topic that comparatively has gained much space in the debates, and which is addressed in the chapter in this book on ownership.

Many people in the health sector, particularly in Europe, find the very concept of the "hospital as a business" to be somehow disturbing. However, in fiduciary terms, using *economic* resources—and perhaps particularly public ones—in a responsible way is in fact a perfect match to ensuring that the appropriate *clinical* choices are made. Far from compromising the public service ethos, understanding and acting on the *appropriateness* of business models are entirely consistent with both economically and ethically appropriate service delivery operations.

Essentially, a business model is a story of how (and why) enterprises succeed or fail (Magretta 2002b). The idea flows from earlier writing by multiple management authors, including Peter Drucker and Michael Porter. Although much of this early writing was not as such centred on healthcare, some has been. Porter in particular has explored "value-based healthcare", which puts forward the idea that healthcare institutions should be paid for the value they create and not for the activity they carry out (Porter and Teisberg 2006; Kaiser and Lee 2015). Porter has also specifically explored the degree to which healthcare needs to be re-arranged around "Strategic Business Units". This analogizes to the way that major corporations have focused activities within dedicated units. To recognize the way that healthcare should operate compared with other industries, for healthcare, he dubs them "Integrated Practice Units" (Porter and Lee 2018).

A generally accepted formulation for business models draws from work done by Christensen, and is summarized graphically in Fig. 4.1:

The value proposition implies a profit formula, which determines the processes used, and those require certain resources to be gathered and

[2] A revealing example: two decades (and a world economic crisis) after their start, the evaluation of European experiences in hospital reform is far from complete.

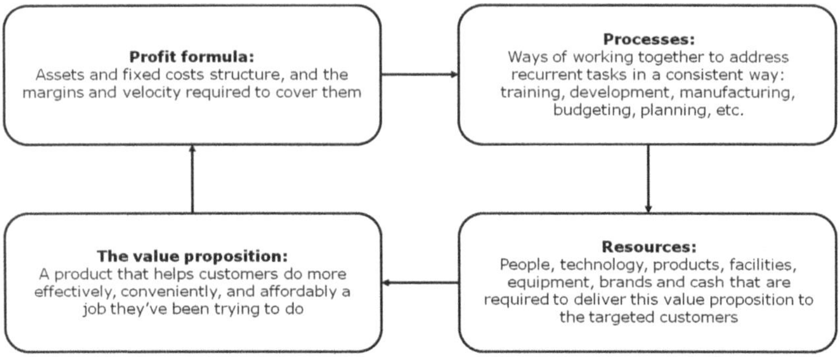

Fig. 4.1 The four components of a business model (Hwang, J., & Christensen, C. M. (2007). Disruptive Innovation in Healthcare Delivery: A Framework for Business-Model Innovation. *Health Affairs, 27*(5), 1329–1335. https://doi.org/10.1377/hlthaff.27.5.1329)

deployed—and then iterate. Analysing the cycle in a retrospective way for pedagogic purposes:

- The cycle of business model development starts with the *value proposition* (the product or service that helps "get a job done effectively, conveniently and affordably" for some defined group of users).
- To make that possible, managers bring together *resources or factors of production* (importantly, but not limited to, human capital, intellectual property, physical capital in the form of assets and equipment).
- Resources are linked via technical *processes* (in the parlance of healthcare and in this book, Chap. 3, "the model of care").
- The capability of the business model to deliver to its stakeholders determines the *profit formula*—the "surplus" that it yields. The business model idea has primarily been worked up in commercial sectors, including the main healthcare markets in the US, where accounting "profit" is a highly relevant managerial issue. For non-profit systems, a surplus should still be created over current costs, and will consist of reimbursement of the capital employed, or probably be captured in forms other than cash and by other players, including, notably, by the users.[3]

[3] This is essentially the idea of "consumer surplus" in economics, rather than "producer surplus", which is closely related to profit.

What Then Is Not *a Business Model?*

The very concept of the applicability of the business model to healthcare and hospitals is not well understood. Intuitively, it seems reasonable that there are different ways to organize a service entity to serve different groups of end-users. However, in reference to business models, terms are typically used without defining them too well or distinguishing properly between them. In this context, an observer could talk about "hospital business models", while referring variously to the product, the setting, the processes of care, the payment systems, the ownership or even the strategy. In fact, *none* of these terms per se is a description of a business model—though all are somehow linked, in ways which need to be elaborated:

- Saying that the business model is "a product" (Accenture 2019) (in healthcare, that could be hospital care) or speaking about a setting (the fact of being something called a hospital, compared to a clinic or primary care centre) are simply tautologies.
- Speaking about "processes of care" limits the definition to a physical, not a business or economic, idea. *Healthcare processes* are what in this book we call "models of care" (Chap. 3), and in turn they constitute one of the key components of business models as in the figure above (Oosterholt and Simonse 2016).
- A business model is not equivalent to *ownership*, as the same healthcare actions can be carried out by entities owned by either private or state agents. Ownership concerns whether the capital employed, which can be human or physical, is owned or controlled by private sector agents (including for-profit, PPP and not-for-profit actors) or by the state—and *this does not necessarily have any direct bearing on what hospitals do* (see Chap. 5 for a discussion on this).
- Payment systems (e.g. capitation or block budgets or fee-for-service) are not specific, because they can equally apply to hospitals operated in different ways, or to many settings other than hospitals. They are part of the various tools for making a business model viable or not (as explained in Chap. 1, they need to be consistent with the objectives that make the business model appropriate; for a full discussion, see Chap. 6).
- A strategy, finally, is a notion incorporated into the organizational world from military jargon and refers to the *achievement of goals*.

> A *strategy* would include, among other things, *the choice of a particular business model*, and therefore is key, but it definitely covers more ground than just the business model proper (Casadeus-Masanell and Ricart 2009).

Remarkably, only a limited number of authors have dwelt extensively on the concept of business models in the health field (Christensen and Raynor 2003; Christensen et al. 2017). This chapter leans on their work, although—as it will be seen—it parts company in important respects (Boxes 4.1 and 4.2).

Box 4.1 Business Models in Healthcare and Hospitals

Christensen et al. identify (only) three archetypical business models, drawn from experience and analysis of other sectors, but applicable in healthcare:

- Model 1, "solution shops", institutions built to diagnose and solve unstructured problems. Consulting firms, research and development organizations and many law firms use this model, which diagnoses the cause of complex problems and proposes appropriate solutions by relying on the high human capital endowments of the people they employ. Christensen's suggestion is that almost all healthcare, at all levels, is "still" like this;
- Model 2, "value-added processes" transform in repeatable and closely controlled, disciplined ways standardized resource inputs to deliver high-quality and efficient services and products at low cost. Processes themselves are the key identifiers. Production-line sectors (automobile assembly, hydrocarbon refining, restaurants etc.) are like this. In the auto industry, the ideas were further extended by Toyota "lean production". Some systematized healthcare institutions do employ this business model, and there is also a truly enormous amount of discussion about applying lean in healthcare (for a Cochrane systematic literature survey, see Rotter et al. 2017).
- Model 3, "facilitated networks" are organizations in which users/consumers are also producers. Telecommunication companies provide a platform, facilitating calls/data transfers. Social care could be regarded as a facilitated user network, dependent on the

user to structure his/her own experience, with boundaries, a value proposition, resources and processes constituting the business model. Although it might feel intuitively harder to think of examples in healthcare, on reflection, it is all-pervasive: integrated care systems (patient-centred care) are one example. In general, "the patient as producer of his own care" happens everywhere, given that most people do most of the management of their own health status.

It should be emphasized that the typology of models as envisaged by these authors is limited just to the above three business models. Within the established health sector, however, they do not split the way it might be expected. Traditional general and teaching hospitals, for example, very often use a "solution shop" model, but the other main setting of care (independent medical practitioners, whether primary care practitioners or specialists) usually follows the same model as well. That is, there is not a *hospital business model* to be compared with an *independent practitioner business model*: both are often "solution shops" and operate as relatively unsystematic, craft-type organizations. This insight has profound implications for the efficiency and scalability of care, and the feasibility of transferring care between settings; transferring care from one solution shop (the hospital) to another solution shop (the GP) is unlikely to yield dramatic improvements.

While most hospitals do perhaps tend to be solution shops, it is evident that they also include significant elements of value-added processing. In fact, case-mix indices for tertiary hospitals are not much higher than for general hospitals; both carry out many interventions which are, or at least could be, standardized. Thus, even tertiary care institutions do (often on a near-production-line basis) uncomplicated work in areas such as cataract removal, joint replacement, hernia repair and kidney dialysis that are now so routine that they could easily be carried out in other settings, taking up few highly qualified physicians, specialized pieces of equipment, and so on. One reason is that university hospitals use the activity surplus to cross-subsidize their sophisticated work; payment systems typically allow a real cash surplus over and beyond the resource costs required to carry out the activities for standard procedures, whereas the tariff revenues for open-ended complex investigations and treatments are often inadequate to cover costs

(Cash et al. 2011[4]; Bojke et al. 2018). These connections would have to be reformed before one could be sure that care is being placed at the most appropriate level. Perhaps the case-mix index of a hospital ought to be merely a preliminary guide as to whether it is (or should be) a tertiary institution. The expectation would be that the hospitals with the highest index would be tertiary, on the concomitant expectation that hospitals with simpler workloads should be operating principally with value-added processing.

Business models do change—according to these authors—through "disruptive innovation". This foresees that a simple technology starts in a sub-market originally served by, but increasingly unattractive to, an incumbent, which eventually abandons it until the disruptive technology gets better and eats the lunch of the incumbent. Examples include mini-mills in the steel industry dominating over integrated blast-furnaces, digital imaging taking over from chemical films, and micro (PC) computers displacing mini-computers. The disrupting technology started off as primitive, convenient and cheap in its low-value niche, but gradually became dominant.

How Have These Features Worked Out in Reality? Uneven Responses to Pressures for Change in the Hospital Scene So Far

Changing Care and Changing Settings

As written in Chap. 1, the common prognosis in relation to current—mostly financial—pressures is that hospitals could end up in a dead-end if changes are not introduced. Since hospitals will for quite some time still occupy various "business niches" but technologies will change their operations, the "evidence-based" line of work to rethink the business models needs to be better identified. Although the "business model" idea is indeed powerful and seems a necessity to understand the manifold problems faced by hospitals, there are neither unique nor simple answers.

Now that many medical technologies are transportable, hospitals have seen parts of what was their *traditional* workload removed. Better anaes-

[4] The study indicates that, in France, the introduction of DRG payment ("T2A") meant price reductions for public hospitals and steady prices for private ones, since tariffs are based on average costs in areas where the private sector had a competitive advantage (ambulatory surgery) and already had a profit margin.

thetic, laparoscopic procedures, and less invasive surgical techniques plus more efficient organizational schemes have made interventions (e.g. gastro- and rectoscopies, minor surgeries) and the like amenable to other locations, such as outpatient or day care.

Either bloodless (computerized scanner, magnetic resonance, endoscopy, echography, etc.) or unaggressive diagnostic devices (digital angiography, biopsies by punction) facilitate and/or permit the diagnosis of many medical processes under outpatient conditions, without hospital admission. Certain elective/programmed surgeries, dialysis and so on are also no longer exclusively inpatient-based treatments carried out by hyper-specialized professionals. This has entailed the remarkable result that, increasingly, hospital inpatients are the elderly, while younger adults have been shifted to be treated as day cases. Patient satisfaction measures are already adopted in many countries with reference to patient rights, including being consulted on the treatment to be received; in an increasing number, patients are allowed to choose a public facility with virtually no restrictions (Winblad and Ringard 2009).

Technology allows, in addition, care to be provided to a bigger number of patients by increasingly technologically competent, but less formally qualified, "highly health specialized" staff (e.g. medical engineering and technical physicians). In addition, technical innovation allows them to work under less supervision—as, every day, opticians demonstrate in relation to eyesight tests. Some years ago, clinical directors of the English Department of Health reviewed emergencies, maternity and mental health, and concluded that most hospital services could be provided in primary care centres, intermediate institutions similar to "polyclinics", and even at home—especially if telemedicine support were provided (Imison et al. 2008). Thus, a dominant factor in initially pushing doctors to enter hospitals (clinical progress) now questions their concentration in an exclusive building.

Moreover, almost no modern hospital is self-sufficient anymore in key areas, irrespective of technology and staff. When treating diseases (e.g. acute crises of diabetes, hypertension or COPD in an obese patient), hospitals have to coordinate with other levels of care (Barnett et al. 2012); dealing one by one with those co-morbidities was easier in the past than managing their continuum of care in coordination with institutions over which the hospital has little or no control. Differences in culture, rules and regulations, and distinct administrative and financial frameworks compared to primary care and/or rehabilitation sometimes seem insurmountable barriers (Oxman and Glasziou 2008). The demands of quality scientific research also go beyond the scope of any single institution, as major clinical trials often require collaboration between several hospitals and non-hospitals, national and international (Leatt et al. 2006).

For the purpose of our discussion, the point at stake here is the emerging possibility of major changes in the service delivery location, plus all the processes, resources, value propositions and profit formulae attached to it.

Productivity and Cost of Services

Another issue to be considered is the response to cost increases. Such increases in healthcare during the last few decades, in absolute figures per capita and as a fraction of the GDP (i.e. at (bigger) growth rates compared to the growth of the economy), have been remarkable in virtually all health systems worldwide. The underlying causes of such an historical increase are likely to have been multiple. In Europe, technology availability as a cost driver (see also Chap. 1) is probably responsible for some 50% in recent decades (Pammolli et al. 2005). The picture is completed by higher public expectations (partly linked to societal increase in wealth), higher input costs and—to a rather lesser degree—the greying of the population as a cause of disability and disease, plus other difficult-to-quantify determinants (Busse et al. 2011).

Constituting the biggest single locus of expenditure in the health sector, hospitals have been high in the systems' response to cost pressures. For years, action on a number of variables has been frequent (first and foremost, reduction in the number of beds), as explained in the previous chapter. But a study in Canada showed that bed reductions in hospitals were accompanied by increases in the number of occasions the emergency services became congested, as measured by their inability to accept ambulance-led emergency admissions (Schull et al. 2001). An arguable defence of "efficiency" has also been popular under the slogan of "sweating resources": new technologies and models of care were introduced based on high utilization and occupation rates, but they often created more problems than they solved (frequent bottlenecks between operating theatres and wards, and between emergency and regular care, as well as, from time to time, increases in nosocomial infections).

Domiciliary (hospital) care is a scheme under which a healthcare professional actively treats a patient who otherwise would need to be admitted to a hospital. A study in the United Kingdom (Shepperd et al. 2009) shows that, for some particular patient groups, this type of domiciliary services—"Hospital at Home Programme", HaHP—produces results comparable to those that would be obtained with an inpatient stay, with similar or even reduced costs through hospital "admission avoidance". In this context, hospital admissions become a support instrument in the relationships between hospital specialists and patients, to be used whenever necessary (but for the shortest possible time). Outpatient departments have also shifted their preferred objective from being a follow-up of previously admitted patients to a pivotal element around which a given specialty's activities get structured.

Korea offers a rather different example of services efficiency. A context of de-regulation made the number of acute care hospitals jump from 973 in 2003 to 1084 in 2005, translated into increased competition and a sharp fall in providers' income. Hospitals responded by specializing in particular services. Small and midsize hospitals, in particular, developed specialized services to compete with bigger ones. Specialization strategies led to a reorganization of services according to those existing in the environment, and to cost containment, by sticking to a restricted service range and eliminating low-volume services.

This hospital specialization process led to the delivery of quality services at reduced costs, yet inpatient and outpatient activity volumes were not statistically relevant for determining the overall efficiency of each centre. The study suggests that the "number of beds" and "staff" are significant variables, though not in an intuitive direction—such as linked to economies of scale. Efficient hospitals had *fewer* beds (average of 95) than less efficient hospitals (average of 324), and had fewer doctors and nurses (averages of 23.3 and 61.4, respectively) than less efficient hospitals (averages of 107.1 and 164.0, respectively) (Lee et al. 2008).

The main point here is that healthcare very often possesses features of a "handicraft industry", such as little room for labour-saving technologies and great dependence on human resources. This phenomenon was analysed when studying difficulties with improving productivity in certain activities—the same number of musicians are still needed today as in the nineteenth century to play a Beethoven symphony, while real salaries are much bigger (Baumol and Bowen 1966). That might explain why healthcare has proved less able than other economic sectors (e.g. telecommunications, cars, travel, electronics, computers, etc.) to generate productivity improvements, and has responded only poorly to cost increases in the sector.

Exploring New Business Models: Process Flow Versus Craft, and Integration of Care with Other Settings

A powerful proposition for a business model replacing *medical specialty-defined hospital wards* would be the possibility to group patients according to *medical needs and dependence level(s)*, such as critical care, intermediate care,[5] minimal care and so on. For that, however, a way would need to be found to link such groupings with prices, costs and financing in order for it to become replicable and scalable. Patients could arrive after referral from, for example, a rapid assessment/triage unit, perhaps staffed by nurses; a study in the London's St Mary's Hospital Trust assigning particular surgical services to *surgical care practitioners*—specialized teams of nurses—showed a considerable reduction of waiting times for minor surgery processes, with good results in terms of quality, without eroding patient satisfaction (Martin et al. 2007). Related proposals are the "*one-stop shops*" able to provide services without unnecessary repetition visits, sometimes integrating PHC/ambulatory clinical services with those of hospitals (Singh 2008), or functioning almost as a polyclinic (Imison et al. 2008, op. cit.).

Some facilities, albeit remaining along with the majority of hospitals as *solution shops* as per Christensen models, are already being built and operated with innovative inspirations that play differently with surfaces and relationships. The University Hospital of Trondheim, in Norway, for example, categorizes its activities by body organs, placing patients in the same building when they have corresponding symptoms and diseases (for example, abdominal—urology, nephrology, gastroenterology and gastrointestinal surgery). This allows the hospital to overcome the division between medicine and surgery and other organizing activities innovatively in one "abdominal clinic" and another "renal and urinary tract clinic". An explicit objective is to concentrate health services in smaller blocks around the patient, thus reducing their need to be transported inside the hospital,

[5] The term *intermediate care* (Steiner A (2002) *Intermediate care—a good thing? Age Ageing* 2002, 30–S3: 33–39) describes those services related with these patients in their transition from hospital to home, as well as from medical and social dependence to functional independence, in an attempt to prevent the risk of new hospital admissions. These services play the bridging role between social and primary as well as specialized care.

for which it uses fewer, more qualified staff per patient (Solumsmo and Aslaksen 2009).

Some *value-added process* institutions are undoubtedly emerging, perhaps as a reflection of so many hospitals being solution shops, indeed a globally inefficient status. The Coxa Hospital for Joint Replacement in Tampere, Finland, offers a regional service of joint prostheses and started operating in 2002 as a self-contained unit in purpose-built facilities. It has grown into a significant institution in its field, especially after a change in the Finnish Health Care Act in 2014 allowed patients to choose freely a specialized healthcare provider among the public hospitals in the country. Its work is based on integrated flow systems and systematized healthcare protocols, collaboration between the concerned institutions, and a very sophisticated ITC platform. One-fifth of total patients in 2015 were people exercising their freedom of choice (Coxa Hospital 2019).

There are well-analysed proposals emphasizing the *processes of care* rather than *functional departments* (mainly radiology and internal medicine), with the hope of achieving more patient-centred care, cost reductions and quality improvements. Hospitals as diverse as the University of Wisconsin Hospitals and Clinics in the US, the Flinders Medical Center in Australia, the Leicester Royal Infirmary in the UK or the A Gemelli Policlinic in Rome have tried during the last few decades to shift from *functional* organizations to an *orientation towards processes* at the time of delivering healthcare to specific patient groups—by means of, for example, focusing on *clinical pathways* or *care pathways* (Vos et al. 2011). In Sweden, the implementation of integrated care pathways for patients with hip fractures led to a significant reduction in hospital stays and improvements in the quality of care (Olsson et al. 2006).

Two approaches to higher *process orientation* have been described (Vera and Kuntz 2007; Gemmel et al. 2008):

1. implementing coordination mechanisms—for example, matrix structures by product lines. *Healthcare activity sequences* (related to diagnosis, consultation, treatment, etc.) get established, and responsibilities are assigned to all professionals involved in care of logistically homogeneous groups of patients—that is, those who need the same type of healthcare activities in a given sequence (*product lines*). By doing this, each professional concerned knows what is expected of him/her in current, previous and following stages; and

2. re-structuring the organizations based on processes. Departments thus become multidisciplinary, based not on professional specialization, but rather on patients' needs, aspiring to tackle healthcare processes almost without the need to involve other departments. But this may not necessarily be the best option in all environments, as consistency with the hospital production structure may be affected because of scale issues (poor critical mass). Also, each specialty has its own values, problem-solving mechanisms and language, and these are reflected in each professional's attitudes. Cultural barriers between medical specialties need to be ameliorated; indeed, participating in a multidisciplinary team calls for flexibility towards other colleagues' territories (Vos et al. 2009).

Evidence, however, seems to show that achieving a process orientation across an entire secondary or tertiary hospital requires a much bigger effort than implementing isolated projects. Coxa, for example, specializes just in musculoskeletal issues, and is attached to a much larger tertiary hospital (University of Tampere), which is not by any means organized the same way. Establishing flow processes across organizational boundaries is also a major challenge (Institute for Healthcare Improvement 2005). If inter-level flow is to be improved and hospital bottlenecks are to be prevented, well-meant (but often only arguably effective) "clinical guidelines" need to be significantly refined. Hospitals need a balance between, on the one hand, optimizing healthcare processes and, at the same time, giving response to, for example, questions such as how to handle scarce resources with different groups of patients.

"Visits" from mobile, previously rigid technologies and doctors from several other units and/or "circulating" from one to another department, in contrast with the classic practice of moving the patient to technology-concentration areas and making him/her wait the rest of the time for the doctor's visit in a room, are becoming increasingly feasible. The Martini hospital in Groningen in the Netherlands reflects that approach, by grouping outpatient departments. Outpatient clinics have, in addition, their surfaces structured by zones, with those of "high intensity" close to intensive and coronary care and next to day-nursing, providing a flexible space for nursing wings to be expanded or reduced in case of need with beds from the adjacent wings (Rechel et al. 2009). The NHS University Hospitals Coventry and Warwickshire includes an acute care hospital, a clinical sciences building and a mental health centre with beds. The separation of children by ages and the assembling of all the "*hot-floor*" spaces (emergencies, operating theatres, coronary units and cardiology) in one critical matrix in order to benefit more from common spaces and synergies are among its many innovative features (Guenther and Vittori 2007). The institution usually receives high scores from both patients and staff (Waters 2015).

Sometimes, however, the supposedly decisive advantages brought by these schemes are less conclusive in practice. Dealing with the continuum of care of hypertension, diabetes and COPD in an obese patient with reduced mobility, visual problems and so on means it is much more difficult for classical hospital units to integrate services from outside and inside the hospital than solving acute crises one after another within its own walls.

Similarly, although healthcare adjusts itself to the widely applied 80/20 Pareto rule (Magretta 2002a), the specifics are less clear-cut. For example, chest pain, breast lumps, rectal bleeding and other frequent processes adjust reasonably to ***standardized protocols***, and some conditions benefit from *care by groups of professionals* (e.g. coronary diseases benefit from the collaboration between internal medicine specialists and cardiological surgeons; cancer from joint approaches by oncologists, radiologists and surgeons; gastrointestinal haemorrhages from the collaboration between internal medicine doctors and surgeons), and so on. However, other disease processes (e.g. AIDS or diabetes, psychiatric problems, epilepsy) do so to a much lesser extent (Rechel et al. 2009).

There are also examples of ***facilitated networks***, with the "insight" to customize practical solutions via that approach. Sets of facilities and professionals of various types are specifically able to integrate active patients in their search for shared lessons. With transportable and cheaper technologies, "medical cabinets" and similar institutions with a bigger resolution capacity than the current ones are expected to proliferate. Ambulatory-facility types could facilitate the integrated management of people with the same morbidity to be visited by a medical team at one time. Many would function as a network rather than independently, although their degree of concentration/connectedness and the implementation of the business model will depend on a proper network in which diagnosis would play a secondary role compared to the advantages emanating from sharing knowledge and experiences between associated members (Eisenmann et al. 2006). ***Shared medical appointments*** are an innovative alternative for patient care related to networks. Conceived to increase both patient access to care and the productivity of doctors with very busy agendas, shared appointments treat simultaneously in one single consultation a group of chronic patients with very similar conditions (who have given their consent in advance). Studies confirm high satisfaction rates in, for example, chronic cardiac morbidity (Bartley and Haney 2010), hypertension (Watts et al. 2009), diabetes (Kirsh et al. 2007) and obesity-related patients (Kaidar-Person et al. 2006).

The implementation of a particular business model may depend also on other health system features; that is, choices will have to be made between the widespread model of, for example, "intermediate-care" surgical facilities or dialysis stations (Castoro et al. 2007).

Guidelines and Possible Tests for New Business Models

The discussion to this point in the chapter reveals useful principles—but has serious limitations. There is a difference between, on the one hand, knowing the evolution of changes in hospitals and, on the other, controlling them today (the diagnosis needs to be refined but the treatment is in any case rather untested). The conclusion, all the above things taken into account, is that a better analysis of the *specific mechanisms* through which hospitals have changed and are likely to change is indispensable in order to propose adequate solutions, adapted to particular governance contexts (process flow versus craft, isolated solutions versus chains or networks approaches, etc.). Christensen's three-model construct is a useful start, but it is only a *Gedankenexperiment*. What is needed is *consensus around a way of analysing various alternative models for particular circumstances.*

Using as a guide *only*, the three-model typology provided exposes major problems in changing the healthcare and hospital business models which have arisen over the decades. It is likely that systematic simulation modelling of business models will be required, to find out the appropriate balance for operations between solution shops, value-added processing and facilitated networks (or hybrid business models which could emerge). The implications of this proposition is elaborated much further in Chap. 9. A number of questions remain. *Hospital reform efforts will continue to be incoherent and partial without an ability to articulate and address some specific questions.* Some guidelines for deploying the business model idea suggest the need to consider:

1. What could be the **metrics** to evaluate hospital business models? Similarly, how to "model business models"? In what cases will we be able to hypothesize that a hospital business model is ripe for incremental (evolutionary) technological and social change, or for the hypothesised "disruption" which inevitably seems to attach itself to the very concept of business models?
2. For value-added processing, which aspects of healthcare and hospital operation are **separable**, such that they can be developed as stand-alone units (perhaps off-site), and operated both efficiently and at high-quality levels?
3. Can we explore the **process technologies** which exist (especially in value-added processes) which will satisfy specified value proposition(s)? The many sets of existing technologies will probably represent the entry possibilities into different parts of the system.
4. Can we specify the "**profit**" formulae (that is, value propositions) that could incentivize the introduction of new business models, and identify who will be able to access them? What payment mechanisms need to be (further) developed to support these "possibly viable" profit formulae?
5. Beyond the three Christensen models, what other or better archetype business models could there be in health and hospitals?
6. Are there specificities that would orient the efforts *preferably* towards certain socioeconomic environments—for example, middle-income countries?

Box 4.2 Reflecting on Christensen, Critically

How do business models change? Are there hybrid forms?

Christensen et al. deal almost entirely with the US hospital/healthcare industry, where at least a facsimile of a market exists. This is less true in Europe and elsewhere. Their contributions are also predicated on *new market entrants,* in whatever sector, using a different business model that "disrupts" the incumbent (such disruption is supposedly "inevitable"). But counterexamples of economic sectors with a stable business model for decades are oil refining and petrochemicals, construction, farming, fishing (still largely a hunting activity!), banking, movies (pre-Netflix, anyway), luxury goods, insurance and education. In other words, business models are *not* synonymous with disruption—they may be stable over decades or longer, simply because nothing sufficiently intrusive disrupts them, or the incumbent is powerful enough. In all cases, of course, dramatic changes with technology, and in demand and tastes, have occurred; simply that the business model, as defined, has not changed anything like as dramatically.

Also, the authors assert that organizations which attempt to run two business models simultaneously almost invariably achieve neither well, or at what would be regarded as optimum levels of quality and efficiency. This means that hospitals worldwide are failing, not because medical trends have rendered them redundant but rather because, with the same facilities and staff, they try to do repeatable and scalable activities simultaneously with complex and open-ended ones. This mix does not work (well enough), it is claimed, opening the discussion of whether only pure or also hybrid business models should be the future for hospitals and healthcare. A way of illuminating this issue starts from the reasons why healthcare is different from (most) other service activities (see also Chap. 3). Healthcare cannot satisfactorily operate as a true market, and certainly not one which is "perfectly competitive", as explained before (Arrow 1963). Hospitals' and doctors' practices are focused on problems of multiple contingencies, typical of uncertain underlying processes. As scientific understanding increases, there could in principle be increasing standardization and streamlining—moving some activities from solution-shop business models to value-added-processing ones. As Castano 2014 writes, this is dependent on *separability* of activities, to pull out the combination of a value proposition, resources and processes in relevant areas such that clinical activity for these areas takes on a demand-side mindset. What does the patient as customer want to get, and how to arrange the production of that?

That business models have to represent pure archetypes is also challengeable. For example, the "full service network carriers" in aviation (FSNC, the flag national airlines) were disrupted two decades ago by "low cost carriers", LCC (e.g. Southeast Airlines in the US and Ryanair and Easyjet in Europe). A solution shop transport system was thus financially devastated by a process-oriented proposal: a capital-intensive model of no-frills service, short distance point-to-point legs, and standardized jet types. The LCC are now differentiating their service offer (pay more for a package, get more) and extending into long-distance city pairs, while the FSNCs are adapting their model in the LCCs' direction (unbundled pricing of some extras, lesser reliance on hub airports, tight cost control at the cost of quality). As a result, almost all carriers in aviation are becoming hybrids somewhere along a spectrum, and the image of a pure business model has not held. Another example might be in retail, where Ikea revolutionized the furniture industry. But its business model has *always* been a hybrid of sophisticated mass production and retailing of the components (value-added processing), together with getting the customer to do the assembly work (network facilitation). It is likely that there will be multiple viable and stable hybrid business models in healthcare too—rather than expecting to see "pure" hospital systems.

Will hospital business models be disrupted? Classic examples showed a specific single new technology—for example, mini-mills in the case of steel—emerging to take dominance over a single dominant incumbent technology and process route (blast furnaces). No analogue disruptive technology seems obvious in healthcare, however. To start with, there is neither a single identifiable incumbent technology, nor any incoming universal disruptor (at present, information technologies—the obvious example—do not appear to be disruptive enough). That health and hospitals will be dragged down such a simple disruptive innovation path is in fact a cause for scepticism. The suggestion is that disruption in the health and hospital sector is inexorable, as simple efficient-process technologies gradually render the elaborate technology of general and teaching hospitals redundant. However, the theory is peculiarly silent on the time dimension, insofar as it applies to medicine. In fact, the true *key questions* are as follows:

- What are the business models for hospitals, and healthcare in general?
- Under what contingencies are business models stable?
- Are there features of health business models that do not look like the proposed paradigm?

Just as important, health status typically carries much more individual value to persons than the majority of industrial, commercial and consumer products, and the mode of payment is very different. The picture of a dominant existing technology steadily improving the high-level part of the total "market" but being undercut in simpler areas is just wrong; technologies improving any part of care will in fact be adopted by the health sector (maybe well, or maybe badly), if only because the patient cares but rarely pays for it. Hospitals get better and better at doing things which patients want as soon as they find out about it; somebody else pays for it; and there is no obvious and easily accessible chink in the market that a new entrant can exploit.

So in summary, the supply doesn't want disruption, and the demand doesn't know that it wants it either. The difficulty is to imagine—outside of the private sector US medical market—which value proposition could bring about disruptive change in the sector.

A visible disruptive bundle of technologies has actually already been adopted in part of the hospital market. It has not been introduced by new entrants, but in fact taken up by incumbents: those supporting day-case procedures such as short-duration anaesthetics, laparoscopic instruments and so on. There was such strong evidence of efficacy, and to a certain degree cost-effectiveness without too much loss of tariff, that the positive case for the introduction of increasing levels of day-case activity, and generally a reduction in average length of stay, was overwhelming. Even here, however, the rates of introduction and success vary sharply across regions, countries and continents.

Decision-Making About Hospitals-in-Healthcare Systems as a Way to Maximize Efficiency

A central part of this book is the argument about understanding "capacity" of the hospital system (and from there, the possibility to use new business models via appropriate governance arrangements). It is emerging in the book that the key to that is the ability to model the hospital as a complex flow system but, as indicated in Chap. 1, the ability to understand hospitals as flow systems is so poor that it constitutes a major problem.

Healthcare almost everywhere does involve exceedingly complex flow processes, and hospitals in turn can be regarded as the most complex single units within healthcare. Patients pass along what are often ill-defined paths, which operate at different speeds, reverse themselves periodically and use multiple processes—sometimes several at the same time (especially for co-morbid patients). The elements to deliver those processes, as was indicated, are made of human and physical capital, of varying vintages and efficiency: they somehow need to be coordinated and this is a non-obvious, often "wicked" problem.

Any complex flow system like this can be modelled, and cannot efficiently be managed without modelling. These issues will be addressed much more fully within Chap. 9 on decision-making.

References

Accenture. (2019). The Product as a Service Business Model. *Outlook, Accenture's Journal of High Performance Business.* Retrieved from https://www.accenture.com/us-en/insight-outlook-buy-own-thats-yesterdays-model.

Arrow, K. (1963). Uncertainty and the Welfare Economics of Medical Care. *American Economic Review, 53*, 941–973.

Barnett, K., Mercer, S. W., Norbury, M., Watt, G., Wyke, S., & Guthrie, B. (2012). Epidemiology of Multimorbidity and Implications for Health Care, Research, and Medical Education: A Cross-Sectional Study. *Lancet, 380*, 37–43.

Bartley, K. B., & Haney, R. (2010). Improving Access to Care, Health Outcomes, and Patient Satisfaction Are Primary Objectives for Healthcare Practices. *The Journal of Cardiovascular Nursing, 25*(1), 13–19.

Baumol, W., & Bowen, W. (1966). *Performing Arts, the Economic Dilemma: A Study of Problems Common to Theater, Opera, Music, and Dance.* New York: Twentieth Century Fund.

Bojke, C., Grašič, K., & Street, A. (2018). How Should Hospital Reimbursement Be Refined to Support Concentration of Complex Care Services? *Health Economics, 27*(1), e26–e38.

Busse, R., van Ginneken, E., & Normand, C. (2011). Re-examining the Cost Pressures on Health Systems. In M. McKee & J. Figueras (Eds.), *Health Systems: Health, Wealth, Society and Well-being* (pp. 37–61). Maidenhead: Open University Press. Retrieved from http://www.euro.who.int/__data/assets/pdf_file/0007/164383/e96159.pdf?ua=1.

Casadeus-Masanell, R., & Ricart, J. E. (2009). From Strategy to Business Models and to Tactics. *Harvard Business School.* Working Paper 10-036, 2009. Retrieved July 18, 2018, from https://www.hbs.edu/faculty/Publication%20Files/10-036.pdf.

Cash, E., Cash, R., & Dupilet, C. (2011). *Étude sur la réactivité des établissements de santé aux incitations tarifaires*, vol. 106. Drees, Série Études et Recherche.

Castano, R. (2014). Towards a Framework for Business Model Innovation in Health Care Delivery in Developing Countries. *BMC Medicine, 12*, 233. Retrieved from https://bmcmedicine.biomedcentral.com/articles/10.1186/s12916-014-0233-z.

Castoro, C., Bertinato, L., Baccaglini, U., Drace, C. A., & McKee, M. (2007). *Day Surgery: Making It Happen*. Copenhagen: European Observatory on Health Systems and Policies. Policy Brief.

Christensen, C. M., & Raynor, M. E. (2003). *The Innovator's Solution*. Boston: Harvard Business Review Press.

Christensen, C. M., Grossman, J. H., & Hwang, J. (2017). *The Innovator's Prescription*. New York: McGraw Hill.

Cochrane, A. (1971). *Effectiveness and Efficiency. Random Reflections on Health Services*. London: The Nuffield Provincial Hospital Trust. Retrieved from http://www.nuffieldtrust.org.uk/sites/files/nuffield/publication/Effectiveness_and_Efficiency.pdf.

Coxa Hospital. (2019). *Hospital Website. History*. Retrieved March 12, 2019, from https://www.coxa.fi/en/about-coxa/history/.

Department of Health. (2016). *Operational Productivity & Performance in English NHS Acute Hospitals: Unwarranted Variations*. Lord Carter of Coles Independent Report for the Department of Health. Retrieved from https://assets.publishing.service.gov.uk/government/uploads/system/uploads/attachment_data/file/499229/Operational_productivity_A.pdf.

Dixon, A., Robertson, R., Appleby, J., Burge, P., Devlin, N., & Magee, H. (2010). *Patient Choice; How Patients Choose and How Providers Respond*. London: The King's Fund.

Eisenmann, T. R., Parker, G., & van Alstyne, M. (2006). Strategies for Two-Sided Markets. *Harvard Business Review, 84*(10), 92–101.

Engström, S., Foldevi, M., & Borgquist, L. (2001). Is General Practice Effective? A Systematic Literature Review. *Scandinavian Journal of Primary Health Care, 19*, 131–144.

Gemmel, P., Vandeale, D., & Tambeur, W. (2008). Hospital Process Orientation (HPO): The Development of a Measurement Tool. *Total Quality Management and Business Excellence, 19*(12), 1207–1217.

Guenther, R., & Vittori, G. (2007). The Coventry Hospital. In *Sustainable Healthcare Architecture* (pp. 208–216). Hoboken: John Wiley and Sons.

Ham, C., Dixon, A., & Brooke, B. (2012). *Transforming the Delivery of Health and Social Care; The Case for Fundamental Change* (p. ix). London: The King's Fund.

Herzlinger, R. E. (2004). *Consumer-Driven Health Care: Implications for Providers, Payers, and Policymakers*. San Francisco: Jossey-Bass.

Imison, C., et al. (2008). *Under One Roof: Will Polyclinics Deliver Integrated Care*. London: King's Fund.

Institute for Healthcare Improvement. (2005). *Going Lean in Health Care*. Cambridge: Institute for Healthcare Improvement.

Kaidar-Person, O., Swartz, E. W., Lefkowitz, M., Conigliaro, K., Fritz, N., Birne, J., et al. (2006). Shared Medical Appointments: New Concept for High-Volume Follow-Up for Bariatric Patients. *Surgery for Obesity and Related Diseases, 2*(5), 509–512.

Kaiser, L. S., & Lee, T. H. (2015, October 8). Turning Value-Based Health Care into a Real Business Model. *Harvard Business Review*.

Kirsh, S., Watts, S., Pascuzzi, K., O'Day, M. E., Davidson, D., Strauss, G., et al. (2007). Shared Medical Appointments Based on the Chronic Care Model: A Quality Improvement Project to Address the Challenges of Patients with Diabetes with High Cardiovascular Risk. *Quality & Safety in Health Care, 16*(5), 349–353.

Leatt, P., Baker, G. R., & Kimberley, J. R. (2006). Organization Design. In S. M. Shortell & A. D. Kaluzny (Eds.), *Health Care Management. Organization Design and Behavior* (p. 339). Stanford: Thomson Delmar Learning.

Lee, K. S., Chun, K. H., & Lee, J. S. (2008). Reforming the Hospital Service Structure to Improve Efficiency: Urban Hospital Specialization. *Health Policy, 87*(1), 41–49.

Maarse H. & Normand C. Market Competition in European Hospital Care in Rechel, B., Wright, S., Edwards, N., Dowdeswell, B., & Mckee, M. (2009). *Investing in Hospitals of the Future. European Observatory on Health Systems and Policies*. Observatory Studies Series No. 16

Magretta, J. (2002a). *What Management Is: How It Works and Why It's Everyone's Business*. New York: The Free Press.

Magretta, J. (2002b, May). Why Business Models Matter. *Harvard Business Review*.

Martin, S., Purkayastha, S., Massey, R., Paraskeva, P., Tekkis, P., Kneebone, R., et al. (2007). The Surgical Care Practitioner: A Feasible Alternative. Results of a Prospective 4-Year Audit at St Mary's Hospital Trust, London. *Annals of the Royal College of Surgeons of England, 89*(1), 30–35.

Nolte, E., & McKee, M. (2008). Integration and Chronic Care: A Review. In E. Nolte & M. McKee (Eds.), *Caring for People with Chronic Conditions: A Health System Perspective*. Maidenhead: Open University Press.

Nolte, E., Pitchforth, E., Miani, C., & McHugh, S. (2014, December 30). The Changing Hospital Landscape. An Exploration of International Experiences. *RAND Health Quarterly, 4*(3), 1. eCollection.

O'Connell, T., et al. (2008). Health Services Under Siege: The Case for Clinical Process Redesign. *Medical Journal of Australia, 17*(Suppl. 6), 9–13.

OECD. (2017). *Health at a Glance 2017: OECD Indicators – Chapter 7*. Health Expenditure. Last updated 9-Oct-2017. StatLink. https://doi.org/10.1787/888933604438.

Olsson, L. E., Karlsson, J., & Ekman, I. (2006). The Integrated Care Pathway Reduced the Number of Hospital Days by Half: A Prospective Comparative Study of Patients with Acute Hip Fracture. *Journal of Orthopaedic Surgery and Research, 1*(3), 121.

Oosterholt, R. I., & Simonse, L. W. L. (2016). Service Pathway: A Case Study of Business Model Design in Healthcare. *ServDes.* Fifth Service Design and Innovation Conference. Retrieved from http://www.ep.liu.se/ecp/125/052/ecp16125052.pdf.

Oxman, A. D., & Glasziou, P. (2008). What Should Clinicians Do When Faced with Conflicting Recommendations? *British Medical Journal, 337*, a2530.

Pammolli, F., Riccaboni, M., Oglialoro, C., Magazzini, L., Baio, G., & Salerno, N. (2005) *Medical Devices, Competitiveness and Impact on Public Health Expenditure.* Florence: University of Florence. Study Prepared for the Directorate General Enterprise of the European Commission. Retrieved August 3, 2017, from http://www.cermlab.it/_documents/MD_Report.pdf.

Pan, Z. X., & Pokharel, S. (2007). Logistics in Hospitals: A Case Study of Some Singapore Hospitals. *Leadership Health Services, 20*(3), 195–207.

Porter, M. E., & Lee, T. H. (2018, September 5). What 21st Century Health Care Should Learn from 20th Century Business. *NEJM Catalyst.*

Porter, M. E., & Teisberg, E. O. (2006). *Redefining Health Care: Creating Value-Based Competition on Results.* Harvard Business School Press.

Rechel, B., Wright, S., Edwards, N., Dowdeswell, B., & Mckee, M. (2009). *Investing in Hospitals of the Future.* European Observatory on Health Systems and Policies. Observatory Studies Series No. 16.

Rotter, T., Plishka, C. T., Adegboyega, L., Fiander, M., Harrison, E. L., Flynn, R. et al. (2017, November 3). Lean Management in Health Care: Effects on Patient Outcomes, Professional Practice, and Healthcare Systems. *Cochrane Database of Systematic Reviews.* https://doi.org/10.1002/14651858.CD012831.

Schull, M. J., Szalai, J. P., Schwartz, B., & Redelmeier, D. A. (2001). Emergency Department Overcrowding Following Systematic Hospital Restructuring: Trends at Twenty Hospitals Over Ten Years. *Academic Emergency Medicine, 8*(11), 1037–1043.

Shepperd, S., Doll, H., Angus, R. M., Clarke, M. J., Iliffe, S., Kalra, L., et al. (2009). Avoiding Hospital Admission Through Provision of Hospital Care at Home: A Systematic Review and Meta-Analysis of Individual Patient Data. *CMAJ, 180*(2), 175–182.

Singh, D. (2008). *How Can Chronic Disease Management Programmes Operate Across Care Settings and Providers?* Copenhagen: WHO Regional Office for Europe. A Policy Brief.

Solumsmo, A. O., & Aslaksen, R. (2009). St. Olav's Hospital Trondheim, Norway. In B. Rechel, J. Erskine, B. Dowdeswell, S. Wright, & M. Mckee (Eds.),

Capital Investment for Health. Case Studies from Europe. European Observatory on Health Systems and Policies. Observatory Studies Series No. 18.

Starfield, B. (1994). Is Primary Care Essential? *Lancet, 344*, 1129–1133.

Vera, A., & Kuntz, L. (2007). Process-Based Organization Design and Hospital Efficiency. *Health Care Management Review, 32*(1), 55–65.

Vos, L., van Oostenbrugge, R. J., Limburg, M., van Merode, G. G., & Groothuis, S. (2009). How to Implement Process-Oriented Care. *Accreditation and Quality Assurance, 14*, 5–13.

Vos, L., Chalmers, S. E., Dückers, M. L. A., Groenewegen, P. P., Wagner, C., & van Merode, G. G. (2011). Towards an Organisation-Wide Process-Oriented Organisation of Care: A Literature Review. *Implementation Science, 6*, 8.

Waters, A. (Ed.). (2015, July 22). Best Places to Work. *Health Service Journal*. Retrieved July 12, 2018, from https://www.hsj.co.uk/leadership/best-places-to-work/hsj-reveals-the-best-places-to-work-in-2015/5087434.article#.VgJD8ejkJv4.

Watts, S. A., Gee, J., O'Day, M. E., Schaub, K., Lawrence, R., Aron, D., et al. (2009). Nurse Practitioner-Led Multidisciplinary Teams to Improve Chronic Illness Care: The Unique Strengths of Nurse Practitioners Applied to Shared Medical Appointments/Group Visits. *The Journal of the American Association of Nurse Practitioners, 21*(3), 167–172.

Winblad, U., & Ringard, Å. (2009). Meeting Rising Public Expectations: The Changing Roles of Patients and Citizens. In J. Magnussen, K. Vrangbaek, & R. B. Saltman (Eds.), *Nordic Health Care Systems. Recent Reforms and Current Policy Challenges* (pp. 126–150). New York: Open University Press, McGraw Hill.

CHAPTER 5

Hospital Care: Private Assets for-a-Profit?

Patrick Jeurissen and Hans Maarse

Introduction

The governance of hospitals and the business and care models they pursue are at the heart of this book. The ownership of hospital assets is a crucial element of an individual hospitals' governance; it also is an important precondition in how governments shape the workings of their hospital sectors. In the nearer future, evidence abounds that the context in which hospitals have to operate will change drastically in Europe, and indeed almost everywhere else. All countries face a rapid digitalization that might further disrupt current business models of hospitals (e-health); epidemiological pressures such as increase in multi-morbidity, prevalence of oncological diseases, and more frail elderly that need attention; and in many (yet

P. Jeurissen (✉)
Radboud University Medical School, Nijmegen, Netherlands

Ministry of Health, Welfare and Sports, Hague, Netherlands
e-mail: Patrick.Jeurissen@radboudumc.nl

H. Maarse
Faculty of Health, Medicine and Life Sciences, University of Maastricht, Maastricht, Netherlands
e-mail: H.Maarse@maastrichtuniversity.nl

A. Durán, S. Wright (eds.), *Understanding Hospitals in Changing Health Systems*, https://doi.org/10.1007/978-3-030-28172-4_5

not all) countries, fiscal challenges continue—putting pressure on the budgets, including for capital, of most (public) hospitals.

For a long time, policymakers have advocated a strategy of substitution of hospital care by primary care and other outpatient settings in order to increase efficiency, tackle rising costs, and bring care closer to the people. However, this solution brings its own challenges: cross-subsidies by straightforward elective and chronic care that now help to cover for the otherwise unmet costs of expensive hospital assets come under threat. Public hospitals might lack the political room to manoeuvre around the coming challenges. At the same time, a healthcare sector where hospitals do not dominate its core infrastructure seems 'unthinkable' for many reasons. Hospitals hold strong political constituencies, with very strong negotiating powers versus payers, and they are and will remain paramount for the treatment of complex diseases of high-need, high-cost populations and for the introduction of new capital-intensive technologies such as robotics.

Historically, hospitals have evolved from places where the poor and needy were cared for with minimum resources to organizations that could facilitate (almost) all possibilities of modern medicine to (almost) everybody. Thus, hospitals became increasingly attractive for medical specialists as a preferred place to practice. As private practitioners could generally not support the investment needs of these hospitals, the state stepped in or orchestrated social insurance schemes and, for many years, private commercial hospitals declined in importance. Self-pay markets did shrink and many states supported public hospitals directly with the capital they needed. Depending on country, specific regulations, and orchestration of this process, private (for-profit and non-profit) and public hospital markets varied in the ways they experienced and responded to these trends. However, in almost all countries the public and not-for-profit hospital sectors strengthened versus the proprietary sector for many years after the end of World War II.

Over the past decades, many countries have shown significant increases in for-profit hospital market share, often without any specific ideological government policies in that direction, although exceptions exist such as in Eastern Europe after the fall of the Berlin Wall. We also witness alternative ways of (private) funding for hospital assets, such as public-private-partnerships (PPP), lease constructions of expensive equipment, and outsourcing of human resources. Standard economic theory and new public management concepts suggest that for-profit hospitals are more efficient than both not-for-profit and public hospitals. Profits in principle are a strong motivator of efficiency, and people with property rights take better care of their assets, both of which increase future revenues. The higher costs of private equity and the larger financial risks that come with it by themselves are strong incentives to strive for efficiency. Opponents of such logics of 'perfect markets' emphasize real world problems, such as restricted access for those unable to pay, cherry-picking strategies, and interference of professional management with clinical autonomy. Essentially, most opponents state that in hospital care, a perfect market does not hold, and that the feasibility of even a workable market is doubtful at best. This raises important questions on private entrepreneurialism for the future of hospitals, in Europe and elsewhere. Is this a feasible strategy to tackle the broader upcoming challenges of the hospital sector?

In this chapter, we categorize the arguments pro and con for-profit hospital assets, and seek empirical evidence on such viewpoints. The Section "Different Ownership Models of Hospital Assets" elaborates different aspects of ownership in the field of hospital care. The Section "Trends in the Ownership of Hospital Assets" presents recent trends in ownership in a representative number of European countries. The Section "Hospital Ownership: Evidence from Empirical Studies" covers the empirical evidence on hospital performance according to type of ownership as well as constructions of private-public-ownership. The Section "The For-Profit Hospital Sector: Case Studies on Its Governance" presents three short case studies of the for-profit hospital sector from Germany, the UK, and the Netherlands. We then discuss what the presented evidence might imply for the governance of the hospital sector in the Section "United Kingdom: A Private Sector Independent from the NHS". The Section "Germany: Privatization Because of Tight Public Investment Budgets" concludes.

Different Ownership Models of Hospital Assets

Generally, three different types of hospital ownership are distinguished: private for-profit (FP), private not-for-profit (NFP), and public (PH):

- For-profit ownership is defined by a bundle of proprietary rights that represents formal control of the hospital and makes the distribution of profits as well as the assets of the company possible. Most notably, (1) the right to receive the remaining residual after all contractually committed payments have been respected; (2) the right to terminate or revise the ownership of the hospital; and (3) the right to sell the rights specified in the preceding two points (Jeurissen 2010). Note that these rights do not need to be distributed according to the financial stake of the owners in the firm, as, for example, is the case in most cooperatives.

- The defining characteristic of not-for-profit hospitals is that the ones who control it—including its board members, directors, and officers—are prohibited from receiving the organizations' net earnings (non-distribution constraint). This (should) serve to demonstrate the trustworthiness of not-for-profit organizations, and this might be important, for example, with regard to developing a complementary partnership between the public and private sector; seeking aspects of 'unobservable' quality of care; or tapping into the markets of volunteers and workers with a pro-social motivation (Jeurissen 2010). However, note that not-for-profits might own for-profit subsidiaries, although any possible returns according to the stake of the non-profit hospital go to the trust. Increasingly not-for-profit hospitals choose to operate for-profit subsidiaries, for example, to run parking lots and other commercial activities, but also ambulatory surgery centres and so on. In contrast to the profit-maximizing paradigm of the standard firm, to date, there is no specific theory on the goals non-profits seek that resembles this. Feldstein showed that the behaviour of not-for-profit hospitals clearly diverges from profit maximization (Feldstein 1979). Henry Hansmann pointed to the difference between 'donative' and 'service-oriented' or 'commercial' non-profits (Hansmann 1980). Pauly and Redisch (1973) saw not-for-profit hospitals as physicians' cooperatives, mainly working for the interests of the medical staff. Not-for-profit law often tends to be enabling law that is poorly enforced, and allows stakeholders to maximize control (Jeurissen 2010).
- Like not-for-profit hospitals, public hospitals are bound to the non-distribution constraint. However, the use of the available proprietary rights depends on the outcome of a political process. Initially, (local) politicians were in direct charge of the running of a public hospital. The closing of a hospital, even if it cannot be sustained financially, is generally a political no-go area. Thus, there exist quite some struggling public hospitals, with few if any financial resources. In such cases, privatization might become an attractive option. Indeed, many countries saw waves of privatization. We might think, for example, of Germany after reunification or Eastern Europe after the break down

> of communist rule. More moderate governance models are also feasible. Today few public hospitals run as specific bureaus of the government. Presently, public hospitals are generally organized as separate public co-operations; public health systems might commission part of their services to the private sector.

It is important to distinguish between formal and effective control. In hospital care, ownership rights are generally constrained by many public regulations, professional autonomy, and social expectations. The differences between formal ('do as you please since you are the owner') and effective ('what you can in practice do') are considerable. Policies might force hospitals to comply with so-called "certificate-of-need" regulations of one kind or another and with all kinds of reimbursement requirements. It is generally unacceptable to fail to provide necessary care to those patients unable to pay. Physicians control large parts of the working processes, and they hold professional goals such as maximizing quality of care, but they also might seek to maximize their income. The central place of physicians in the governance of hospitals might allow them to do both, and thus increase the level of costs beyond an optimal from the societal perspective.

Another involvement of private entrepreneurism in the hospital sector is that of public-private partnerships (PPP), that see their origin in the thinking of new public management from the early 1990s onwards. Public-private partnerships are more or less permanent (i.e. usually at least decades-long) co-operations between public and private actors, through which joint products or services are developed and where risks, costs, and profits are shared according to certain stakes (Klijn et al. 2007). The concessions and contracts under these partnerships generally tend to run for many years, as is the case with toll roads and airports, and also with hospitals. The main underlying idea is that the private sector can perform some tasks (most notably operational management and efficiency) better than the public sector and thus should deliver these on behalf of the public sector in order to increase overall efficiency. An important prerequisite to prevent rent-seeking strategies is that specific and enforceable contracts between public and private parties are feasible. Montagu and Harding (2012) see four types of hospital PPPs[1]:

[1] There are several other available typologies for PPP—see, for example, Barlow et al., Health Affairs, 2013. Some prominent PPP types such as a now almost famous Alzira model would not fit easily into the Montagu/Harding structure.

- Facilities and finance PPPs focus on mobilizing capital and creating new hospital buildings and equipment. The Private Finance Initiative in the UK stands as a model for this type of PPP; private companies provide capital and develop and operate hospital facilities and perhaps equipment.
- In another model, services themselves are the core of the partnership; private companies deliver part of the services—such as facility management, but extending into clinical services—but also the management of a complete hospital, for a fee.
- In a third model, public hospital services are tendered out to private operators. For example, private hospitals tender for a certain number of hip-replacements.
- Finally, private companies can make payments to public hospitals to capitalise on the value of public assets. An example might be the renting of a separate wing and surgery facilities to a private clinic that caters for a better-off clientele.

Trends in the Ownership of Hospital Assets

Over the last couple of decades, for-profit hospitals have seen a substantial rise in many countries, although not everywhere. Table 5.1 illustrates that the current market-share of for-profit hospitals varies greatly between countries. In the Nordic countries and in the Netherlands, their presence is still negligible, but in many countries in Southern and Eastern Europe as well as in Germany and France the stake of for-profit hospitals is larger even than in the US. Reasons lay in historically strong private parallel systems in Southern

Table 5.1 For-profit hospital beds, percentage of total (2000—most recent year)

	2000	*2005*	*2010*	*2013*	*2016*
Austria	7.2	9.0	11.1	13.1	13.5
Denmark	0.8	1.4	2.1	2.1	2.5[a]
Finland	3.3	3.7	4.4	4.2	4.7
France	19.8	20.5	23.4	23.7	24.0
Germany		26.2	29.7	29.8	30.3
Italy		28.1	28.0	28.2	29.0
Spain	18.0	19.7	18.2	18.8	19.0
US	13.1	13.8	15.1	16.5	16.9[b]

Source: OECD (2018)

[a]2017

[b]2015

Europe, where the National Health Services (NHS) do not always have the funds to be attractive to a more prosperous clientele, and in mass privatizations of (outdated) public hospitals in Eastern Germany and the rest of Central and Eastern Europe after the fall of the Wall.

The rise in for-profit ownership only partly illustrates the growing involvement of the private sector with hospital care. Reliable comparative statistics are lacking, but we also see in many countries a steep rise in the number of independent treatment centres, walk-in clinics, and clinics that specialize in ambulatory surgery. These clinics are very commercially-aware, and concentrate on a smaller bundle of services than once was the exclusive domain of the hospital.

Another trend is that of an increase in private-public-partnerships. Mostly countries that rely on a national health service seek partnerships with private companies to spur the efficiency of their public delivery system. However, this sometimes is also a way to circumvent strict rules of public capital budgets that amortize all investment costs at once, not allowing for depreciation over a long period of years that for hospitals typically varies between 30 and 50 years.

Hospital Ownership: Evidence from Empirical Studies

Over the past couple of decades, more and more studies have researched the whereabouts of for-profit hospitals on real world markets. A meta-review by Mark Schlesinger and Bradford Gray (2006) on US evidence found that not-for-profit hospitals hold an advantage or faced no significant performance differences in 179 out of 220 individual comparisons. However, methodology differs substantially between these and other studies with respect to the measurements of important variables, such as quality of care and community benefits, as well as the handling of the (bigger) profit margins of for-profit hospitals. Besides, most studies follow a cross-sectional design and thus longitudinal aspects are not taken into account.

Here we summarize an earlier review on US studies (Jeurissen 2010). These studies show that adjusted costs per service do not differ widely between hospital ownership types. So from this perspective, pro or con for-profit ownership does not seem to matter much. However, cost structures do in fact differ substantially. For example, US for-profit hospitals consistently do allocate more resources to capital investments and to the reimbursement of medical staff and management. However, their expenses for nurses and other workers are substantially lower than other ownership types (Carter et al. 1997). Another typical feature is that for-profit hospitals generally charge higher (adjusted) rates to payers, operate with higher margins, and hold stronger balance sheets. In other words, it is not so much the differences in the economic performance that count, but the allocation of the resources: who gets, what, when, and how.

Due to many methodological difficulties, such as unobservable outputs and case-mix differences, the available evidence with respect to quality of care should be taken with caution. Variations in quality of care seem to be at least as large within as between ownership types (Eggleston et al. 2006). However, in comparison to for-profit hospitals, private not-for-profit facilities do seem to deliver somewhat better measurable quality of care while public facilities seem to lag somewhat behind. Longitudinal studies capture important aspects of the business model of for-profit hospital chains. They illustrate that for-profits are (much) more active in the purchasing and acquisition of other hospitals. This probably increases their efficiencies of scale. They also typically buy struggling facilities and seek a turnaround. If successful, this does contribute to the improvement of social welfare (Herr 2008). For-profit hospitals also seem to be more responsive to reductions in demand, including the closure of redundant facilities (Hansmann et al. 2002).

A recent review from countries in the European Union on the performance of private (both for-profit and non-profit) versus public hospitals, which includes 45 studies from Italy, Germany, the UK, France, Greece, Austria, Spain, and Portugal, broadly confirms these findings. Public hospitals seem to be at least as efficient as private hospitals, although the specific context might matter (these particular studies mainly represent the situation in Germany and Italy). The authors also remark that accessibility might be a problem in private provision and that, especially in Beveridge countries with private parallel private systems such as the UK, Italy, Spain, and Greece, high-income people get better access to such facilities. Studies on quality of care showed mixed results, although private hospitals seem to do relatively well on observable outcomes in comparison to structure and process indicators (Kruse et al. 2018).

Both the above reviews conclude that private (for-profit) hospitals seem to be more responsive to all kinds of incentives, as shown by responses to changes in demand, to changes in reimbursement practices, up-coding practices, as well as observable quality indicators (where German and Italian for-profit hospitals seem to perform better) (Kruse et al. 2018).

This holds important implications for policymakers. A careful design of incentives might foster the potential superior efficiency of the private sector, but a suboptimal design might very well lower social welfare and give way to opportunistic behaviour such as cherry-picking and increasing the amounts of low-value services.

The evidence on PPP initiatives is less well structured, but lies in line with the above results. A recent report by the National Audit Office in the UK was very critical of the financial rationale of private finance initiative (PFI) and merely saw it as a way of off-budget funding of hospital infrastructure where (substantially higher) costs were shifted to the future (NAO 2018). Also recently, a study of the outsourcing of hospital cleaning services in the NHS found that this was associated with lower economic costs, but also with greater incidence of hospital-borne meticillin-resistant *Staphylococcus aureus* (MRSA) infection (the additional treatment costs were not included in the economic analysis) (Toffolutti et al. 2017). A study on Spain's Alzira model concluded that its 2015 performance was statistically worse for the majority of indicators than a public peer group, although in some areas of care, such as adjusted mortality improvements after percutaneous coronary interventions, its results have been outstanding (Comendeiro-Maaloe et al. 2018).

The For-Profit Hospital Sector: Case Studies on Its Governance

There exists a huge diversity in for-profit ownership types across both countries and time. For example, Germany and some Central and Eastern European countries witnessed steep rises in the share after the fall of communism. The UK developed an independent sector following the birth of the NHS. In the US, Medicare's initial capital reimbursements were very favourable in the case of for-profit hospitals. Other countries witnessed moderate trends in such hospital types. The comparatively well-funded health systems of the Nordic countries and their egalitarian cultures and structures never allowed for more than a niche position for private hospital providers. The same holds for the Netherlands and Belgium. Still, other countries have large historic stakes of for-profit ownership (Spain, Italy, and France among them). This section illustrates how differences in access to capital and their regulations as well as the interest and organization of physicians explain much of this diversity. We analyse below three country cases in more depth.

United Kingdom: A Private Sector Independent of the NHS

In the UK, most of the private sector resembles a parallel system to the NHS. It delivers elective care and amenities to those willing to pay its lavish rates. If the NHS fails to live up to people's expectations, the attraction of the independent sector and the willingness-to-pay for these services increases. However, over time the private sector was enabled to grow as a result of the recurring waiting list problems of the NHS and the underfunding of its infrastructure. Notably, NHS consultants are allowed to treat those willing to pay both in NHS pay-beds ('private patient units') and/or the private sector (Jeurissen 2010). Private insurance companies depend for their business models on the private sector, and in the past have facilitated the emergence of private hospital chains. Chains of small hospitals and clinics form the dominant business model of the private sector. The care model increasingly incorporates focused pathways for elective surgeries.

The governance of the NHS bears the marks of fierce political battles that induced all kinds of reforms. For example, in the 1970s, the Labour government tried to phase out NHS pay-beds, only to find consultants much more willing to refer these patients to the independent sector (Laing & Buisson 2007). Then the Conservatives followed a policy that contained the costs of the NHS while providing at the same time generous tax breaks to the private sector (Higgins 1988).

The purchaser-provider split gave backing to the idea that the NHS might also commission private providers. The number of private beds peaked at around 6 per cent of the total in 2000. Large investments by the Blair governments increased the positive image of the NHS. Under the PFI, many new public hospitals were developed. Private companies could gain contracts to treat NHS patients on condition that they had an acceptable level of efficiency compared to the NHS; and that the use of NHS employees to deliver these commissioned services was limited. This somehow spurred a second business model where private hospitals delivered care on the conditions of the NHS, quite aside from the existing business model where insurance companies and self-pay patients were, and are, the main clients. These 'independent sector treatment centres' were units set up largely to cut NHS waiting lists/times, and the client was entirely the NHS (Naylor and Gregory 2009). Because of austerity policies, the prospects of private companies to earn NHS business on favourable conditions worsened after 2008: private providers faced difficulties to live up to the financial standards of their NHS commissioners. To date, the UK private hospital sector still holds a niche position and, without a major turnaround of its business and care models, seems unlikely to be a feasible alternative for the NHS under current governance arrangements.

Germany: Privatization Because of Tight Public Investment Budgets

In Western Germany, regulations favoured self-regulation and pluralist hospital ownership. However, for a long time the for-profit sector had virtually no access to funding by sickness funds, and no access to public capital subsidies—the latter were reserved for the larger public and not-for-profit hospitals that were included in state hospital plans (Simon 2000). Between 1972 and 1989, 200 small private clinics closed doors (Jeurissen 2010). In an effort to sustain a private sector, private insurance companies supported the start of private hospital chains just as in the UK.

The for-profit hospital sector really took off after German reunification in 1989. Many public hospitals in Eastern Germany were acquired by newly found for-profit chains. Special capital subsidies from Western Germany, through a reunification fund, made major redevelopments of the outdated hospital infrastructure possible. In the West, the opposite happened, but with the same outcome: the amount of publicly available capital declined, and this gradually led to a so-called *Investitionsstau* among public hospitals (Augurzky et al. 2007). This put pressure on public hospitals that could not pursue the necessary investments and often bore annual deficits. Many cities and municipalities decided to privatize these clinics, further accelerating the growth of private chains. The highest profile acquisition was that of the university clinics in Marburg/GieBen by Rhön-Klinikum in 2006. Between 1992 and 2007, the market share of for-profit hospital beds almost tripled (Jeurissen 2010). A lot of this for-profit sector growth was fed through acquisitions of public hospitals.[2] As a result, the German for-profit hospital sector resembles the scale and scope of public and non-profit facilities more than in most other countries (Augurzky et al. 2015). Recently, the sector has entered harder territory: the market of mergers and acquisitions has now matured, and German hospitals have only a small share of the fast-growing market for outpatient treatments, where private physicians dominate.

[2] According to Barlow et al. (2013) (footnote 1, above) these hospitals would be closer to a PPP than a 'true' private hospital: they are registered and committed to certain services in the state *Krankenhausplan* (hospital plan), contracted for the *Krankenhausplan* (sickness funds), and paid at the same DRG rate as public hospitals.

The Netherlands: Market Reforms Without For-Profit Hospital Ownership

In the Netherlands, the distribution of rewards for equity capital (i.e. dividends) is still forbidden. The 1971 Hospital Facilities Act restricted all access to social insurance funding of any for-profit hospitals, although at the time no such facility actually existed. Private insurance companies and physicians held no strong interest in the building of a for-profit hospital sector. Private patients were treated in not-for-profit hospitals that delivered all kinds of extra amenities. In contrast to Germany and the UK, Dutch hospital doctors were self-employed and profited from the higher fees of such patients themselves (Jeurissen 2010).

The year 2006 saw a big reform of the Dutch healthcare system. Insurance companies and all providers had to compete on regulated markets. Among other things, regulations on the setting of insurance premiums, purchasing models, provider reimbursement and certificate-of-need were severely deregulated, making the Netherlands an international front-runner in the liberalization of the healthcare market. Remarkably, profit-making stayed highly controversial, and to date the ban on this still exists among large parts of the purchaser and provider markets. Nevertheless, the Netherlands is witnessing the emergence of a for-profit sector in disguise. A rapid rise in the number of independent treatment centres is one illustration. Also, three struggling community hospitals have been bought by an investor. The anticipated lifting of the ban on for-profit hospital ownership, however, is still failing to materialize. In late 2018, these hospitals went into default because of difficulties that possibly relate to the lack of clear business and care models.

Discussion

As discussed throughout this book, hospitals should not be understood by what they have (beds, doctors etc.), but ideally by what they do and how they do it, in the setting of the wider healthcare system. This implies that hospitals should be articulated around the notions of business and care models, their governance, and the context in which they operate. In many countries of the world, the historic function of for-profit hospitals was to provide care to a richer (self-paying) clientele and to offer senior physicians the possibility to take their private patients to these facilities. This shaped the business and care models of these facilities: comparatively small, with a broad spectrum of all kinds of elective services and rather good amenities. However, they had a limited role in the broader pattern of governance of the healthcare sector.

The coming of universal health coverage put that model under pressure, and the challenge for the private for-profit hospital sector then became to get access to these new and growing markets. This affected their business and care models, which now depend less on diversity of services and more on standardization and an economic proposition for the public purse. They have increasingly succeeded in getting this access, although with a lot of variety between countries. For example, as indicated, in Germany, for-profits now fulfil an essential role, in the UK they still hold niche positions and still rely heavily on their role as a private parallel system for the well-off, and in the Netherlands they until now have failed to play any important role.

Within current health systems, the typical for-profit hospital can be defined as a smaller facility, but now part of a bigger commercial chain with a lot of muscle to negotiate with its payers and subcontractors. Financial positions of for-profit chains are generally strong, especially in comparison with public hospitals in NHS-type systems. This gives them more firing power for investments, although most governments can generally attract capital more cheaply (i.e. pay a lower interest rate) from the markets. Most for-profit clinics contain rather focused business and care models that are shaped to maximize operational efficiencies of a spectrum of elective treatments, next to the provision of other profitable services and amenities. They are generally not big all-services-under-one-roof hospitals, although some are. In other words, they are complementary to large public hospitals that seek to provide the entire spectrum of specialist care.

Most studies show that for-profit hospitals do not deliver superior performance in terms of quality-of-care and costs to public payers and social insurance funds (static efficiency), but they seem more flexible and responsive to changes in their context (dynamic efficiency). The market share of for-profit hospitals has primarily improved because of:

1. A shortage of capital in the public sector (indebted governments and public providers with worse margins);
2. Their appeal to physicians (better remuneration and the prospect of sharing in the growing value of the company); and
3. The coming of new technologies that favour other and more specialized business and care models (minimal-invasive surgery, digitalization, and e-health).

For-profit hospital chains bring additional benefits such as scale in procurement strategies, negotiating power with payers, and more dense reference networks. Future hospitals will have to operate with very different models of care. The focus of inpatient stays will be on complex treatments and on patients who are frail or suffer from many co-morbidities. The importance of digitalization and outpatient treatments will only continue to rise in coming years and be more compatible with different business and care models, also serviced by the private sector. This asks for models of experimental governance that includes private provision; together with the structural growth of healthcare as an increasing sector of the larger economy which will attract private companies.

Important questions will focus on the governance arrangements needed in hospital markets with mixed ownership types:

- The first is a robust arrangement for universal coverage of state-of-the-art healthcare services. This not only implies a financial sharing of risks, but also acceptable waiting times and access to an adequate hospital infrastructure with all the modern equipment.
- An important remaining question is raised by the not only theoretical possibility that social models will be gradually dismantled, as a result of politics of further privatization, and where for-profit companies might be tempted into rent-seeking behaviour such as cherry-picking and gaming public payers and reimbursement models. This calls for sound governance and institutions with respect to access of care, reimbursement, and a radical improvement of the 'contractability' of the services at stake.

We think a fruitful strategy might be to recognize that, in a mixed market, it makes sense to use different constraints for different types of providers. For example, countries in Europe might follow US tax regulations that allow fewer tax breaks to for-profit hospital companies (while tax law in Europe mostly allows at present a sizeable tax break for institutions offering community services, such as hospitals). Another regulation might be an independent valuation of public or not-for-profit assets before allowing their acquisition by a for-profit company. Both give to the taxpayer control over unobservable and hard to prevent rent-seeking strategies.

Summary

This chapter has analysed the logic of for-profit ownership for hospital assets. The for-profit hospital sector is on the rise in many European countries, generally not as the result of intended policies in that direction. It most probably will continue doing so. Four arguments seem to trump the current mixed empirical evidence on their cross-sectional performance:

- First, healthcare will keep on growing over the next decades, and leaving the for-profit sector out of this growth will be very hard as it will eventually hamper the model of an open economy;
- Second, many countries and public hospitals lack the capital resources for the necessary investments to make hospital care fit for the future (infrastructure, equipment, and digitalization);
- Third, there is a growing need for business models that rely on value-added processes (focused factories), and this logic fits well with the strong points of private for-profit providers, as do care models that depend on digitalization;
- Fourth, the private sector is more responsive to changes in context—that is, is able to work with more agility. Such agility is needed to handle the many current and future technological and epidemiological challenges.

That is not to say that a further increase of private for-profit assets is without problems. Some of them could be severe, as follows:

- Governments need to guarantee universal access across the different ownership types and increase the level of 'contractability' and 'accountability' of the services at stake. The latter are important because this stimulates business and care models that focus on operational excellence and the increase of dynamic efficiencies;
- Governments also should protect the interest of the taxpayer in bail-out procedures of public or non-profit assets by for-profit companies; this includes the interests of other stakeholders, such as healthcare workers. A high quality and trustworthy public sector is an important prerequisite for further privatization of the hospital market. An equal market might depend on unequal preconditions between ownership types;

- Finally, some complex risks that come with high asset specificity (e.g. university clinics) are simply too expensive to cover on the financial markets, and should continue to reside under public ownership.

References

Augurzky, B., Engel, S., Krolop, C., Schmidt, M., & Terkatz, S. (2007). *Hospital Rating Report 2006, Approaches to the Sustainable Financing of Patient Care and Treatment – Development of German Hospitals up to 2010*. Essen: RWI-Heft 33.

Augurzky, B., Pilny, A., & Wübker, A. (2015). *Krankenhäuser in privater Trägerschaft 2015*. Essen: RWI Materialien 89.

Barlow, J. G., Roehrich, J. K., & Wright, S. (2013). Europe sees Mixed Results from Public-private Partnerships for Building and Managing Health Care Facilities and Services. *Health Affairs, 32*(1), 146–154.

Carter, R. B., Massa, I. J., & Power, M. L. (1997). An Examination of the Efficiency of Proprietary Hospital Ownership versus Non-Proprietary Hospital Ownership Structures. *Journal of Accounting and Public Policy, 16*, 63–87.

Comendeiro-Maaloe, M., Ridao-Lopez, M., Gorgemans, S., & Bernal-Delgado, E. (2018). A Comparative Performance Analysis of a Renowned Public Private Partnership for Health Care Provision in Spain Between 2003 and 2015. *Health Policy*. https://doi.org/10.1016/j.healthpol.2018.11.009.

Eggleston, K., Shen, Y. C., Lau, J., Schmidt, C. H., & Chan, J. (2006). *Hospital Ownership and Quality of Care: What Explains the Different Results?* NBER Working Paper 12241.

Feldstein, P. J. (1979). *Healthcare Economics*. New York: John Wiley & Sons.

Hansmann, H. (1980). The Role of Nonprofit Enterprise. *Yale Law Journal, 89*, 835–890.

Hansmann, H., Kessler, D., & McClellan, M. (2002). *Ownership Form and Trapped Capital in the Hospital Industry*. NBER, Working Paper 8989.

Herr, A. (2008). Costs and Technical Efficiency of German Hospitals: Does Ownership Matter? *Health Economics, 17*, 1057–1071.

Higgins, J. (1988). *The Business of Medicine: Private Healthcare in Britain*. London: Macmillan.

Jeurissen, P. P. T. (2010). *For-Profit Hospitals. A Comparative and Longitudinal Study of the For-Profit Hospital Sector in Four Western Countries*. Rotterdam: Erasmus University. Dissertation.

Klijn, E. H., Edelenbos, J., & Hughes, M. (2007). Public-Private Partnership: A Two-Headed Reform. A Comparison of PPP in England and the Netherlands. In C. Pollitt, S. van Thiel, & V. Homburg (Eds.), *New Public Management in Europe Adaption and Alternatives* (pp. 71–89). New York: Palgrave Macmillan.

Kruse, F. M., Stadhouders, N. W., Adang, E., Groenewoud, S., & Jeurissen, P. P. T. (2018). Do Private Hospitals Outperform Public Hospitals Regarding Efficiency, Accessibility, and Quality of Care in the European Union? A Literature Review. *International Journal Health Planning and Management, 33*(2), e434–e453.

Laing & Buisson. (2007). *Laing's Healthcare Market Review 2007–2008* (20th ed.). Bedfordshire: Newnorth Print Ltd.

Montagu, D., & Harding, A. (2012). A Zebra or a Painted Horse? Are Hospital PPPs Infrastructure Partnerships with Stripes or a Separate Species. *World Hospitals and Health Services, 48*(2), 15–20.

NAO – National Audit Office. (2018). *PFI and PF2, Report by the Comptroller and Auditor General*, January 12, 2018. Retrieved from https://www.nao.org.uk/wp-content/uploads/2018/01/PFI-and-PF2.pdf.

Naylor, C., & Gregory, S. (2009, October). *Briefing: Independent Sector Treatment Centres*. London: Kings Fund.

OECD. (2018). *OECD Stat*. Retrieved April 1, 2019, from https://stats.oecd.org/Index.aspx?DataSetCode=HEALTH_REAC.

Pauly, M. V., & Redisch, M. (1973). The Non-Profit Hospital as a Physicians' Cooperative. *American Economic Review, 63*, 87–99.

Schlesinger, M., & Gray, B. H. (2006). How Nonprofits Matter in American Medicine, and What to Do About It. *Health Affairs*, w287–w303.

Simon, M. (2000). *Krankenhauspolitik in der Bundesrepublik Deutschland, Historische Entwicklung und Probleme der Politisches Steuerung stationärer Krankenversorgung*. Wiesbaden: Westdeutscher Verlag.

Toffolutti, V., Reeves, A., McKee, M., & Stuckler, D. (2017). Outsourcing Cleaning Services Increase MRSA Incidence: Evidence from 126 English Acute Trusts. *Social Science and Medicine, 174*, 64–69.

CHAPTER 6

Hospital Payment Systems

Paolo Belli and Patrick Jeurissen

Introduction

Why a chapter in this book on payment systems (PS), purchasing arrangements, or methods of payment when tens of books and hundreds of articles have already been written on the topic? The simple answer is: we have wanted to include it because payment systems occupy a key place in ***adjusting*** the role that hospitals play in intermediating between payers and recipients of care (see Fig. 1.1 in Chap. 1). Such is the case for all modern hospitals, irrespective of their size, specialism, location, and so on, and therefore payment schemes have an almost universal importance in the arrangements of contemporary health systems.

A definitive initial statement is that payment systems (PS) are connected—and indeed should be in line with—the business model(s) that

P. Belli (✉)
The World Bank, Nairobi, Kenya
e-mail: pbelli1@worldbank.org

P. Jeurissen
Radboud University Medical School, Nijmegen, Netherlands

Ministry of Health, Welfare and Sports, Hague, Netherlands
e-mail: Patrick.Jeurissen@radboudumc.nl

A. Durán, S. Wright (eds.), *Understanding Hospitals in Changing Health Systems*, https://doi.org/10.1007/978-3-030-28172-4_6

have emerged and may emerge for hospitals in the health system in the context of a given governance arrangement (i.e. PS are indispensable in how they contribute to "make true" the assumptions about how the organization will perform in creating value for stakeholders—and in particular to its value proposition).

Christensen (2009) writes that, if hospitals would become "separable" by function and their payments were likewise tailored according to their business model (refer to the corresponding Chap. 4), the payment system for each type would have to be different—that is, "solution shops" would be paid in a different fashion from "value-adding processing" facilities and from "facilitated networks". When he wrote his book, Christensen predicted that such a three-way split would occur rather soon, but this is not in fact yet visibly occurring. In any case, little is known of the evolution of the issue in the real world, although there are signs in that direction, especially in the payment to value-adding chains, day care centres, and the like.

This chapter explains how few elements in hospitals can be analysed simultaneously as both the source of serious problems in creating wrong incentives and as a recurrent candidate to become the "miraculous remedy" that would solve the above problems. Experience shows that no matter how complex and sophisticated the design of payment systems may be in order to avoid them being gamed, sooner rather than later health professionals and administrators alike find a way to circumvent them, opening yet another episode of disappointment, and so on. Besides, reforming the reimbursement of hospitals is a very political endeavour, and this makes it very difficult to create a neat PS that fits with theoretical propositions such as the ones from Christensen or others.

After this introduction, the structure of this chapter is as follows:

- First, concepts, and the various categories;
- Second, hospital payment system reforms over time;
- Third, key trade-offs in design of payment systems;
- Fourth (and despite the remark in the paragraph above), some suggestions about the intersection of payment systems with potential business models of hospitals;
- Finally, broad conclusions.

Some Concepts and the Various PS Categories

Resource allocation, purchasing arrangement and payment systems (PS) define the criteria according to which funds within the health system, collected through different revenue sources and pooled together, flow eventually to reach service providers including hospitals.[1] A PS is defined as a set of rules establishing the criteria according to which a provider of health services receives financial compensation. These, as will be seen, can be variously linked to inputs, the number of patients, their diagnosed health-related condition, the type and the cost of care given, outcome, a combination of the above, and/or other factors.

PS play a particularly important role in the health sector, due to the peculiar interplay of demand and supply. More than in most other markets, when demanding health services, individuals are largely uncertain about the appropriateness of the service they are receiving. Any health service is an *experience* good, one for which appropriateness and quality can be ascertained only ex post. Even ex post, the quality of any individual health service is difficult to assess precisely because the patient often receives a multidimensional service (diagnosis, advice, treatment, etc.), and because the final outcome ("good health" or "health improvement", which are what people really demand) depend in uncertain ways on factors other than the kind of care received and the output produced. The lack of information and the particular psychological condition of patients produce crucial consequences for the interaction between demand and supply. It is the doctor, and not the patient, who generally chooses the amount and the type of services that the latter receives, and these knowledge asymmetries and agent/principal disconnects are important.

Four observations should also be made at this point:

- First, payment systems not only define the criteria for allocation of resources for given services, but also determine the total amount that is paid. In other words, the combined "how much to purchase" and "at what prices?" questions (i.e. the total revenue) are as important as the "how to pay?" question. In economic/financial terms, for an individual hospital, there is an incentive to provide

[1] Note that health financing includes both the alternative ways to gather the funding for health services, by collecting and pooling resources for health, and the criteria for distributing resources across purchasers and providers.

any service, as long as the payment it receives for each case treated is higher than its marginal cost. Since hospitals incur significant fixed costs and relatively less significant marginal costs, this helps explain why a fee-for-service PS which reimburses above marginal cost can lead to incentives to overproduce services and escalate costs quite substantially.

Taking an intertemporal view, in Chap. 1 and elsewhere, this book has emphasized the developments in technology (in the broadest sense) and medical science knowledge which progressively transformed Middle Age "alms houses" into modern hospitals. However, equally important in making possible such a concentration of qualified staff and asset-specific capital stock embodying technology in what we call modern hospitals has been the increasing level and concentration of financial resources, created by economic growth and facilitated by the development of massive/universal pre-payment and risk-pooling mechanisms. It would be impossible to conceive, for example, that a system entirely dependent on patients' out of pocket expenditures could ever have generated modern hospitals. This highlights the importance of governance as a facilitating and fostering factor.

- Second, in presenting various PS for hospitals, one key distinction is between "retrospective" and "prospective" payment systems. A payment system is retrospective when the cost of the activities implemented (in terms of volume of inputs and unit cost of service) are reimbursed ex post. It is prospective, when the amount given is determined ex ante (e.g. according to the population covered), and not directly linked to the actual costs to be incurred. Note that retrospective PS isolate the hospital from the risks associated with input costs, demand uncertainty, and any other risk influencing costs of service delivery (they are paid on cost, or perhaps cost-plus). An immediate implication is that payment mechanisms should have at least some prospective elements, which will incentivize the hospital towards new and more cost-effective types of services for the population, and in addition help to control the cost for any given model of care. We will return to this element, the links of which with governance also have severe ethical resonances.
- Third, an ample literature shows that payment system reforms per se are not able to move the needle decisively towards better results (whether in terms of equity, quality or efficiency results). They need to operate in synchrony with other reforms which include broader system redesign and governance and accountability reforms.

- Fourth, it is important to emphasize the distinction between PS for individual providers (e.g. doctors) and those for provider facilities (such as hospitals, clinics, or health centres). Some PS are the same for both institutions and individual providers and, in general, the criteria for paying the latter are very much influenced by those for the former—yet this is not necessarily the case. For example, in several countries of Western Europe, physicians employed in hospitals and other facilities have continued to receive time- and seniority-based compensation, even after the reimbursement criteria for their provider facility had been radically changed. This chapter limits its focus to PS for provider facilities, and specifically for hospitals.

When analysing the principal payment systems for providers, the health economics literature has indicated the associated incentives. Hospitals, as with other parts of health systems, are paid for the economic resources they use in a variety of ways, dependent on the prevalent policy goals. Table 6.1 categorizes those various methods and the features inherent in them.

Hospital Payment System (PS) Reforms

Given the variety of PS in existence, it is not surprising that administrations have shifted between them in search of policy impact. Until two decades ago, across OECD and developing countries, two prevailing PS would in general be found:

- In health systems with public sector hegemony, hospitals were mainly reimbursed according to line-item budgets and historical expenditure. Financing was distributed separately for the different line items of the hospital's budget (i.e. so much for salaries, so much for capital, so much for consumables, etc.). The total budget was generally rolled over from year to year with minor adjustments. It is no surprise, therefore, that because at any level of activity the amount received by any hospital depended on its "size" in terms of personnel, capital, and other inputs, the incentive was to expand these inputs beyond the technically efficient level.
- In health systems where the insurance function is held by the private sector of one kind or another rather than the state, as a matter of contrast, hospitals were mainly paid retrospectively (i.e. with full cost

Table 6.1 Comparison of hospital payment methods: from payer (ministries of health, local authorities, national health insurance funds, private health insurance companies) to hospitals

Line-item budget: Allocation based on the inputs (personnel, medicines, utilities). Budget comes segregated by economic classification					
Country examples: Spain, Ukraine, most public hospitals in low income countries	Goals: Expenditure Control Minimize financial risk to payer	Incentives to hospitals: Increase inputs (staff, beds)	Disadvantages: Rigid, no incentive for efficiency or performance	Management capacity of the purchaser and provider required: Low	Transaction cost: Low
Per diem: The hospital receives a set tariff per patient-day spent in the hospital					
Country examples: European countries in the 1970s–1980s. Several missionary hospitals in Africa today	Goals: Pay according to some simple measure of output	Incentives to hospitals: Increase average length of stay	Disadvantages: Unnecessary hospitalization	Management capacity of the purchaser and provider required: Low	Transaction cost: Low
Global budget: A fixed amount to cover the aggregate costs of a hospital providing a set of services					
Country examples: Australia, Canada, Norway, Iceland[a]	Goals: Expenditure control. Minimize financial risk to payer	Incentives to hospitals: Provide care within a budget ceiling	Disadvantages: Less care (under-treatment), low transparency. Cream-skimming (cherry picking of patients). Long waiting lists	Management capacity of the purchaser and provider required: Low	Transaction cost: Low
Capitation: A risk-adjusted amount per patient covered to provide a set of services					
Country examples: Thailand, Spain (Valencia)	Goals: Expenditure control. Minimize financial risk to payer	Incentives to hospitals: Provide care within a budget ceiling	Disadvantages: Less care (under-treatment), low transparency. Cream-skimming (cherry picking of patients). Long waiting lists	Management capacity of the purchaser and provider required: Low	Transaction cost: Low

(*continued*)

Table 6.1 (continued)

Diagnosis-related groups (DRG)[b]: Hospitals get paid fixed amount per admission or per diagnosis regardless of actual cost or expenditure					
Country examples: Most West European countries, Brazil, Hungary, Croatia, Russian Federation	Goals: Improve internal efficiency. Expenditure control	Incentives to hospitals: Increase admissions, shorten length of stay, reduce unpaid services	Disadvantages: Focus on more profitable activities (gaming, up-coding). Selection of less severe patients case-mix (cherry picking)	Management capacity of the purchaser and provider required: Advanced	Transaction cost: High
Fee-for-service: Hospital get paid for each individual service provided					
Country examples: US, Japan, China	Goals: Increase service supply and access	Incentives to hospitals: Increase service provision	Disadvantages: Supply-induced demand (over-treatment). High expenditure	Management capacity of the purchaser and provider required: Moderate	Transaction cost: High
Pay-for-quality/performance: Payment based on quality/performance measures (clinical process, patient experience, health outcome, safety)[c]					
Country examples: US (Medicare)	Goals: Improve performance and care quality	Incentives to hospitals: Improve performance and care quality	Disadvantages: Difficult to design the incentives, may fail to work	Management capacity of the purchaser and provider required: Advanced	Transaction cost: High

Source: Belli, adjusted from "Global Experiences of Hospital Global Budget Reform", draft, World Bank 2018

[a]Some people include the Netherlands in this category, and for reasons of contracting convenience, they have a point. Formally however, the system is a 4000+ DRG-based system that is being transformed into some form of budget

[b]Under DRG-based PS, each patient is classified in a specific "diagnostic" group according to his/her principal diagnosis and, correspondingly, a fixed reimbursement is given to the hospital for treating the patient

[c]There are narrow P4P programmes on such indicators and much broader types such as ACO (capitation plus). The broad ones (although generally based on US evidence) seem to perform better

reimbursement), on a fee-for-service (FFS) basis, directly by patients and/or indirectly by indemnity insurers. Countries such as the USA where FFS PS were widespread then experienced as a result a pronounced growth in hospital and in total health expenditure, in absolute terms as well as a proportion of GDP. One stream in the USA health economics literature has underlined that, when reimbursement to providers is activity-and-cost-based (as in a fee-for-service system), there is no incentive to focus on any actions that could lead to less costly treatments. Hospitals gain by making use of ever more costly treatments and equipment, and even by inducing demand and supplying services above the level that would be clinically justified. The first empirical study of this phenomenon was that by Roemer (1961), who found a strong correlation between supply and utilization of health services (by examining the cross-sectional correlation between bed-supply and utilization, Roemer found that "a bed built is—roughly—a bed half-filled"). The phenomenon was named "supply-induced demand"; see Evans (1974), Fuchs (1978), Robinson and Luft (1985), Dranove (1988), and Mooney and Ryan (1993). Over the last four decades, the phenomenon of supply-induced demand (in fact applicable across both private and state systems) has been widely studied and documented, ceasing to cause debate.

In response to these problems, the general trend of hospital PS reforms has been to move away from both input-based and fee-for-service PS towards case-based payment systems. The intention with these reforms was that part of the financial risks for unexpected increases in unit costs and volumes of service, and the responsibility for managing them, would be shifted to hospitals.

In mostly publicly funded health systems, the developments described above were part of a broader set of reforms meant to achieve more efficient and client-oriented delivery of publicly financed services, with greater emphasis on engagement of the private sector in service provision (and at the same time, in many cases, the interposition of a health purchaser/agency between patients and health providers to mimic market).

The premise here was the recognition that "incentives apply to governments and not just to markets" (Stiglitz 1999), explicitly factoring in the governance factor. Professional purchasers within a purchaser-provider split are better informed, and have a greater bargaining power, than patients; thus, they would "organize specific types of health care for a designated population (whether defined by geography, employment type or voluntary enrolment)" (Rice and Smith 2000). They would potentially enhance health providers' sensitivity to quality and/or cost. Finally, there could be a role as well for these strategic purchasers in supporting universal health coverage, as a population insurance function; the purchasing power of purchasing agencies, unlike that of patients, can be easily equalized by financing/subsidizing population groups. This necessarily involves such a purchasing agency being an active purchaser, and not just passively passing funds through to the service providers.

The reform trend mentioned above in many countries was accompanied by an increase in the level of autonomy of individual hospitals or groups of hospitals. According to the economic theory behind the purchaser/provider, pseudo-market reforms (Enthoven 1985), the government would then retain only the two roles of (partially) financing health services and of externally regulating the quality of care (expressed in the slogan "steering rather than rowing").

As mentioned in Table 6.1, a line-item budget has limitations in being inflexible, linked to inputs rather than outputs, and creating perverse incentives. In other words, line-item budgets cut completely the link between the resources which hospitals (and other budgetary units) receive and their ability to attract "customers". Regardless of all other possible forms of regulation and control, the only true guarantee that hospitals will take into account patients' preferences in their choices is to allow patients to leave them when they are dissatisfied, and to penalize financially those hospitals that are not able to attract patients. Under line-item reimbursement, this is not possible.

In moving away from line-item budgets, several countries initially adopted "global budget PS" (in UK terminology, "block payments"). These guaranteed hospitals greater internal autonomy and flexibility in the use of resources. Global budgets had several advantages for the payers as well:

- administrative simplicity and low transaction cost;
- clear limits on total expenditure by hospital;
- by linking funding to service targets, instead of to inputs, global budgets could also help align health service provision with health sector goals and strategies; and
- incentivization of providers and health professionals not to supply unnecessary or low-value care.

However, global budgets—as with line-item budgets—isolate the revenue hospitals receive from their ability to attract patients. As a result, hospital payment mechanisms in several countries then evolved further from global budgets towards case-based payment systems exemplified by diagnosis-related groups (DRGs).

It is important to note that this clearly political development marked a convergence of destination between Europe (where progress to a degree was from FFFs to line-item budget to global budget to DRG) and US hospital PS reforms (FFS direct to DRG). A DRG system is conceptually simple (care which is diagnostically similar is grouped and paid at the same rate), but complexity tends inexorably to rise—when the new DRG-based PS was introduced in the US Medicare system, pathologies were classified in 468 different DRGs (Chilingerian 2008), but since 1983 the number of DRG categories has been expanded several times.[2] In the late 1980s and 1990s, case-based PS were also adopted in several developing and former socialist economies to pay for inpatient care (the first government to adopt them in Latin America was Brazil, and among Former Soviet Economy (FSE) countries, the first was Hungary). In some cases, they used the US classification system, but in other cases they used, for example, the Nordic or the Australian classification variants. With the intention to reduce administrative costs, prevent manipulation, and provide stronger incentives for cost control, some middle-income countries have sought to experiment with case-based PS based on simpler classifications than US DRGs. However, in reality, once institutions learn to game the system, DRGs turn out to be closer to FFS in not optimizing care using the latest processes and not sharing care across other parts of the health system (Busse et al. 2013).

Note that there have also been several attempts to introduce "pay for performance" (P4P) or "outcome-based payment models" (OBPM), where outcomes and quality of care are explicitly measured and contribute to determine the remuneration of providers—either "narrow" for one provider type or disease area or "broad" across budgeting arrangements and different provider groups (Vlaanderen et al. 2018). These "outcomes" have included service coverage targets, quality dimensions and also process quality variables.

[2] Presently, DRG codes are based on the 11th revision of the International Classification of Diseases.

Payment Systems: The Major Trade-offs

The "optimal" PS will invariably be at most a second-best equilibrium—that is, a balance involving important trade-offs associated with provider payment systems. The relevant trade-offs are between:

- on the one hand, creating the incentive to enhance quality and, on the other, containing costs (note that many of the PS, and especially OBPM, are based on the idea that raising quality reduces costs, which if true results in a happy circumstance);
- the objectives of avoiding risk selection and stimulating productive efficiency;
- the aims of containing providers' surplus and inducing them to supply an optimal service level; and
- administrative accessibility and convenience, and ability to flexibly respond to individual circumstances and provide complete information.

It is also of course true that policymakers need to tread a path between placing contingencies on providers to incentivize desired behaviour whilst avoiding at all costs destabilizing them to the point that their survival is threatened—healthcare does not take gracefully to riskiness.

We have judged that the first of the above is potentially the most important, and so the rest of this chapter will focus on it.

In typical hospital PS reforms, both purchasers and hospitals are increasingly subject to prospective funding in order to create the proper incentives for cost control, and they have to bear the extra costs associated with unexpected increases in the volumes of activity and/or in the unit cost of treatment. Unfortunately, there is no single reimbursement system that is plausibly able to provide incentives for cost containment without at the same time creating incentives for quality-skimping; the hospital is induced to reduce the quality of services supplied if at any time the payment it receives for those quality-enhancing investments does not fully cover the cost of providing them (supply-side moral hazard effect).[3] The position

[3] Several models in the literature have analysed the problem of finding the PS able to "optimally" balance the provider's (the agent's) cost reducing and quality enhancing efforts, in the context of a "hidden action" or "(supply side) moral hazard" principal-agent model. The authors of these models include the following: Ellis and McGuire (1986), Ellis and McGuire (1990), Allen and Gentler (1991), Holmstrom and Milgrom (1990), Glazer and McGuire

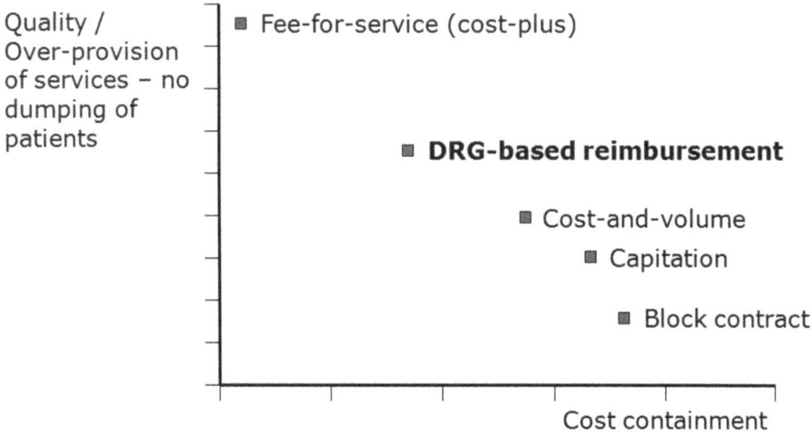

Fig. 6.1 Providers and type of reimbursement (Belli 2002)

where the different PS stand along the lines of this trade-off can be represented, *in highly stylized form*, as follows (Fig. 6.1).

Moving from fee-for-service towards DRG-based reimbursement, cost-and-volume contracts, capitation[4] funding and block contracts progressively increase the part of providers' payment that is fixed ex ante. In other words, the incentive to contain costs increases, but at the same time so does the incentive to skimp on quality and dump those patients who are relatively costly to treat. If the hospital was overproviding services under FFS arrangements, such a change might be positive.

Note that in this regard, the for- or not-for-profit nature of hospitals is important because it influences their objective function (in the conceptual models, increasing or decreasing their genuine concern for quality). A truly "benevolent" hospital (*if such exists*, noting that it would by definition be a not-for-profit) will do what a welfare maximizing agent would want it to do with a fixed budget—this being the definition of "benevolence" in this context—and, in this case, a pure block contract in fact

(1994), Hodgkin and McGuire (1994), Ma (1994), Rogerson (1994), Chalkley and Malcomson (1995, 1998), and Ma and McGuire (1997). They have achieved different degrees of success.

[4] It can be argued that, when the size of the population served is known, there is little or no difference between capitation and block budgeting.

achieves first-best results (Chalkley and Malcomson 1998). However, it should be said that the interaction of ownership with PS is not an easy one to disentangle. Reviewing the evidence for performance between for-profit, not-for-profit, PPP, and public hospitals, the accompanying Chap. 5 (Section "Hospital Ownership: Evidence from Empirical Studies") in this volume shows mixed comparative results. However, none of this large body of empirical work was anyway carried out controlling for the relevant payment mechanism—which would indicate that the weight to be reliably placed on real-world ownership results in terms of quality or cost control is rather limited.

Again, in theoretical terms, it can be shown that a cost-per-case or fixed-price payment system can induce the hospital to choose both an efficient (first best) cost-reducing effort as well as an optimal (first best) quality of services (Holmstrom and Milgrom 1990). But many of these and similar results depend on very strong assumptions (Ma and McGuire 1997), which will not in practice be met. Such assumptions are violated if any of the following circumstances occur, if: (1) there are capacity constraints on the supply side (e.g. beds are already fully utilized); (2) patients' perception of quality is uncertain; (3) there is a moral hazard effect on the demand side (patients tend to overconsume health services when insured because they do not face the full marginal cost) that makes it optimal explicitly to ration the volume of services; (4) patients are constrained in their choice of hospitals; or (5) the volume of demand for treatment and quality are substitutes in patients' demand (if patients make up for a lower quality by consuming more, for example, by visiting doctors more frequently).

In *normal circumstances, one or all of the above constraints will apply*, so the only way to achieve an optimal level of quality of services is directly to reimburse, separately from the prospective payment system, part of the quality-enhancing costs sustained by the hospital (by introducing a retrospective component in the total payment). This is what is increasingly being done in several OECD countries through "performance or quality-based top-ups" to the existing payment system.

The main, and important, conclusion which is acceptably robust found in this literature on optimal payment systems is that the second-best PS is generally **neither** fully prospective **nor** fully retrospective, and that it should include an explicit payment for the quality of care dimension.

Payment Systems, Business Models, and Governance

One of the major suggestions of this chapter is that payment systems (just as with ownership considerations, Chap. 5) are highly political and in that sense determined by the governance situation. This should not paralyse the discussion, but it frames the degree to which purely technocratic solutions around PS could work.

In the terms of this book, a PS should be evaluated in the context of the *business model*, and *model of care*, being followed by (or mandated for) the hospital concerned, and the given *governance context*. Further, any interaction with the type of institutional ownership is not an obvious one—to recapitulate a message from Chap. 4, a hospital can be NFP, FP, PPP or public, yet follow the same business model, governance context permitting. No PS should therefore be directly attached to an ownership structure, as such. This is to say that the more important dimension in deciding on the payment system is the value proposition being followed by the hospital: in what way is it trying to meet functional *goals*? The business model typology of Chap. 4 included "solution shops" (or "medicine as craft"), "value-added networks" (or "medicine as process activity") and "facilitated networks" (or "medicine as a co-production between providers and the population"). In this framing of the discussion, what is sought are payment systems which are compatible with the business model of the hospital, or those that the government (where the public sector controls the direction of the healthcare system) wants to encourage, or at least permit.

In this context, the following could be hypothesized:

- The PS for solution shops should, directionally and relatively speaking, place less weight on prospective elements and more weight on retrospective elements (to incentivize the hospital to maintain a large capacity to do work, even if that is perhaps under-used, in both physical capital stock and human capital), plus governance-induced quality/performance top-ups. We should not expect a site performing like this to run lean. Notably, most hospitals in most health systems are already like this;
- Value-added networks should—again, directionally and relatively speaking—have a balance in their PS more towards prospective elements, which have a known positive effect on cost control where process efficiency is the determining factor (this is, after all, what this type of hospital is all about); and

- Facilitated networks might have a balance in their PS tilted more towards an integration with other settings of care (under a "bundle payment system"). In part, this is because that is how they will work, and in part because it seems likely that facilitated networks should be paid more on outcomes, rather than outputs or, still less, inputs. In addition, they might need extra PS elements designed to attract patients, because health(care) systems are known to be difficult to adapt for care integration.

One implication of this discussion concerns "hybrid" business models. Christensen et al. suggest that an efficient business model will be a pure one, where management is not distracted by trying to run simultaneously different value propositions and different process answers within the one organizational framework. Chapter 4 maintained that this was over-simplified, even in the context of the other industrial or economic sectors which are used as business model exemplars (airlines, retail, etc.), and that hybrid business models are in fact to be expected and can be quite stable. Being confused about the business model being run, however, would no doubt be terminal! Hybrid models appear to be demonstrably valid for the health sector and particularly hospitals. If hybrid business models in fact do apply—where, for example, a hospital is carrying out solution shop activity for complex problems but operates as a value-added network for more standardized activities (e.g. cataracts and joint replacement)—one might expect that the PS should be calibrated towards that. This would alter the balance between retrospective (e.g. FFS) and prospective (not complex DRG, capitation and other types of bundled payments) Payment System design.

It is evident that the material in this book is exploratory in many senses, and needs more work before it can be treated as operational. But it may provide some help in shedding light on why payment systems are so seductive but end up not fulfilling their promise in the real world.

Conclusions

The main conclusions that can be drawn from this review of payment systems are as follows:

1. First, there is no unique "solution" to the ubiquitous problem of optimal payment systems and trade-offs—it depends on the objectives which policymakers want to pursue. In any case, any solution

will always be a "second-best", and subject to continuous refinements as hospital administrators and physicians learn and react strategically to the incentives given to them. An implication is that there are still perhaps too many people ready to sell the next payment system as the "magic bullet" able to address all incentive challenges simultaneously.

2. One of the key suggestions in this book is that, despite hospitals being extremely varied in size, functions, ownership, and so on, the problem of their "intrinsic identity" (i.e. the very reason of our call for more attention) deserves more attention. Associated with that, more research on the issues of governance, models of care, and models of business would throw some light or open "some opportunities" on the type of payment system which would best be suited to achieve different objectives.
3. At the same time, PS are far from "irrelevant" and may have a serious influence on results. Different payment systems produce different results in terms of incentives for quality enhancement, cost reduction, equity, and efficiency, because of the peculiar demand-supply interaction that characterizes the health sector. Yet, measured by their results, in many countries, hospitals do not seem to show adequate interest in doing things properly; invariably, they are fully paid, so to speak, which is unfortunate, especially concerning poor countries where each "dollar matters" and hospitals absorb a lion's share of the total budget for health. Without dramatizing the situation, there is an urgent need to support an evolution of PS in poor countries similar to what European countries underwent in the decade of the 1990s—that is, open up the "black box" of hospitals ("we know how much is going in but have no way of measuring what is coming out") and make hospitals more efficient and responsive.
4. What permits hospitals to progress is their "governance context". Payment mechanisms need to be consistent with/and as much as possible tailored to good governance, in the sense of transparent control and accountability mechanisms of the institution (e.g. not allowing rent making, etc.).
5. Hospital PS which disconnect hospital revenue from their ability to "attract patients", such as under line-item budgets or rigid global budgets, are not recommended, given the strict assumptions necessary for such a PS to be efficient (cf. Fig. 6.1). Hospitals which are

subject to these PS have little or no interest in changing their models of care and innovating in general. At the opposite side of the spectrum, FFS is not a viable PS either, because it takes away any incentive for efficiency and cost control.

In summary, hospital payment systems are highly political and should have both prospective and retrospective elements, some elements explicitly rewarding quality improvements, and in addition, the ability to attract patients. ***Such an albeit idealized package would incentivize each hospital to push the institution towards new and better types of services, including models of care across population needs, in addition to controlling costs.*** New "bundled" PS like this, which go beyond the individual hospital situation and attempt to reward holistic case management and new prevention strategies, could open significant opportunities to align PS with frontier medical knowledge and innovation.

References

Allen, R., & Gertler, P. (1991). Regulation and the Provision of Quality to Heterogeneous Consumers: The Case of Prospective Pricing of Medical Services. *Journal of Regulatory Economics, 3*, 361–375.

Belli, P. (2002). *Incentives and the Reform of Health Care Systems*. London: London School of Economics, PhD thesis.

Busse, R., Geissler, A., Aaviksoo, A., Cots, F., Hakkinen, U., Kobel, C., et al. (2013). Diagnosis Related Groups in Europe: Moving Towards Transparency, Efficiency, and Quality in Hospitals? *BMJ (Clinical Research ed.), 347*(7916), 1–7.

Chalkley, M., & Malcomson, J. (1995). *Contracting for Health Services with Unmonitored Quality*. Discussion Papers in Economics and Econometrics 9510, University of Southampton.

Chalkley, M., & Malcomson, J. (1998). Contracting for Health Services When Patient Demand Does Not Reflect Quality. *Journal of Health Economics, 17*, 1–20.

Chilingerian, J. (2008). Origins of DRGs in the United States: A Technical, Political and Cultural Story. In J. Kimberly, G. De Pouvourville, & T. D'Aunno (Eds.), *The Globalization of Managerial Innovation in Health Care* (pp. 4–33). Cambridge: Cambridge University Press. Retrieved from https://www.cambridge.org/core/books/globalization-of-managerial-innovation-in-health-care/origins-of-drgs-in-the-united-states-a-technical-political-and-cultural-story/708E309A8ED8C6C018C45C160356EABD.

Christensen, C. (2009). *The Innovator's Prescription a Disruptive Solution for Healthcare*. New York: McGraw Hill.

Dranove, D. (1988). Demand Inducement and the Physician/Patient Relationship. *Economic Inquiry, 26*(2), 281–298.

Ellis, R., & McGuire, T. (1986). Provider Behaviour Under Prospective' Reimbursement. *Journal of Health Economics, 5*, 129–151.
Ellis, R., & McGuire, T. (1990). Optimal Payment Systems for Health Services. *Journal of Health Economics, 9*, 375–396.
Enthoven, A. (1985). *Reflections of the Management of the NHS.* London: Nuffield & Provincial Hospitals Trust.
Evans, R. (1974). Supplier-Induced Demand: Some Empirical Evidence and Implications. In M. Perlman (Ed.), *The Economics of Health and Medical Care.* London: Macmillan.
Fuchs, V. (1978). The Supply of Surgeons and the Demand for Operations. *Journal of Human Resources, 13*, 35–56.
Glazer, J., & McGuire, T. (1994). Payer Competition and Cost Shifting in Health Care. *Journal of Economics and Management Strategy, 3*, 71–92.
Hodgkin, D., & McGuire, T. (1994). Payment Levels and Hospital Response to Prospective Payment. *Journal of Health Economics, 13*, 1–29.
Holmstrom, B., & Milgrom, P. (1990). Multitask Principal-Agent Analyses: Incentive Contracts, Asset Ownership, and Job Design. *Journal of Law, Economics, and Organization, 7*, 24–52.
Ma, C. (1994). Health Care Payment Systems: Cost and Quality Incentives. *Journal of Economics and Management Strategy, 3*, 93–112.
Ma, C., & McGuire, T. (1997). Optimal Health Insurance and Provider Payment. *American Economic Review, 87*(4), 685–700.
Mooney, G., & Ryan, M. (1993). Agency in Health Care: Getting Beyond First Principles. *Journal of Health Economics, 12*, 125–136.
Rice, N., & Smith, P. (2000). *Strategic Resource Allocation and Funding Decisions.* Copenhagen: European Observatory on Health Care Systems. Paper presented at the European Observatory on Health Care Systems' Project on Funding Health Care: Options for Europe.
Robinson, J. C., & Luft, H. S. (1985). The Impact of Hospital Market Structure on Patient Volume, Average Length of Stay, and the Cost of Care. *Journal of Health Economics, 4*(4), 333–356.
Roemer, M. (1961). Bed Supply and Hospital Utilization: A Natural Experiment. *Hospitals, 35*, 36–42.
Rogerson, W. (1994). Choice of Treatment Intensities by a Non Profit Hospital Under Prospective Pricing. *Journal of Economics and Management Strategy, 3*, 7–51.
Stiglitz, J. (1999, June). *Incentives and Institutions in the Provision of Health Care in Developing Countries: Towards an Efficient and Equitable Health Care Strategy.* Rotterdam: International Health Economic Association. Presented at the iHEA II Meetings, Rotterdam.
Vlaanderen, F. P., Tanke, M. A., Bloem, B. R., Faber, M. J., Eijkenaar, F., Schut, F. T., et al. (2018, July 5). Design and Effects of Outcome-Based Payment Models in Healthcare: A Systematic Review. *European Journal of Health Economics.* https://doi.org/10.1007/s10198-018-0989-8.

CHAPTER 7

Hospitals in Different Environments: A Messy Reality

Tata Chanturidze and Richard B. Saltman

Introduction

We aim here at a better empirical grounding, looking particularly at non-European geographies, for the ongoing practical discussion of how the models of governance (Chap. 2), the models of care (Chap. 3), and the models of business (Chap. 4) might be brought together by policymakers—in their own national and health system contexts—in a more effective and sustainable manner than has been visible in recent debates on the place of hospitals.

This book opened with a subsection in Chap. 1 called "Confusion About What a Hospital Is", followed with the subsection in Chap. 2 called "Misleading Labels for Hospitals". This reinforced that the reality of hospitals is less clear than the words normally used would seem to suggest at first sight.

T. Chanturidze (✉)
Oxford Policy Management, Oxford, UK
e-mail: Tata.Chanturidze@opml.co.uk

R. B. Saltman
Department of Health Policy and Management, Rollins School of Public Health, Emory University, Atlanta, GA, USA
e-mail: rsaltma@emory.edu

A. Durán, S. Wright (eds.), *Understanding Hospitals in Changing Health Systems*, https://doi.org/10.1007/978-3-030-28172-4_7

Evidently, our analysis of the birth of hospitals, as well as their shaping up and rather stealthy conquest of centre stage in healthcare, was mostly focused on Europe. European hospitals were created in a context of substantial urbanization and in an era when traditional feudal relationships were replaced by bourgeois, capitalist social organization. There was at most loose government control over the development of hospitals. Provision was haphazard, with a mixture of ownerships (public-municipal, state, university, charity etc.). There was no central guidance until after World War II.

In contrast, in the United States, the spontaneous rather than centrally planned character of hospital development through until current times, and the diverse character of institutional ownership and purpose, helps to explain the considerable range in focus, facilities, and capacities across different parts of the country. There was a peculiar combination of public and private institutions that are at once charities and businesses, social welfare institutions and icons of science, wealth, and technical achievement. Hospitals were developed in successive layers as the country and its population expanded; key in that process were the waves of differing immigrants through the nineteenth century, the development of new population centres as the country grew westward, the establishment of federally owned hospitals to care for the veterans of twentieth century wars, and the emergence of for-profit hospitals in the South and Southwest in the late twentieth century.

Reflecting confessional preferences, early settled cities like Boston and New York have large hospitals set up first by Protestant, then Catholic, then Jewish immigrants, in many cases close to each other, all either public or not-for-profit in character. Subsequent territorial expansion and immigration shifts then led, for instance, to Swedish Hospital, now one of the largest in Seattle, Washington State, on the West Coast. In the twentieth century, as first private insurance and then Medicare arrived, residual publicly owned hospitals became safety net institutions for the indigent and uninsured, resulting in such institutions as the New York Hospitals Corporation, Boston City Hospital, Cook County Hospital (Chicago), and Los Angeles County Hospital (Stevens 1993).

Still in the United States, the introduction of the newly developed PPBS (planning programming budgeting system) model in the early 1960s to steer publicly operated institutions was seen as the gold standard for eliciting effective outcomes and efficient performance. This applied to both public and private sector institutions alike, including the

Veterans Administration (then a nearly 200-hospital-system funded and operated by the US federal government) (Kissick 1967).

The adoption in 1983 by the US Congress of the diagnosis-related groups (DRGs) approach that introduced case-based (rather than per-diem-based) payment as the framework for Medicare reimbursement to both private and public hospitals alike was hailed as a breakthrough, which would simultaneously generate higher-quality care to patients as well as reduce public sector costs (Kahn et al. 1990). The subsequent DRG-based measurement of hospital productivity was later on adapted and adopted in many Western European hospital systems (see Chap. 6) as the state-of-the-art basis for efficient management (EuroDRG 2019). As a result, both in Europe and in the United States, there were hospitals of many levels of specialization, many sizes, many organizational arrangements, and so on (more on this below).

In summary, this chapter will try to review the kaleidoscopic patterns generated by these and other issues. Attention will be paid to different environments, with emphasis now on developing countries and the ex-Soviet and associated countries.

Hospitals in Developing Countries

A complete representation of hospitals in developing countries—a vast range of physical, cultural, economic, political and social arrangements—exceeds the scope of this chapter but, for example, some basic features are worth noting to illustrate the global picture. For decades in the underdeveloped world, a definition similar to the standard ones recorded in Chap. 1 of this volume would have conceptualized hospitals as places where people generally go when they or their children feel sick, because only there they can find—most times—a doctor or a nurse, and some medicines. If they are lucky, they may also find some functioning equipment, such as an X-ray machine, and have a basic lab test carried out. Hospitals in developing countries (many of them originally formal or informal colonies) were established through a combination of initiatives by the colonial/master power and by charity institutions, often to improve the living conditions of particular groups (mother and children, people affected by specific infectious diseases, public servants, and so on).

By their political economy logic and their governance environment, hospitals as institutions were mostly developed as an intrinsic part of the public sector in districts or equivalent territories (English et al. 2006). They were overseen by different levels of government. Comparatively, private sector hospitals remained small and poorly equipped, as only rarely—until recently—would owners have been able to raise the capital required for the necessary investments. Hospitals were often surrounded by a multitude of solo practice, or nurse-run, primary care centres, most of them badly operated and not interacting much with each other. Vertical programmes (mainly mother and child, but also disease-based such as tuberculosis [TB], etc.) added to the picture.

In many countries, the situation has evolved substantially in the last few decades. Better-trained professionals and improved technologies were often incorporated. However, the health sector soon became trapped in inertia, with institutions—rather irrespective of tradition or political orientation—directly run by the authorities of the state. Public hospitals were funded as budget institutions, paid on the basis of line item, or—in countries where the fiscal outlays to hospitals frequently collapsed—mainly financed through out-of-pocket (OOP) expenditures. An emerging formal private sector largely skimmed off the profitable part of the market in urban areas, usually on OOP payment bases from those who could afford to pay.

In contrast, the urban poor and rural areas were served by nurse-run primary care centres and an informal private sector (at best, traditional medicine in its various forms, but often "quacks" or "renegade" doctors). Isolated solo practices and single-purpose programmes, usually with vertical delivery structures, financed by donors and charities, were also characteristic. One feature linked to poverty is that the poor either did not and still do not adequately access healthcare or, even when they do, the income consequences can be dire (hence in part the efforts led by the World Health Organization (WHO) in Universal Healthcare and the typology mentioned in the introductory chapter of this volume on health systems with objectives that include responsiveness and fair financial contributions [WHO 2011]).

At the risk of caricaturizing, modern hospitals in the developing world now include two different "branches":

1. In many senses, the above-mentioned features have created a heavy weight for the public sector hospitals to bear, in that they may consume a much higher fraction of available health system resources (sometimes significantly above 50%) and still fall far short of delivering the needed care. For example, the WHO estimates that 5% of births clinically may require a caesarean section, but in East African countries in 2005 less than 1% of women had access to it (Alkire et al. 2015).

The 25 countries in the African Surgical Outcomes Study had 0.7 surgeons, obstetricians and anaesthetists per 100,000 people on average; the rich world more than 40. Half the district hospitals in one study of eight African countries had no anaesthesia machine. Around 40% of donated surgical equipment in poor countries is out of service—yet a caesarean section costs between \$15 and \$380 for every year of disability (DALY) averted, cataract surgery \$50 and hernia repair between \$10 and \$100 (all these are extremely low figures, implying good returns to the interventions). For reference, anti-retroviral treatment for HIV/AIDS costs \$900 per DALY; again rather cheap in the Western world, less so in less-developed countries. In 2010, 17 million lives were lost in Africa from conditions needing surgical care, whereas HIV/AIDS involved 1.5 million, TB 1.2 million and malaria also 1.2 million; roughly one-third of the gross burden of disease (GBD) measured by DALYs is from conditions requiring surgery. Such metrics rely on assumptions which can be contested, but they do suggest that basic procedures can have large benefits at low cost (The Economist 2018).

Globally, 1 billion women would not get the urgent care they would need in the event of complications with a pregnancy; nine in ten people living in developing countries do not have access to safe and affordable surgical care. About 60% of operations around the globe are concentrated in countries with only 15% of the world's population (IHME 2019). When compared with the global average, patients in Africa are twice as likely to die after surgery. Again, from the African Surgical Outcomes Study (cohort study of patients over the age of 18 years undergoing any inpatient surgery in 25 African countries, February–May 2016), complications occurred in 1977 for 10,885 patients, and 239 of 11,193 patients died. Infection was the most common complication (1156 of 10,970 patients), of whom 112 died. There is clearly a need emerging from these figures to couple initiatives to increase access to surgery in Africa with improved surveillance and the resources necessary to achieve this objective. As a rule of thumb, there will be about 5000 operations per 100,000 people every year in rich countries; according to the African Surgical Outcomes Study on 25 African countries, the median rate on that continent is just 212 per 100,000; some 25% of operations in rich countries are for emergencies, compared with 57% in developing ones (Madiba and Biccard 2017).

2. However, the above is not any more the picture in *all* hospitals in low- and middle-income countries. In parallel, a change has affected many sectors and virtually the entire world by which, in many countries of Asia, Africa and Latin America, a booming private sector is hosting world-class hospitals—that perhaps a couple of decades back would not have been conceivable. Many least developed countries thus now have state-of-the-art hospitals staffed by personnel highly qualified in virtually all medical specialties. Although the unmet need for services is far greater still, to that end, essential legal and regulatory reforms have been carried out in Africa (over 45 policies and legislative instruments developed across the region) in the last few years, with a corresponding investment in hospitals (Rogo 2018).

Something similar applies to Asia and Latin America:

- In India in particular, the total expenditure on healthcare as a proportion of GDP in 2015 was 3.89%, of which the out-of-pocket expenditure as a proportion of the current health expenditure was about 65% in 2015; governmental health expenditure was just about 1% of GDP. In that context, the private sector owns 58% of the hospitals in the country, with 81% of doctors and 29% of hospital beds. Some offer world class "frugal innovation", with low price and high quality, such as the Aravind Eye Care System and the Narayana Hospitals (WHO 2012).
- In Brazil, whilst of course there are top-notch hospitals in many cities, in an unusual situation some 56% of public spending on hospitals is directed to private facilities under contract with the Unified Health System—SUS in Portuguese—therefore private ownership, public payment. Approximately 38% of hospitals (30% of beds) are public, and the remainder are split between non-profit (25%) and for-profit (37%) facilities. The state of Sao Paulo went so far as to set up a pioneer experience with PPP in a number of general hospitals located in low-income neighbourhoods of heavily urbanized municipalities, averaging 200 beds and offering basic specialties, including surgery, gynaecology and obstetrics, internal medicine, paediatrics, and psychiatry; all maintain intensive care and neonatal units, offer emergency care, and most provide outpatient care (La Forgia and Harding 2009). Contractual agreements specify provisions regarding the use and maintenance of the newly built facility by the operator.

Hospitals in Communist Regimes Before the Collapse

The former Soviet health system also offers an abundance of cases worth mentioning. As is known, the USSR, satellites and associated countries were built with the ideals of Karl Marx and Lenin: that a healthy workforce would result in more productivity, higher labour-force participation and increased economic growth. This would be achieved by government-owned, -managed, -funded and -delivered healthcare. The Soviet Union made health a universal right for all citizens (Article 42, Soviet Constitution, 1936), with healthcare provided as a right to all, funded and delivered by the state. From the early years, it became evident that—although Communist administrations worked with the intention to build a people-oriented system, a combination of underfunding, unequal distribution of resources, low performance, low quality of care and, later, inequality and corruption plagued the system. Discussed in the academic literature mostly with reference to the post-1950 period, these issues were apparent in the USSR from as early as the 1920s and 1930s, and were only exacerbated later (Davis 1983).

Hospitals under the Soviet "Semashko" system were significant politically, regarded as the backbone of the health sector and the main manifestation of the health system's ability to fulfil a caring role (McKee and Healy 2002). The performance of the system was judged by hospital capacity, measured by the increase in the number of beds and physicians, which was expected to achieve universal access (Bonilla-Chacin et al. 2005). The overall design and governance of a totalitarian system, exemplifying boundaries and confinements set for all sectors including health, made this interminable counting of beds and medical personnel an approach "carved in stone". The hospital sector was characterized by central planning and budgeting. For all 15 republics of the USSR, targets were set in Moscow following a planning methodology that involved 2000 indicators (*pakazateli*) and norms (*normative*) classified in 17 groupings. Hospitals, however, had no autonomy at all over how resources were allocated at facility level. Any new approach or idea would typically fail to overcome the multiple hierarchical barriers at federal, republican and institutional levels, and would face the risk of being interpreted as "disobedience", to be severely punished.

Hospitals in this model represented "a multi-tiered system (district, *rayon*, municipal, *oblast* and federal hospitals) with a strongly differentiated network of service providers where each of the five levels corresponded to the severity of the disease and these were all connected by a sound referral system" (Sheiman 2013). Federal level hospitals included republican centres and research institutions, multi-profile university (teaching) hospitals, as well as top mono-profile hospitals (e.g. oncology and "sepsis" centres). These, indeed, were "tertiary level" institutions, handling the most complex services, and also hosting research and teaching activities. Hospital networks at lower levels included general hospitals, mono-profile obstetrics hospitals ("Rod-Dom") and dispensaries such as for tuberculosis (TB) and mental care (psychiatry and narcology). Notably, while in Western Europe and North America the *general* hospital model became prevalent, in the Soviet Union (and later on in Eastern Europe), the *single specialty* hospital gained similar importance.

Rayon and municipality hospitals provided all kinds of care for population catchments from 20,000–100,000 (including inpatient, outpatient, primary health care [PHC], ambulance, public health [hygiene], some social care). In some countries (e.g. Lithuania), they also included small village hospitals with 20–30 beds, village PHC ambulatories and *feldsher* (community nurse) posts. Networks of sanatoria provided non-intensive rehabilitation and spa services, entirely on inpatient basis. One of the main characteristics of this hospital scheme was the low cost of personnel, linked to low salaries, and the limited availability and use of technologies, contributing to the maintenance and, later, to non-reversible growth of an excessive network. The Ministry of Health with its regional and *rayon* (district) health departments ran, funded, staffed and supervised hospitals, as part of a centrally planned and hierarchically organized health system.

After World War II, in a search for political power, the Soviets' quantitative contest for "more and bigger hospitals" started to generate political dividends. Between 1950 and 1986, hospital beds per 100,000 population doubled in the USSR from 557 to 1301 (this was general; in Moldova, for example, it tripled between 1950 and 1978, from 451 to 1166). The density of hospital beds (per 100,000 population) ranged in 1980 from about 650–700 in Poland and Slovenia to over 1200 in the Baltics (Table 7.1). By comparison, the density of nurses—of which 44–69% worked in hospitals—was more consistent across countries.

This nominal capacity growth flourished with the established practice of offering "new hospitals" to constituencies during election campaigns, at the cost of compromised quality standards. As admitted in the *Basic Guidelines for Developing Health Protection of the Population*: "Almost a third of hospital beds have been installed in adapted buildings in defiance of sanitary and

Table 7.1 Hospital beds and nurses per 100,000 population, selected countries, 1980

Countries	*Hospital beds per 100,000 (1980)*	*Nurses per 100,000 (1980)*
Bulgaria	885	513
Czech Republic	1085	731
Estonia	1246	615
Hungary	917	n/a
Latvia	1389	800
Lithuania	1206	763
Poland	667	422
Romania	877	368
Slovakia	857	632
Slovenia	695	442

Rurik and Kalabay (2009)

hygiene standards". In 1990, the State Statistical Committee of the Soviet Union reported that 24% of hospitals lacked plumbing, 19% lacked central heating, 45% lacked bathrooms and showers, 29% lacked hot water, and 15% operated without any water at all (Tulchinsky and Varavikova 1996). Infrastructure in rural hospitals was particularly poor, for example, about 20% had no running water, and only 35% had a supply of hot water (Ryan 1990). In secondary and tertiary hospitals, the use of laboratory investigations was sparse even in cases of major surgery with long inpatient stays (Telen 2014).

In some sense, the Soviets wanted in the period 1945–1990 to reproduce the Western model of hospitals, observing how the West was steadily experimenting with different ways to organize services. To various extents, some of the tendencies in the West (creation of "one-stop shops"; "high-resolution consultations" and "intermediate" specialized centres; super-specialization in search for efficiency or for confronting complexity; development of reference centres; replacing some form of care with others) were reflected in the Communist hospital architecture (e.g. differentiation between secondary and tertiary care, and between mono-profile and multi-profile hospitals), but the Soviets continually fell behind—and kept what in this book we have called their original business, and care, models essentially intact.

Critically, the aspiration to extend hospital capacity was not necessarily accompanied with adequate financing. Estimates suggest that the Soviet Union allocated 3–4% of GDP to the health sector (Schieber et al. 1992), and an argument was made that about half went exclusively to political elites. Government health funding declined in relative terms after 1960, by which time many communicable diseases had been brought reasonably under control yet non-communicable diseases (cardiovascular and cerebrovascular diseases, linked to lifestyle issues and particularly tobacco and alcohol consumption), posed increasing burdens. Defining hospital budgets by demonstrated bed capacity created a largely hospital-centric conceptualization of health service provision and an associated incentive to build more beds. As a result, 60–75% of total health expenditure was designated to inpatient services—up to as high as 80% in Ukraine (Lekhan et al. 2004).

In truth, hospitals suffered from a severe lack of resources and supplies. Salaries were low, consistent with the Politburo classification of medical professionals as among "unproductive sectors" of the economy, and with communism's failure to invest in social sectors (more so as the Soviet economy faltered following agricultural failures and unaffordable expenditure on complex military-industrial initiatives). After the 1980s, hospitals became a "black hole" of a Semashko system, with many facilities to maintain but without autonomy or capability to act towards efficiency objectives. This contributed to an unprecedented growth of de-facto out-of-pocket payments (OOPs) for medical services and pharmaceuticals, causing subsequent social repercussions in many post-Soviet health systems.

More to the point, the USSR increasingly lagged behind the West in its ability to deliver complex interventions, such as modern pharmaceuticals, surgical techniques and equipment (e.g. in 1988, there were 50 computerized tomographic (CT) scanners in the entire USSR, 50 times fewer per capita than in the United States [Schultz and Rafferty 1990]). Political isolation from Western countries served as a barrier to learning from new scientific advances and from the rise of evidence-based medicine (McKee and Nolte 2004). Western knowledge on the realities of the Soviet health system was, from its own side, informed more by the corroboration of disparate facts or factoids than by credible evidence, as summarized eloquently by Christopher Davis (Davis 2006):

> *Studies by Western specialists were constrained by the facts that few of them possessed knowledge of Russian language and that the Soviet Union published only a small amount of information in Western languages. The USSR provided minimal quantities of demographic and health statistics to the UN (for the Demographic Yearbook) and the World Health Organization (but nothing to*

the World Bank and OECD). All WHO publications related to health in the USSR were either prepared by Soviet specialists or vetted by Soviet authorities, and contained even less critical analysis than that found in Russian language sources. Official Soviet books on health published in foreign languages provided some useful basic information, but essentially were propaganda documents.

Most of the USSR/Central and Eastern Europe (CEE) kept on operating at occupancy rates of 80% or above (Georgia and Yugoslavia being outliers), within the vividly inefficient hospital network (e.g. 122 beds per 10,000 population serving a country of 1.4 million in Estonia [Fidler et al. 2009], and high average length of stay [e.g. 18.2 in Latvia, 18.6 in Lithuania, 17 in Russia]; [see the WHO Health for All Database]). Unnecessary hospital stays were triggered by over-diagnosis or over-investigation, or due to a "social responsibility" of hospitals for patients actually requiring long-term or terminal care.

Additionally, Communist hospitals were overspecialized, with emphases mainly on infectious diseases, and some selected non-communicable ones. The 1970s and 1980s saw considerable growth in the network of specialized healthcare facilities, the introduction of specialized consulting rooms in polyclinics, and the conversion of general-medicine units in hospital into specialized units. Some publications explain: "*The intense and in many ways uncontrolled process of specialization had shifted the priorities in health care at the expense of primary health care, with local physicians—the leading figures in the Soviet model—increasingly reduced to mere dispatchers of patients to specialists...These developments failed to halt the increasing impact of non-communicable disease, with several indicators of population health in the Soviet Union beginning to deteriorate from the mid-1960s onwards*" (Lekhan et al. 2004).

As mentioned above, the USSR in addition failed to recognise or exploit the development of evidence-based medicine, which had begun to advance in the West from the 1970s. Medical protocols (official practice guidelines) were based on so-called "expert" opinions rather than empirical evidence. The core medical curriculum had little practical training and failed to reflect the medical advances of the time. Murray Feshbach noted in a 1990 paper: "*According to published surveys, ten percent of Soviet physicians do not even know that cancer is treatable, and eight percent do not know that cardiac problems are treatable*" (Feshbach 1990).

The Soviet systems also missed important trends in Western health systems aimed at increasing patient choice. In short, hospital care in

Communist regimes never generated a robust system, due to issues of ideology and limited resources (and technologies). Exceptional “centres of excellence” could for sure be found in prominent tertiary hospitals in Moscow and Petrograd, but they were outnumbered by many hugely inefficient hospitals, embedded in a rigid and inefficient sector, and offering poor quality.

And Hospitals, After the Collapse of the Communist Regimes

The downfall of the Communist regimes in the early 1990s greatly affected health systems in the USSR, Central and Eastern Europe (CEE), but also beyond (e.g. China, North Korea, Cuba, etc.). Three main types of driver shaped the policy responses that led to the current hospital sector configuration across this disparate cluster:

- political—in some countries, particularly CEE, there was (at least for a while) a strong political appetite to break away from the socialist public sector governance model, and to experiment with new policies. Other countries merely entered a period of prolonged instability (e.g. with civil wars in Tajikistan [1993] and Georgia [1992]);
- economic—the magnitude of economic retardation brought about by the USSR collapse made GDP per capita fall almost threefold in most countries (e.g. at USD purchasing power parity, from $699 [1987] to $218 in Albania [1992]; from $3169 [1987] to $1212 [1992] in Bulgaria, and from $3429 [1989] to $1331 [1999] in Russia). There were, correspondingly, severe health financing constraints; and
- organizational—the distortion inherent in wholly centralized health systems revealed huge gaps in governance and management capabilities in individual settings, which needed somehow to be filled.

These challenges pushed post-Communist states towards experimenting with market-oriented, competitive and capitalist solutions, often with support and/or technical assistance from international development organizations. A wave of reforms focused on decentralization, privatization, pharmaceutical liberalization, and alternative sources of financing and service purchasing patterns in the health sector.

However, for every reform that was carried through, there were other initiatives which were planned or considered but never really pursued. To give only one example, between 2000 and 2016, at least four comprehensive hospital sector analyses and two hospital masterplans were produced in Romania, with associated recommendations—of which only some of the most incremental transformations were implemented (Vladescu et al. 2016). Overall, the above trends carry significant implications in shaping the current hospital systems in former Soviet Union (FSU), CEE and beyond. The challenges involved in such processes made even more visible the pre-existing failures in hospitals. In most of these countries, hospitals as main providers of healthcare but remaining budgetary "black holes" in a context of extremely limited resources, rendered themselves immediate candidates for reforms aiming to contain cost and improve performance.

Concerning rationalization of hospital infrastructure (intended to downsize the excessive capacity and optimize service baskets), the approach took different shapes in various settings, very much influenced by the given societal values and political agenda (Chanturidze et al. 2009). In Central and Eastern Europe, the transition of hospital-based care towards a greater emphasis on primary or ambulatory services became a common component of health policy during the 1990s (Preker et al. 2002).

A decrease in length of stay in hospitals was another prevalent tendency, spreading from the West to CEE and FSU. In many FSU countries, further restructuring occurred in the specialization of hospitals, with hospital departments closed or merged. Decisions on building new hospitals were often made without considering the future of existing hospitals (e.g. in Romania and Kazakhstan). Some publications argue that the process of rationalization should be understood to be driven by the incentives facing hospital owners, rather than purely political decision-making (Saltman et al. 2011).

Many countries proceeded with hospital mergers, re-profiling or closure. Romania provides a recent example of aggressive facility closure, although more than half of the hospitals involved were later reopened, arguably with positive impacts on service organization and governance (Scîntee et al. 2018).

Remarkably, because of the time dependence, only a few countries managed to form a coherent vision of sector-wide rationalization, and even fewer emphasized the development of business models which could effectively deploy resources for desirable outputs and outcomes. Many disregarded the need for capacity planning, pursuing instead sporadic hospital clusters. In Romania, again, though the hospital prototypes are de jure streamlined in five main (and seven sub) categories, de facto differentiation between the baskets of services provided, and human resources and equipment deployed by types I, II and III hospitals, is largely diluted.

A recent OECD study similarly describes 34 hospital prototypes in Kazakhstan, representing a puzzling fusion of Soviet-inherited and modern Western classifications (OECD 2018). In Ukraine, the governments prioritized investments in selected hospitals to create “centres of excellence”, as an alternative to pursuing more consistent sector–wide transformation.

Optimization attempts brought variable outcomes to hospitals. For instance, while Russia orchestrated a slow but significant downsizing of hospital facilities from 11,869 to 5,006 by 2013, the efficiency gains were not made explicit, with hospital closures perhaps resulting in geographic barriers to access in rural areas. Similar trends were observed in countries with significantly difficult topography, such as mountainous areas of Kyrgyzstan and Tajikistan. In many settings, incoherent policy design, outdated and often-disjointed governance frameworks, and cumbersome administrative procedures restricted managerial autonomy and obstructed efficiency gains. In a context of chronicly insufficient funding, misaligned incentives and overly rigid service procurement processes, hospitals struggled to adjust service baskets to the population’s health needs or to overcome financial hardship.

In summary, rationalization efforts revealed above all fundamental limitations in governance in CEE and FSU countries, pointing to the misalignment between the responsibility and decision-making capacity given to hospitals in a questionably conducive context (Duran et al. 2019).

Towards Dynamic Models of Organization in Developed Countries

Questions about the *coordination/alignment*—sometimes called “integration”—of care between hospitals and other system levels are emerging as most countries now consider hospitals as core institutions, but within a wider system. Examples abound from recent transformations affecting hospitals in developed OECD European countries (Duran and Saltman 2015), hospitals in Australia or the United States (Mossialos et al. 2015), rich countries outside the OECD (e.g. Singapore) and upper middle income countries, such as Brazil, Colombia, and so on. The success of these approaches depends on parallel efforts to deliver services outside hospitals, which are challenging for over-fragile patients or patients with chronic conditions whose hospital discharge may mean a risk because of the support required but not necessarily available after interventions.

Calls for increased service coordination at various levels are now ever present. For example, if there is lack of alternative places to refer the patient to—that is, if options are scarce and places in long-stay institutions are too expensive—(acute) bed blockage by delayed discharge after hospital treatment finishes is often the only solution. Modern community psychiatric services are now possible and to a large extent desirable (*de-institutionalization*), but the need for parallel alternative structures to play the social roles previously played by psychiatric centres rings a note of caution. As non-CEE examples, de-institutionalization of long-stay psychiatric patients in Austria led to considerable reduction of costs while preserving high quality standards (Haberfellner et al. 2006), whereas a study in England suggests that many elderly with mental health problems admitted to hospitals or residences would receive more appropriate services in their own homes, at reduced costs, *if only* community services were available (Tucker et al. 2008). Germany is another example of a country which achieved such service substitution correctly, while Hungary has experienced problems (Stubnya et al. 2010).

At the same time, developing new strategies to manage hospitals better is hardly a new topic. In fact, the British government introduced the National Health Service in July 1948 in a principal belief that centrally managed public hospitals—much as had been in place on a de facto basis during World War II—would produce substantial economies of scale and thereby improved efficiencies of operation (Eckstein 1958).

As discussed above in Chap. 2 on governance, in the early 1990s, new public management (NPM) strategies tied to activity-based funding were designed and introduced in public hospitals in England, Sweden and parts of Central Europe, intended to improve both clinical and financial outcomes (Pollitt and Sorin 2011). Similarly, as presented in Table 7.2, multiple strategies to introduce semi-autonomous hospital management were developed across both Northern and Southern Europe in largely tax-funded health systems to enable greater hospital-level managerial decision making and financial control (Saltman et al. 2011).

In the first two decades of the twenty-first century, seeking solutions to the same organizational and managerial problems as earlier efforts, there

Table 7.2 Models of increased hospital self-governance

Country	*Model of increased hospital self-governance*
Czech Republic	Corporations
	Limited Listed Companies
Estonia	Corporations
	Foundations
Israel	Private non-profit
	Governmental
	Private Insurance Principal shareholder
Italy	Azienda Ospedaliera
	Azienda Socio—Sanitaria Territoriale (ASST)
Netherlands	Private non-profit foundations
England	NHS Trust
	Foundation Trust
Norway	Regional Healthcare Companies
Portugal	Public Business Entities EPE
Spain	Public Health Company
	Foundation
	Consortium
	Administrative Concession
Sweden	Public Stock Corporations

Authors' adaptation from Duran and Saltman (2013)

has been a virtual deluge of both new and old solutions and mechanisms, at macro (national), meso (institutional) and micro (clinic) levels, all proposed as the "new best way" to achieve the same old, insufficiently achieved, organizational objectives. Public hospitals have found that "shared governance" now incorporates different and stronger roles for national (Norway, Denmark, Ireland, Italy) or regional (Finland) levels of government (Jakubowski and Saltman 2013). At the same time, NPM styles of contracting, case-based and activity-based management have been increasingly contested by public health activists on the (statistically questionable) grounds that they cost too much to implement and produced unequal healthcare outcomes (Dahlgren 2014).

Seeking new managerial strategies, hospitals in the United States in a currently voluntary arrangement developed by Medicare and in a small number of European pilot projects are experimenting with re-orienting their clinical services to handle new case-based reimbursement structured as "value-based payment". During the post-2008 fiscal crisis period, in Denmark and in some Swedish regional governments (Sorenson and

Burau 2015), existing activity-based hospital budgeting approaches have been dropped in favour of a return to a 1980s model of government-dictated global budgeting.

Similarly, on the structural level of institutional governance, the elimination (Norway 2002) or the cutting back (Denmark) of the prior regional level of elected government has dramatically reduced "shared governance" between levels of government, consolidating (or further consolidating, in the case of Norway) real decision-making and managerial authority in the hands of national government institutions (Saltman 2018). This shift backwards to—essentially—global budgets broadly steered by the national government, in a pattern similar to that imposed in Ireland recently, also has been recently introduced and defended in the name of greater hospital operating efficiency and effectiveness. As this brief historical review suggests, there are still very pronounced core issues in the effective management of public but also private hospitals across many countries that remain beyond the range of current managerial mechanisms and tools. The necessary twenty-first century mix of organizational stability on the one hand, coupled with innovative clinical and custodial re-structuring on the other, has continued to remain mostly beyond standard managerial grasp.

The Way the Wind Is Blowing: The Hospitals That Emerge from Hospital Structural and Management Reforms 1990–2018

Efforts to understand hospital behaviour have produced extensive analyses but few successful or long-lived models. Helpful frameworks suggest thinking of a hospital as "a unified social and political system" based on "multi-faceted collaboration and/or resistance" (Saltman and Young 1981). Similarly, Rouse described modern organizations generally—and health systems specifically—as "complex adaptive systems" (Rouse 2009), a perspective similar to that of defining hospitals as "complex dynamic systems" put forward at the beginning of Chap. 1.

Pursuing these initial characterizations further, large modern hospitals can usefully be thought of for managerial and policy purposes as similar in structure and behaviour to complex living organisms. In this analogy, like real physiological organisms, hospitals at any given historical time are the composite of a long, tightly intertwined series of internal organic and external environmental and cultural factors. Moreover, inevitably, any effort appreciably to alter one dimension of this complex relationship induces a range of compensating and countervailing reactions in an extensive series of other operational parameters, both inside and outside these institutions.

This last point is essential: whether one is talking about large or small hospitals, or about publicly or privately operated institutions, no externally imposed financial or reporting measure by a policymaker or politician nor any internally imposed process mechanism implemented by senior-, mid-level, or clinic-floor-level managers will be free of counter-effects and adjustments that simultaneously both adapt and diminish the impact of the new initiative (Lipsky 1981).

Further, within this complex—"neo-biological"—understanding of hospital behaviour, hospitals typically find themselves responding to two disparate, often contradictory, dimensions of regulatory reform. On the one hand, policymakers typically focus on introducing changes in how their health systems *finance* hospitals: how the money flows (whether operating or capital funding), and how it is accounted for. These financial objectives are set forward as the official intended drivers of newly introduced policy, and typically are then used to seek to achieve a range of complex, sometimes contradictory, cultural, political, and social objectives (Saltman and Young 1981). In addition, however, these specifically financial changes simultaneously generate a wide range of operating and performance changes in the hospital's day-to-day *organizational behaviour*, triggering a complicated and again often contradictory set of behavioural incentives (for both desired and undesired behaviour) that accompany the new measures. These necessarily have a substantial impact on multiple non-financial hospital management dimensions: patient quality, outcomes, and satisfaction; working relations between physicians and nursing personnel; the adequacy of support staff functions; and staff retention rates. There is treatment in greater depth of payment systems and mechanisms—their intentions and results—in Chap. 6, emphasising what are often counter-intuitive results.

In short, while both public and private hospitals normally separate financial from operating policies, the two interact in myriad complex ways that influence overall outcomes and, as a consequence, modulate the success of most of these policy initiatives. This becomes important in the real world when, as described in earlier chapters of this book, the combined mix of financial and operational measures has been insufficient in meeting/facing the challenges that modern hospitals confront, leading to frequent, sometimes rapid shifts in policy and management strategies, particularly in the aftermath of the 2008 financial crisis (Mladovsky et al. 2012).

While many of these changes have not been sufficient to achieve their assigned objectives, they have, to a degree, improved hospital performance. Thus, for financially generated reforms, the increments from per diem payment to case-based payment (DRGs) and (possibly) to value-based payment have largely had specific positive impacts on public as well as private hospital outcomes (better targeting of scarce resources, improved patient outcomes for many clinical conditions, among others). Similarly, shifts from "Taylorized" day-to-day operating arrangements to patient- and outcome-based measures, in particular more sophisticated patient flow measures (better scheduling for clinical support services such as radiology and pathology), have improved both patient and medical staff satisfaction rates.

Within this conceptual context, hospitals in developed countries have since the early 1980s undergone a long and in some cases dramatic range of financial and operational changes. As discussed above and in Chap. 6, reimbursement models have been changed, changed again, and—in some countries—changed back. At the time of writing, once again new models (particularly the value-based payment notion) are under active development in the United States and in Europe (Cattel et al. 2018).

Operationally, a wide range of efforts have been developed and/or are in the process of being introduced, including "e-health" diagnosis and follow-up treatment, electronic internet monitoring of chronically ill elderly at home, tablet-based medical records, and exact-dosing methodologies for bedside drugs (Truitt et al. 2016).

There also has been a variety of administrative efforts to consolidate and better coordinate care across existing delivery providers. Large centrally located hospitals have been designated as the focal point for new networks of smaller regional hospitals. The objective of these administrative consolidations was to maintain some services (typically including an accident and emergency facility) in politically sensitive and sometimes deprived rural areas, while nonetheless consolidating the increasingly high-technology and therefore expensive surgical specialties in a larger central hospital. In tax-funded European health systems, these networks had already begun to emerge in the early 2000s.

In Denmark, for example, smaller rural hospitals were either closed or merged into becoming low-intensity treatment arms for larger institutions (Christiansen and Vrangbaek 2018). A similar process had been underway for some time in England, and a limited version of institutional consolidation was introduced during this time period in Sweden where the national government put in place a programme to require the 21 regional governments that run its health sector to consolidate certain high-technology specialties (such as cardiac surgery for coronary artery bypass grafts, also paediatric ophthalmological oncology) into only a few regional centres (Magnussen et al. 2009).

Rather differently, a rapidly evolving private sector model for institutional consolidation in the hospital sector began to emerge in the early 2000s in the United States, where changes in the reimbursement rates based on DRGs, especially for Medicare which provided about 60% of all hospital funding in 2017, triggered a process of rapid consolidation of smaller suburban and regional hospitals into networks led by large urban hospitals (Cuellar and Gertler 2003). This process of consolidation has been further speeded up by the substantial financial consequences for the hospital sector that emerged from the federal 2010 Affordable Care Act ("Obamacare"), particularly the establishment of localized patient-population-based providers termed "Accountable Care Organizations", which combined hospitals as well as primary and home care elements.

Further, in Europe following the onset of the extended financial crisis that began in 2008, a number of countries introduced similar hub-and-spoke consolidation strategies. In Latvia, for example, smaller hospitals were forced by the national government to merge their specialty services into large central institutions (Taube et al. 2012). In Ireland, the merging of five regional boards into one government-run national body led to a similar process of hospital-level consolidation.

Importantly, in a major expansion of traditional patient discharge patterns and responsibilities, hospitals in a number of countries have not only consolidated their hospital-level services (e.g. horizontally within the hospital sector), but have become increasingly integrated vertically, linking operationally and/or institutionally with non-tertiary providers including primary care, long term care, or home care organizations, in order to improve the quality and reduce the costs (especially of re-admissions) for the rapidly growing numbers of chronically ill patients. Thus, either by statute (the US, the Netherlands) or in practice (Denmark, Norway, Sweden, England), national policymakers have created a vertical consolidation between hospitals and other less-intensive care provider sectors. Policy studies had already begun in the 1990s regarding the importance of this type of vertical integration and, in the early 2000s, hospitals in some countries were increasingly required to take on substantial new obligations to coordinate hospital provision of inpatient care with primary care, as well as outpatient hospital, nursing home, and home care, involving the rapid introduction and expansion of a large number of new technologies, services, and support activities.

A further extension of vertical integration between hospital and non-hospital services was introduced in 2012 in Norway, where national legislation required municipal governments to establish a primary care function inside each public regional hospital (to facilitate and coordinate faster discharge planning) and also set up an MAU (municipal acute unit) with step-down beds that could be used to monitor and treat known elderly patients with a range of standard chronic conditions, thereby keeping those patients out of both the hospital's Emergency Room and its inpatient beds (Hagen et al. 2015). A less ambitious but similar effort to combine hospital, primary and social care in Norrtalje, Stockholm County, Sweden—the Tio Hundra project—has also been considered to be relatively successful.

In social insurance countries like the Netherlands, as well as mixed tax-funded but social health insurance-operated countries like Israel, large hospitals have increasingly found themselves contracting services out to innovative new providers. Examples are Cordaan in the Netherlands, which provides a mix of home, primary and mental health services and, similarly, Natali in Israel, with integrated home care and high-tech internet monitoring services (Saltman 2019).

In the fully tax-funded English NHS, seeking similar efficiencies within the existing configuration of separately operated NHS-funded organizations and budgets, Greater Manchester, starting from 2014, established a pilot cooperation project among some 38 different NHS hospital and primary care trusts, as well as social care agencies (McKenna and Dunn 2015). This pilot has produced preliminary evidence of small but significant improvement in care coordination, along with minor financial efficiencies (discounting, though, the large one-time "innovation" fund of GBP 400 million that the NHS used to entice these organizations into participating in the project).

It is also important to observe, however, that a number of other, less successful reforms have been implemented and appear to have had little real impact on service delivery. As one example, a number of tax-funded health systems in Europe and, increasingly, social health insurance systems as well (Austria and Germany in particular, but also Belgium and France) launched, but then (officially or unofficially) downgraded various nationally trumpeted cooperation initiatives between the health and social sectors. Given continuing structural rigidities and, especially, separate budgetary and reporting lines, many of these less successful efforts appear to have been little more than movement in organizational charts rather than the implementation of significant change in the day-to-day patient-facing behaviour of clinicians and/or care providers.

Reflecting the continued contested status of governmental efforts to improve hospital management and organizational behaviour described here, the next chapter builds on this and goes on to explore two things:

1. What changes have been made over the past several decades in how hospitals are being approached managerially, and what has been the impact of those changes?
2. The degree to which the "stability vs. innovation" conundrum that defines the current hospital dilemma reflects a deeper set of organizational quandaries that continues to affect management of modern hospitals generally, and of publicly owned and operated hospitals in particular. Chapter 8 will thus move on from this chapter's review of the sheer complexities facing hospitals in almost all geographical areas to provide an analysis of why the above initiatives, and their impacts, have been so limited.

References

Alkire, B. C., Raykar, N. P., Shrime, M. G., Weiser, T. G., Bickler, S. W., Rose, J. A., et al. (2015). Global Access to Surgical Care: A Modelling Study. *Lancet, 3*(6), e316–e323.

Bonilla-Chacin, M. E., Murrugarra, E., & Temourov, M. (2005). Health Care During Transition and Health Systems Reform: Evidence from the Poorest CIS Countries. *Social Policy and Administration, 39*(4), 381–408.

Cattel, D., Eijkenaar, F., & Schut, F. T. (2018). Value-Based Provider Payment: Toward a Theoretically Preferred Design. *Health Economics Policy and Law, 27*, 1–19. https://doi.org/10.1017/S1744133118000397.

Chanturidze, T., Ugulava, T., Duran, A., Ensor, T., & Richardson, E. (2009). Georgia: Health System Review. *Health Systems in Transition, 11*(8), 1–116. Retrieved from http://www.euro.who.int/__data/assets/pdf_file/0003/85530/E93714.pdf.

Christiansen, T., & Vrangbaek, K. (2018). Hospital Centralization and Performance in Denmark – Ten Years on. *Health Policy, 122*, 321–328.

Cuellar, A. E., & Gertler, P. J. (2003). Trends in Hospital Consolidation: The Formation of Local Systems. *Health Affairs, 22*, 77–87.

Dahlgren, G. (2014). Why Public Health Services? Experiences from Profit-Driven Health Care Reforms in Sweden. *International Journal of Health Services, 44*(July), 507–524.

Davis, C. (1983). Economic Problems of the Soviet Health Service: 1917–1930. *Soviet Studies, XXXV*(3), 343–361.

Davis, C. (2006). Commentary: The Health Crisis in the USSR: Reflections on the Nicholas Eberstadt 1981 Review of Rising Infant Mortality in the USSR in the 1970s. *International Journal of Epidemiology, 35*(6), 1400–1405. Retrieved from https://academic.oup.com/ije/article/35/6/1400/660128.

Duran, A., & Saltman, R. B. (2013). Innovative Strategies in Governing Public Hospitals. *Eurohealth, 19*(1), 3–7. Retrieved March 5, 2019, from http://www.euro.who.int/__data/assets/pdf_file/0018/186021/EuroHealth-v19-n1.pdf.

Duran, A., & Saltman, R. B. (2015). Governing Public Hospitals. In R. Blank, E. Kuhlmann, I. L. Bourgeault, & C. Wendt (Eds.), *International Handbook of Healthcare Policy and Governance* (pp. 443–461). Basingstoke: Palgrave Macmillan, Chapter XX.

Duran, A., Chanturidze, T., Gheorghe, A., & Moreno, A. (2019). Assessment of Public Hospital Governance in Romania: Lessons From 10 Case Studies. *International Journal of Health Policy and Management, 8*(4), 199–210. Retrieved from https://www.ijhpm.com/article_3581.html.

Eckstein, H. (1958). *The English Health Service Its Origins, Structure and Achievements.* Cambridge: Harvard University Press.

English, M., Lanata, C., Ngugi, I., & Smith, P. (2006). The District Hospital, Chapter 65. In D. Jamison, J. Breman, A. Measham, G. Alleyne, M. Claeson, D. Evans, P. Jha, A. Mills, & P. Musgrove (Eds.), *Disease Control Priorities in Developing Countries* (2nd ed.). Washington, DC: World Bank and Oxford University Press. Retrieved from https://openknowledge.worldbank.org/handle/10986/7242 (License: CC BY 3.0 IGO).

EuroDRG. (2019). *Diagnosis-Related Groups in Europe: Towards Efficiency and Quality Webpage. Publications.* Retrieved January 27, 2019, from http://euro-drg.eu/publications.html.

Feshbach, M. (1990). *The Health Crisis in the USSR.* Boston: Institute for the Study of Conflict, Ideology and Policy, Boston University. Publication Series, No 4. Retrieved from https://www.bu.edu/iscip/pubseries/pubseries-4feshbach.pdf.

Fidler, A., Bredenkamp, C., & Schlippert, S. (2009). Innovations in Health Services Delivery from Transition Economies in Eastern Europe and Central Asia. *Health Affairs, 28*(4), 1011–1021.

Haberfellner, E. M., Grausgruber, A., Grausgruber-Berner, R., Ortmair, M., & Schöny, W. (2006). Deinstitutionalization of Long-Stay Psychiatric Patients in Upper Austria – Utilization of Healthcare Resources and Costs of Outpatient Care. *Psychiatrische Praxis, 33*(2), 74–80.

Hagen, T., Saltman, R. B., & Vrangbaek, K. (2015). New Strategies for Elderly Care in Denmark and Norway. *Eurohealth, 21*(2), 23–26.

IHME – Institute for Health Metrics and Evaluation. (2019). *Global Burden of Disease Study 2016*. Seattle: Institute for Health Metrics and Evaluation, University of Washington. Retrieved from http://ghdx.healthdata.org/gbd-2016.

Jakubowski, E., & Saltman, R. B. (2013). *Recent Health System Governance Reforms*. Brussels: European Observatory on Health Systems and Policies. Occasional Series, 91 [Earlier Version Published as 'Comparative Governance Arrangements in Eleven Countries' in Appendix 4 of Slutbetankande av Statens Vard och Omsorgutredning (Final Report of the Swedish Government's Commission on Health and Social Care), SOU 2012:33, Stockholm, May 2012, pp. 289–374].

Kahn, K. L., Keeler, E. B., Sherwood, M. J., Rogers, W. H., Draper, D., Bentow, S. S., Reinisch, E. J., Rubenstein, L. V., Kosecoff, J., & Brook, R. H. (1990). Comparing Outcomes of Care Before and After Implementation of the DRG-Based Prospective Payment System. *Journal of the American Medical Association, 264*, 1984–1988.

Kissick, W. L. (1967). Planning, Programming, and Budgeting in Health. *Medical Care, 5*, 201–220.

La Forgia, G., & Harding, A. (2009). Public-Private Partnerships and Public Hospital Performance in São Paulo, Brazil. *Health Affairs, 28*(4), 1114–1126. https://doi.org/10.1377/hlthaff.28.4.1114.

Lekhan, V., Rudiy, V., & Nolte, E. (2004). *Health Care Systems in Transition, Ukraine*. Copenhagen: European Observatory on Health Care Systems, HiT, Vol. 6, No. 7. Retrieved from http://www.euro.who.int/__data/assets/pdf_file/0010/96418/E84927.pdf.

Lipsky, M. (1981). *Street Level Bureaucrats*. Washington: Russell Sage Foundation.

Madiba, T. E., & Biccard, B. (2017). The African Surgical Outcomes Study: A 7-Day Prospective Observational Cohort Study. *South African Journal of Surgery, 55*(3), 75.

Magnussen, J., Vrangback, K., & Saltman, R. B. (Eds.). (2009). *Nordic Health Care Systems: Recent Reforms and Current Policy Challenges*. London: Open University Press/McGraw-Hill Education.

McKee, M., & Healy, J. (Eds.). (2002). *Hospitals in a Changing Europe*. Buckingham: Open University Press. European Observatory on Health Systems and Policies.

McKee, M., & Nolte, E. (2004). Health Sector Reforms in Central and Eastern Europe: How Well Are Health Services Responding To Changing Patterns of Health? *Demographic Research, 2*(7), 163–182.

McKenna, H., & Dunn, P. (2015). *Devolution: What It Means for Health and Social Care in England*. London: Kings Fund, Briefing. Retrieved from https://www.kingsfund.org.uk/sites/default/files/field/field_publication_file/devolution-briefing-nov15.pdf.

Mladovsky, P., Srivastava, D., Cylus, J., Karanikolos, M., Evetovits, T., Thomson, S., & McKee, M. (2012). *Health Policy Responses to the Financial Crisis in Europe*. Brussels: European Observatory on Health Systems and Policies, Policy Brief.

Mossialos, E., Wenzl, M., Osborn, R., & Anderson, C. (Eds.). (2015). *International Profiles of Healthcare Systems 2014*. New York: Commonwealth Fund. Retrieved from https://www.commonwealthfund.org/sites/default/files/documents/___media_files_publications_fund_report_2015_jan_1802_mossialos_intl_profiles_2014_v7.pdf.

OECD. (2018). *OECD Reviews of Health Systems: Kazakhstan 2018*. Paris: OECD Publishing. https://doi.org/10.1787/9789264289062-en.

Pollitt, C., & Sorin, D. (2011). *The Impacts of New Public Management in Europe: A Meta-Analysis*. COCOPS Work Package 1 Deliverable 1.1. Research Report. Retrieved from http://www.cocops.eu/wp-content/uploads/2012/03/WP1_Deliverable1_Meta-analysis_Final.pdf.

Preker, A. S., Carrin, G., Dror, D. M., Jakab, M., Hsiao, W., & Arhin, D. (2002). *Role of Communities in Resource Mobilization and Risk Sharing: A Synthesis Report*. Washington, DC: The World Bank.

Rogo, K. (2018). *Redefining Government Role in PPP: Success Factors*. Johannesburg: The World Bank. May 2018 Presentation.

Rouse, W. B. (2009). *Health Care as a Complex Adaptive System: Implications for Design and Management* (pp. 1–9). Bridge: National Academy of Engineering.

Rurik, I., & Kalabay, L. (2009). Primary Healthcare in the Developing Part of Europe: Changes and Development in the Former Eastern Bloc Countries that Joined the European Union Following 2004. *Medical Science Monitor, 15*(7), PH78–PH84.

Ryan, M. (1990). *Doctors and the State in Soviet Union*. New York: Palgrave Macmillan.

Saltman, R. B. (2018). The Impact of Slow Economic Growth on Health Sector Reforms: A Cross-National Perspective. *Health Economics Policy and Law*, 1–24. https://doi.org/10.1017/S1744133117000445.

Saltman, R. B. (2019). Structural Effects of the Information Revolution on Tax Funded European Health Systems and Some Potential Policy Responses. *Israel Journal of Health Policy Research, 8*, 8. Retrieved from https://ijhpr.biomedcentral.com/articles/10.1186/s13584-018-0284-2.

Saltman, R. B., & Young, D. W. (1981). The Hospital Power Equilibrium: An Alternative View of the Cost Containment Dilemma. *The Journal of Health Politics, Policy and Law, 6*, 391–418.

Saltman, R. B., Duran, A., & Dubois, H. F. W. (Eds.). (2011). *Governing Public Hospitals, Reform Strategies and the Movement Towards Institutional Autonomy*.

Brussels: European Observatory on Health Systems and Policies. Observatory Studies Series No. 25, 38.

Schieber, G., Anthony, R., Berman, P., Cleland, C., & Rice, J. (1992). *Health Care Financing in Russia*. Washington, DC: US Agency for International Development.

Schultz, D. S., & Rafferty, M. P. (1990). Soviet Health Care and Perestroika. *American Journal of Public Health, 80*(2). Retrieved from https://ajph.aphapublications.org/doi/pdf/10.2105/AJPH.80.2.193.

Scîntee, S. G., Vlădescu, C., Sagan, A., & Hernández-Quevedo, C. (2018). The Unexpected Outcomes of the Closure of 67 Inpatient Care Facilities in 2011 in Romania. *Health Policy, 122*(11), 1161–1164. https://doi.org/10.1016/j.healthpol.2018.08.010.

Sheiman, I. (2013). Rocky Road from the Semashko to a New Health Model. *Bulletin of the World Health Organization, 91*, 320–321. https://doi.org/10.2471/BLT.13.030513.

Sorenson, M.-L., & Burau, V. (2015). Why We Need to Move Beyond Diagnosis-Related Groups and How We Might Do So. *Journal of Health Services Research and Policy, 21*(1), 64–66. https://doi.org/10.1177/1355819615586444.

Stevens, R. (1993). *In Sickness and in Wealth: American Hospitals in the Twentieth Century*. New York: Basic Books.

Stubnya, G., Nagy, Z., Lammers, C. H., Rihmer, Z., & Bitter, I. (2010). Deinstitutionalization in Europe: Two Recent Examples from Germany and Hungary. *Psychiatria Danubina, 22*(3), 406–412.

Taube, M., Mitenbergs, U., & Sagan, A. (2012). The Impact of the Crisis on the Health System and Health in Latvia. In S. Thomson, J. Figueras, T. Evetovits, M. Jowett, P. Mladovsky, A. Maresso, J. Cylus, M. Karanikolos, & H. Kluge (Eds.), *Economic Crisis, Health Systems and Health in Europe: Country Experience*. Brussels: European Observatory on Health Systems and Policies.

Telen, M. J. (2014). Teaching Evidence-Based Medicine in the Former Soviet Union Lessons Learned. *Transactions of the American Clinical and Climatological Association, V125*, 88–103.

The Economist. (2018). An Affordable Necessity. Both in Rich and Poor Countries, Universal Health Care Brings Huge Benefits. *The Economist*, 26 April, Special Report: Universal Health Care. Retrieved May 20, 2018, from https://www.economist.com/special-report/2018/04/28/both-in-rich-and-poor-countries-universal-health-care-brings-huge-benefits.

Truitt, E., Thompson, R., Blazey-Martin, D., NiSai, D., & Salem, D. (2016). Effect of the Implementation of Barcode Technology and an Electronic Medication Administration Record on Adverse Drug Events. *Hospital Pharmacy, 51*, 474–483.

Tucker, S., Hughes, J., Burns, A., & Challis, D. (2008). The Balance of Care: Reconfiguring Services for Older People with Mental Health Problems. *Aging & Mental Health, 12*(1), 81–91.

Tulchinsky, T. H., & Varavikova, E. A. (1996). Addressing the Epidemiologic Transition in the Former Soviet Union: Strategies for Health System and Public Health Reform in Russia. *American Journal of Public Health, 86*, N3. Retrieved from https://ajph.aphapublications.org/doi/pdf/10.2105/AJPH.86.3.313.

Vladescu, C., Scîntee, S. G., Olsavszky, V., Hernández-Quevedo, C., & Sagan, A. (2016). Romania: Health System Review. *Health Systems in Transition, 18*(4), 1–170. Retrieved from http://www.euro.who.int/__data/assets/pdf_file/0017/317240/Hit-Romania.pdf?ua=1.

WHO – World Health Organization. (2011). *World Health Report 2010. Health System Financing; The Path to Universal Health Coverage*. Geneva: World Health Organization.

WHO – World Health Organization. (2012). *WHO Country Cooperation Strategy: India 2012–2017*. New Delhi: WHO – World Health Organization. Regional Office for South-East Asia. Retrieved from https://apps.who.int/iris/handle/10665/161136.

CHAPTER 8

Why Is Reform of Hospitals So Difficult?

Richard B. Saltman and Tata Chanturidze

A Plethora of Easy Solutions

Hospitals are concentrations of human and technological healthcare capital which embody diverse models of care and business models, are governed with very diverse decision-making regimes in both the public and the private sectors, and are managed by teams with very diverse qualification and competence.

A useful guide to understanding hospitals, as presented in Chap. 7 and before, is an analysis of their "societal goals and functions changing through history":

- from a first phase, protection in alms houses, shifting towards
- a second phase based on curative care, with emphasis on clinical technology—diagnostics and surgery—now towards

R. B. Saltman (✉)
Department of Health Policy and Management, Rollins School of Public Health, Emory University, Atlanta, GA, USA
e-mail: rsaltma@emory.edu

T. Chanturidze
Oxford Policy Management, Oxford, UK
e-mail: Tata.Chanturidze@opml.co.uk

A. Durán, S. Wright (eds.), *Understanding Hospitals in Changing Health Systems*, https://doi.org/10.1007/978-3-030-28172-4_8

- a third phase spinning around an—as yet—rather unresolved position in an era dominated by chronic multi-morbidity, moving from "industrial" processes to "digitalization and ICT technologies, genome sequencing, personalized medicine", and so on.

This last phase raises questions about the coordination and alignment ("integration") of care between hospitals and other system levels—a necessity for patients who will be moving frequently between settings and whose data needs also to travel continually, reliably and securely with them. Substantial changes are occurring in the way medicine in general is practised and health systems are organized. For example, immunizations have consolidated their decisive role in all countries[1] (Summers and Yamey 2015) and improvements in health results have occurred at many levels, while some activities have been taken out of earlier forms of hospitals (Robertson et al. 2014).

Present-day emphasis on collective population-based social determinants of health and their link to individual illness experience may be blurring the major challenges faced by hospitals. The way in which health systems have articulated their functions (service production, financing, stewardship and input generation) has necessarily generated country variations of outputs and outcomes. That is, different organizational and institutional features, availability of means, geographical and economic accessibility, incentives for professionals, and service utilization patterns all have a clear influence on services and results (Sparkes et al. 2017), although that influence has not yet been quantified by research in sufficiently comparative detail.

This amalgam of features is perhaps why standard messages on hospital reform tend to be only apparently simple. They mix issues pertaining to different categories of systems, ownership, and governance. Aspects typically covered may include an unclear focus on ownership and/or governance issues (both governmental/regulatory-macro-level and management/operational-meso/micro at institutional level) and efficiency/appropriateness operating issues that affect hospitals of all types once they reach a certain size. Much of the available literature and the issues analysed actually focus on the predominant ownership arrangement in particular parts of the world, namely, public hospitals in Europe and private hospitals in the US; this

[1] But even that is threatened, perhaps, by the "anti-vaxxer" movement now.

over-focuses on both the issues of the developed world and of ownership as a factor (see Chaps. 5 and 7).

Perhaps all the above reasons together explain, however, how it is often not easy to clarify what exactly the now-standard messages on hospital reform deal with. In many texts and as described in our introductory Chap. 1, contents get blurred between issues pertaining to (1) all hospitals of all ownership types and health systems (e.g. US as well as Europe, developed as well as developing countries, etc.); (2) public hospitals in publicly funded health systems (e.g. mostly in Northern/Southern European tax-funded health systems); (3) modified/re-structured/semi-autonomous publicly owned hospitals in tax-funded health systems—but also in Central European hybrid/state-attached social health insurance models, (4) privately owned—not-for-profit (e.g. Netherlands) and (5) for-profit (Germany, the US) hospitals, not to mention multiple structural variations found in China, India and other countries.

While improvements in health are being pursued in a context of *globalization*, hospitals in the developing world are criticized as delivering, at high-cost, services which are poorly accessible and of insufficient quality, and this is hard to accept in the light of so many other areas of resource scarcity. Yet in developed countries, hospitals now account on average for only a third, or a bit more, of total health systems cost (ranging broadly from 30–45%, although hospital pharmaceuticals and potentially capital expenditures are not always systematically included in those figures).[2]

Confirming It's Not Easy: The Erratic Path in Ex-Centrally Planned Economies

Privatization

Private hospital beds achieved a significant presence in most Western European countries between 1995 and 2013, as Table 8.1 shows (see also Chap. 5).

Chapter 7 has shown that the 1990–2010 rationalization reforms made some remarkable impacts on health systems, dramatically so in Central and Eastern European (CEE) and former Soviet Union (FSU) countries. The post-collapse reforms shaped the current configuration of public-hospital infrastructure there, with significant downsizing in the number of

[2] See Box 1.1, hospital expenditure, in Chap. 1

Table 8.1 For-profit hospital beds, some European countries, selected years

		1995	*2000*	*2005*	*2010*	*2013*
Austria	Total beds	67,853	63,674	63,248	64,008	56,347
	% for-profit	6.9	7.1	9.0	11.1	15.1
Czech Rep.	Total beds	87,784	79,985	77,309	73,746	67,888
	% for-profit				13.7	17.7
Denmark	Total beds		22,927	20,902	19,405	17,241
	% for-profit		0.1	1.4	2.1	2.1
Finland	Total beds	41,483	39,026	37,000	31,395	26,429
	% for-profit	3.3	3.3	3.7	4.4	4.2
France	Total beds		484,279	455,175	416,710	413,206
	% for-profit		19.8	20.4	23.4	23.7
Germany	Total beds			698,303	674,473	667,560
	% for-profit			26.2	29.7	29.8
Italy	Total beds			234,375	215,980	203,723
	% for-profit			28.1	28.0	27.6
Netherlands	Total beds	81,437	76,859	72,698	76,980	
	% for-profit	0	0	0	0	
Poland	Total beds			248,860	251,456	252,281
	% for-profit			17.0	24.3	26.8
Spain	Total beds	154,644	148,081	145,863	145,199	138,153
	% for-profit	19.4	17.9	19.6	17.7	18.8

OECD Data, 18 January 2016, extracted from Jeurissen et al. (2016)

hospitals, number of hospital beds, and the average length of stay. Few European countries in ex-centrally planned economies (CPEs) or for that matter elsewhere have actually built wholly new public hospitals after 1990, and to the extent that there was major expenditure, the aim was substitution of obsolete infrastructure with new buildings, rather than extending overall hospital network capacity. It should be noted that the opposite trends were observed with private hospitals, discussed in the sections below.

In a number of Eastern European countries, there were constructive hospital rationalizations. Estonia showcases a best-practice example, achieving remarkable improvements in efficiency, quality, and patient satisfaction without compromising access and utilization (Box 8.1). Careful consideration of the sector-wide rationalization objectives; redesigning the models of care with the emphases to PHC, day care and long-term care; and innovative hospital business models—all well aligned with the proposed governance arrangements—produced this success in Estonia.

Box 8.1 Hospital Sector Rationalization in Estonia After Independence

At the time of independence, Estonia inherited 120 public hospitals with more than 17,000 beds, thus 122 beds per 10,000 population, serving a country of 1.4 million (Fidler et al. 2009). In 1991, a year after independence, hospitals were given semi-autonomous status, providing hospital managers with decision-making authority. New health policies appealed to increased market exposure, creating opportunities for investment (Habicht et al. 2011).

Between 1995 and 2000, the average length of stay in acute care fell by 30% (Habicht et al. 2018). Private investment in hospitals throughout the 1990s resulted in improvements in medical technology, evidence-based clinical practice, and financial incentives. The Estonia Health Insurance Fund (EHIF) was formed and emphasized cost containment, as well as quality of service improvement. After introduction of licensing standards in the 1990s, a number of small providers facing difficulties in fulfilling new criteria were transitioned into specialty care and outpatient centres. In 2012, there were 65 licensed hospitals in Estonia, including 19 acute care hospitals and 35 nursing and rehabilitation hospitals (NIHD 2018). By 2016, this number decreased to 30 hospitals (Statista 2019). Hospital discharge rates, length of hospital stay (acute care) and hospital beds per 1000 inhabitants have decreased (OECD 2018). The hospital governance arrangements were improved (Saltman et al. 2011). Patient satisfaction increased, with patient choice and low waiting times cited as reasons for high satisfaction (Polluste et al. 2012).

By 2015, Estonia had experienced remarkable improvement in health outcomes. Life expectancy at birth had increased from 71 years in 2000 to 78 years; premature deaths from cardiovascular disease were reduced by 24% over the period 2009–2015, albeit that they remain relatively high (Habicht et al., op. cit., Habicht et al. 2018). This was achieved despite health spending lower than in most EU countries (6.5% of GDP in 2015 OECD 2017), though arguably future improvement will require an uplift in spending, which is currently being developed.

In many post-Soviet countries, private investments helped modernize and upgrade hospital infrastructure (Transparency International 2012), with part of the excess facilities being re-profiled (e.g. into Long Term Care) or turned into profit-making institutions. The private sector in post-Soviet countries today largely encompasses specific services, such as dental care, pharmaceuticals, and service provision for foreigners (Rechel et al. 2014). In some countries, privatization took place at a greater scale; for example, all healthcare facilities were converted to joint-stock companies in Armenia (Bonilla-Chacin et al. 2003), and most of the pharmaceutical, PHC and hospital facilities were privatized in Georgia (Chanturidze et al. 2009).

Pharmaceutical markets were liberalized to address supply shortages in the 1990s. While some researchers believe that this objective was largely achieved, others contend that the better supply of medicines was accompanied by increased prices and aggressive politics substituting expensive drugs for generics, reducing access in some cases. In 2010, around 80% of Russian inpatients still paid for a portion of their medicines (Marquez and Bonch-Osmolovskiy 2010), and in 2011, 62.7% of inpatients in Moldova reported purchasing pharmaceuticals on their own when the hospital was unable to provide them (Turcanu et al. 2012). Although some policy reforms have attempted to address these challenges, many physicians still have considerable distrust of generics (e.g. in Romania), and the pharmaceutical industry remains powerful in some liberalized markets in some FSU countries (e.g. Kazakhstan, Georgia, Russia) (Richardson et al. 2014).

On a positive side, privatization helped some hospitals to define a "niche" which they can successfully occupy. Mono-profile tertiary hospitals (e.g. neurosurgery) and mono-profile hospitals producing "low technology/high turnover" services (e.g. cataract surgery) survived rather well in some countries (e.g. Georgia). While the quality, effectiveness, and volume of services were improved, these transformations happened without governments having any leverage to influence prioritized service baskets, reflecting a gap in sector-wide planning, and negatively affecting access to other hospital services that are financially unattractive to private actors.

Theoretical claims for positive effects of private ownership stem from public choice and property rights theories, which revolve around competition and public management/ownership arguments (Blom-Hansen 2003). Health systems have in practice developed new ways of organizing their relationships with private providers (Saltman 2003). Recent policy discussion has shifted to the optimal balance between public and private provision, replacing prior debate solely on the role of the private sector in health. In this context, competition between public and private hospitals for state funding became inevitable. To date, it remains widely discussed whether the private sector supersedes public institutions in terms of economic performance and quality, as shown in a recent review of 17 studies representing more than 5500 hospitals across Europe (Tynkkynen and Vrangbæk 2018).

In practice, governments' approach to health sector privatization sometimes translated into negative outcomes. In a number of former FSU countries, governments fell short in preparing the regulatory environment to monitor an expansive private sector, though this was more in dental care, pharmacies and medical manufacture than in hospitals themselves (Footman and Richardson 2014). Inadequate accountability and oversight processes enabled private providers to pursue profit-driven practices, without addressing broader population-based health needs. Here, the case of Georgia's hospital system—contrasting starkly with that of Estonia in Box 8.1—provides an illustrative example (see Box 8.2).

Box 8.2 Implications of Hospital Privatization in Georgia

In the absence of rigorous regulations, and with poor implementation and oversight capabilities, 40% of hospitals in Georgia ended up owned by insurance companies, 30% by individuals, and 20% by pharmaceutical companies and other entities (Transparency International 2012). Over time, large companies dominated their respective markets: for example, the Georgia Health Care Group, the largest health service provider in Georgia, which owns pharmaceutical distributors, hospital and diagnostic networks and outpatient facilities, operates at a 26.6% market share, and is also the largest medical insurer in Georgia with a 38.4% market share.

Other pharmaceutical companies, once becoming hospital owners, controlled the drug supply and prescription in their hospitals. In these cases, instead of improvements in quality or efficiency, hospital privatization increased out-of-pocket payments and made healthcare less accessible, particularly for the uninsured (Rechel et al. 2014).

An important lesson is that one key challenge for having good hospitals starts by creating a robust governance context (cf. Chap. 2). Many post-Communist countries have simply replaced "rigid" with "poorly regulated", with detrimental consequences. Factors affecting this failure reflected the social and technical inability of countries to set up robust governance systems and practices.

Decentralization and Fragmentation

Alongside privatization, the transition period brought about a decentralization of responsibilities to regional and municipal governance structures. Since newly independent countries were faced with a myriad of health challenges, in some cases health officials were eager to associate inherited failures with (excessive) government intervention, and therefore sought to separate health sector development from central oversight (Barr and Field 1996). There was a consolidation of central government authority in the early 1990s, leading in turn to the creation of new regional and district governance structures. Despite formal operational decentralization, much decision-making authority was transferred to national health policy and legislative processes as well as to ministries of finance (Rechel et al. 2014).

One important additional dimension of decentralization created an opportunity for increased autonomy of hospitals and the ability of hospital management to make decisions concerning administrative, financial and human resources issues. As discussed in Chap. 7 and shown particularly in Table 7.2, some hospitals transitioned to locally controlled hospital governance structures, with hospital boards consisting of political representatives which could further the interests of the local community (Saltman et al. 2011). Hospitals also strengthened their internal financial management and audit processes. Others started to collect data on patient satisfaction; for example, in Kadan, Czech Republic, emphasis was placed on patient communication to understand how patients experience care. Decentralization of management combined with shifts in payment mechanisms were then implemented to improve performance (Roubal and Hrobon 2011).

In other cases, however, in health systems lacking funding and having only municipal systems able to react to the needs of the surrounding population, decentralization further exacerbated service challenges rather than solving them. The distribution of power and budgets has resulted in weak and uncoordinated pockets of authority amongst local government and health insurance agencies. In addition, while decentralization resulted in the transfer of ownership of health facilities to local governments, regional- and municipal-level administrations were ill-equipped to assume these new responsibilities. Primary care facilities, for example, technically fell under municipal ownership; however, facilities in regional centres were under regional authority. Municipalities also lacked sufficient funding to provide adequate quality care. Inequalities between health financing systems developed as a result of varying levels of taxation that regions could afford, and around which policy was developed (Saltman and Bankauskaite 2006). Many of these inequalities in access to healthcare have persisted from the transition through until today (Rechel et al. 2014).

Lack of regulation and inadequate measures to monitor hospitals and other health facilities had detrimental effects on service provision. Standards and processes for monitoring were uncoordinated and distributed to lower levels of government (Turcanu et al. 2012). In addition, corruption has been frequently observed as a concern in the implementation of health sector activities in FSU countries, especially given the sudden heterogeneity of governance and administration of health facilities (Bonilla-Chacin et al. 2003).

In response to the above challenges, in the last two decades some countries have experienced a push-back from decentralization, seeking to re-institute greater central influence. Russia and Kazakhstan have proposed moving financial (health service purchasing or health insurance) and various administrative functions to central oversight (Katsaga et al. 2012). Moldova and Kyrgyzstan instituted a national pooling of funds in an attempt to provide a more equal resource allocation after the establishment of district-level financing structures resulted in large inequalities in healthcare delivery. Other reforms have focused on governance, such as those that were implemented in Armenia to reduce the authority of village-level leaders over outpatient clinics (Richardson 2013).

Some commentators argue that countries that retained more authority within the Ministry of Health experienced greater efficiency in decision-making and policy reform. In Kyrgyzstan and Moldova, for instance, decentralization was reversed with the removal of regional and district health departments. This enabled them to implement a family medicine model for primary care and a single-payer system, resulting in less inequality in access to health services (Rechel et al. 2013). These examples somehow echo the centralization of Japanese hospitals, discussed in Chap. 2.

Insurance Purchasing and Finance

A parallel wave of transformation in this region was related to the introduction of new financing and service purchasing mechanisms for hospitals. Following the collapse of the Soviet-based Semashko model, a number of countries moved away from funding based on general taxation towards health insurance (or mixed) systems. Arguments for plurality, independence, and market-based competition were discussed as benefits of health insurance (Lawson and Nemec 2003). Many countries in Central Europe and the Balkans, and some elsewhere in the FSU, adopted some form of social health insurance (SHI), with transformations being uneven across countries in terms of onset and duration (McKee and Nolte 2004). Supplementing budgetary allocations for health with these SHI revenues systems created a blending of Bismarck and Beveridge models, in some settings.

The available evidence suggests that the introduction of SHI and accompanied service-purchasing reforms globally had a positive impact on the hospital sector. A study utilizing a difference-in-difference design method between 28 countries from 1990 to 2004 shows that the SHI adoption increased national health spending and hospital activity rates (Wagstaff and Moreno-Serra 2009). Other studies show improvement in contracting and service purchasing (McKee and Healy 2002).

Nevertheless, many systems have been unable to restructure hospital governance and administrative processes in such a way as to implement effectively solutions to the gaps in insurance systems (McKee and Nolte 2004). Out-of-pocket payments (OOP) remain a major unresolved concern, and perhaps the most visible sign of the "unfinished business" of health financing reform.

Figure 8.1 illustrates a mixed progress in addressing OOPs in CEE/FSU between 2000 and 2015. Undeniably, OOPs had a common negative impact on hospitals (especially in poor resource settings) in terms of unpredictable and unsystematized revenues, as well as continued "under the table" payments, affecting the financial performance of hospitals, and the attitude and clinical practice of the medical personnel (Kujawska 2017). A "refusal to seek care" developed among some citizens as an inevitable consequence of OOPs, and was expressed in an overall decline in outpatient visits in the 1990s, with the highest decline in Georgia (−75%), Armenia (−42%), Azerbaijan (−25%) and Tajikistan (−35%) (Bonilla-Chacin et al. 2003; Balabanova et al. 2004). Other signs of persistent OOP challenges were expressed in increased fragmentation, polarization, and, in some cases, exclusion of marginalized patient groups, for example, the Roma population across CEE (Koupilova et al. 2001).

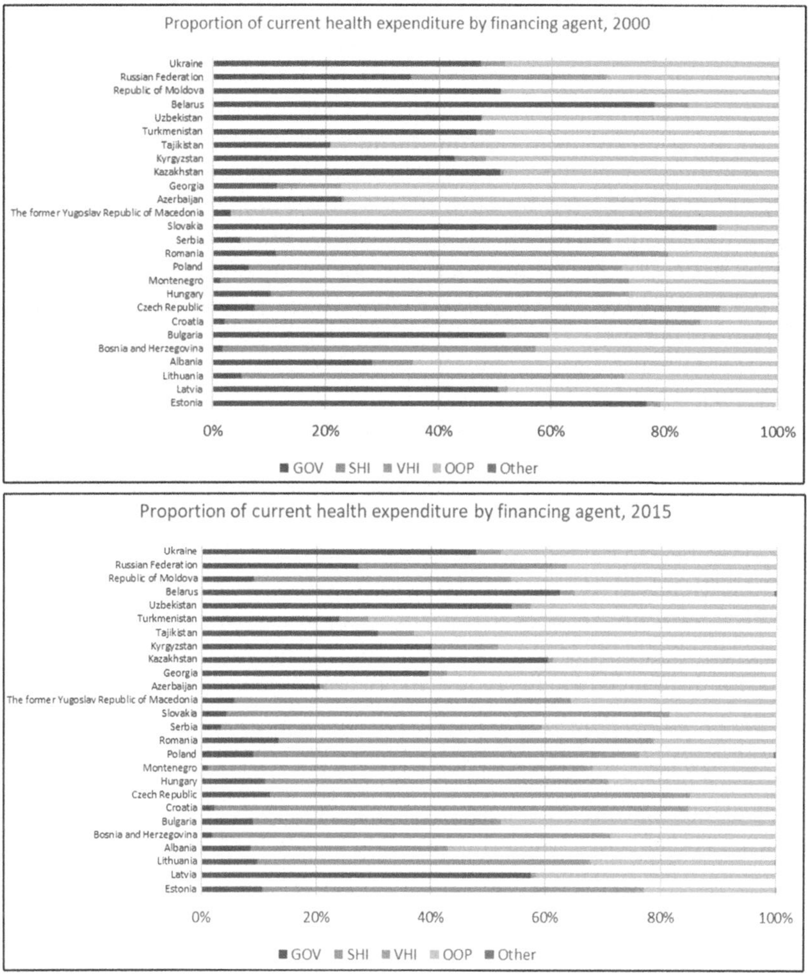

Fig. 8.1 Structure of current health expenditure by financing agent in FSU countries 2000 and 2015 (Adrian Gheorghe (OPM), based on WHO Global Health Expenditure Database. Note: In the first panel (2000), data for Hungary, Poland and Czech Republic are from 2003)

The goal of ***changing provider-payment mechanisms*** was to reduce inefficiencies by lessening the importance of inputs, to increase the importance of population needs in budget-setting and resource allocation, and to put more emphasis on performance outcomes. By the year 2000, most CEE/FSU countries were experimenting with one or more forms of hospital reimbursement mechanisms alternative to the traditional line-item budgets. A decade later, by early 2010, quite a number of countries had moved to nationwide diagnosis-related group (DRG)-based payment systems (Croatia, Estonia, Hungary, Kyrgyzstan, Lithuania, Poland, Romania and the Former Yugoslav Republic of Macedonia), while others were considering or piloting DRGs (Bulgaria, Latvia, Republic of Moldova and Serbia) (Mathauer and Wittenbecher 2013).

Performance-based purchasing, designed to reduce inefficiencies by moving away from input-based funding and emphasizing performance outcomes, was attempted in Kyrgyzstan, Georgia, and Armenia (Bonilla-Chacin et al. 2003). Input-based budget setting, prioritized in Tajikistan, was accompanied by attempts to introduce "per capita payments" for primary healthcare (Rahminov et al. 2000).

Other trends in service purchasing included ***cost-sharing arrangements*** for selected health services. Co-payment structures were introduced and have evolved in various ways, with some involving a central determination of health insurance benefits (e.g. Latvia), and others allowing hospitals to charge co-payments for services in municipal benefit packages (e.g. Georgia). Armenia (later Georgia, 2004) introduced ***means-tested social assistance benefits*** to target those who are low-income rather than only those exhibiting non-income-related characteristics. Subsidies have been shown to be effective when their funding is sustained; however, informal payments have remained a substantial barrier to access (Bonilla-Chacin et al. 2003).

This section of the chapter has shown that contextual specificities did not allow "Semashko" hospitals to come up with something dramatically different from the traditional models of care and business models in the West, despite the evident need to introduce more cost-effective and efficient arrangements. A key dilemma has been the rigidity and poor articulation of overall health system governance, producing rate-limiting shortfalls in the course of quite fundamental and dramatic transformations: privatization, decentralization, and health financing reforms.

Numerous Reforms: Why So Little Real Change in Worldwide Hospital Behaviour and Outcomes; Why Stasis Is the Norm

Why and how *in specific terms* did institutions, some of them visibly successful a few decades before, come to a situation which can be so heavily criticized—in the ex-CPE, the US, Europe and least developed countries (LDCs)? Solutions of all kinds have been tried:

- Reaction to demographic and epidemiological changes: "chronicity" and "consumerism";
- Transferring more power to primary care;
- Participating in "non-traditional" healthcare networks;
- Technological innovation; the possibility of changing the location of care;
- Reduction/readjustment of beds plus partial process reengineering;
- Standardization of processes and creation of hospital chains;
- Deepening specialization;
- Mergers, integrations and hospital convergences;
- Strategic tools to change the position of hospitals in the system;
- Reform of financing and payment methods (payment for performance, P4P, bundled payments, capitation, and shared savings);
- Changing the legal status of institutions (conversion into (semi) autonomous/corporatization of entities);
- Public-private partnerships, in a variety of models; also privatization…

The limited success generally achieved with the shotgun efforts listed above to improve hospital behaviour and performance strongly suggest that modern—especially public—hospitals have fundamental structural characteristics that at a minimum complicate, and at times directly thwart, substantial organizational change.

To some degree, a lack of substantial real organizational change reflects a laudable defensive dimension, reflecting resilience of staff and institutional processes ("stability"). However, it also highlights a less laudable protective barrier, reflecting resistance to both modernization and reform ("stasis")—or, more subtly, it may simultaneously reflect both stability and stasis. To different constituencies, this reflects differing concerns and musters widely divergent degrees of intra- and/or extra-institutional authority, which continues to be a major unresolved issue concerning hospitals for both national policymakers and academic organization theorists alike.

A recent assessment of public hospital behaviour (Edwards and Saltman 2017) provides an opportunity for a deeper understanding of the core structural forces and factors that confound most politically generated efforts to influence and improve the behaviour, most specifically, of publicly operated hospitals. This assessment conceptualizes these hospitals' institutional resistance to reform as reflecting a highly complex, six-part decision environment (see Box 8.3).

Box 8.3 Public Hospital Decision Environment

- Normal organizational dysfunction, plus
- Health professional dysfunction, compounded by
- Governance/political dysfunction

Modified by:

- Clinical/organizational complexity
- Market failures
- Universal anxiety
(Edwards and Saltman 2017)

Each of these six dimensions of hospital-level organization and decision-making generates substantial obstacles to innovative structural or clinical change, and each interacts with the other five dimensions to complicate further and delimit the potential range of organizational and managerial discretion and response. Moreover, these six factors appear to be inherent in almost all twenty-first century hospitals. While the degree of emphasis and the implications for performance may vary between publicly as against privately operated institutions, and between developed as against developing countries, the core characteristics of the hospital policy dilemma remain broadly similar (Edwards and Saltman 2017 op. cit.; Braithwaite et al. 2017).

Among developed countries, the most apparent examples can be found in the tax-funded and publicly operated hospital systems in Northern and Mediterranean Europe (Saltman 2018). Among developing countries, notable examples include China, India, and Russia; Middle Eastern/North African countries, including Egypt, Tunisia, Morocco, and Jordan; Former Soviet Republic countries like Georgia, Kazakhstan, Ukraine and

Belarus; as well as Chile and other South American countries, as cited by Preker and Harding 2003).

The three organizational and three contextual dimensions in Box 8.3 frame what is a core structural dilemma for contemporary hospital development. The constraints placed on hospital responses by these six dimensions effectively delimit a broad range of reform pretensions, whether managerially or politically inspired.

This section briefly reviews the analytic and academic grounding for the six constraining dimensions, linking them directly to current-day hospital behaviour.

The "Normal" Level of Dysfunction That Organizational Theorists Attribute to All Large Organizations

Multiple scholarly efforts in multiple academic disciplines have sought to explain why all large organizations—both public sector and private sector in ownership and operation—have such great difficulty in meeting and maintaining the formal operating objectives they set for themselves. Among the more prominent writers are the following:

- *Max Weber*, a German sociologist writing in the first decade of the twentieth century (Weber 1947), described all organizations—both public and private—as formalistic and "bureaucratic", by which he meant that they operated on a formalistic "legal-rational model" of authority structured as a "system of rules and office", which was seen as a "career" for its inhabitants.
- *Herbert Simon*, a Nobel-Prize-winning economist, theorized that the "limits of rationality" prevented individual managers from adequately analysing more than three or four alternative strategies for any one decision (Simon 1947).
- *Charles Lindblom*, a Yale political economist, expanded on Simon's insight to argue that, in public sector organizations (or, implicitly, organizations with public sector responsibilities), an incremental approach he termed "the method of successive limited comparisons" was both intellectually superior and politically safer than attempting a "rational comprehensive" bottom-up decision analysis (Lindblom 1959).

- *Aaron Wildavsky*, a University of California/Berkeley political scientist, wrote (in concert with Jeffrey Pressman) that public sector organizations typically had "too many decision points" in too many different organizational offices to implement organizational programmes efficiently (or, often, even at all) (Pressman and Wildavsky 1972).
- *Michel Crozier*, a French sociologist, found in two large French public sector bureaucracies that each skill-based group of workers developed their own "group strategy" to maximize their power over day-to-day operating decisions. The group with the most power was that which controlled the most "uncertainty" over the organization's ability to meet its management-established production targets. Only in the case of a major crisis that threatened all employees' jobs could organizational change be successfully introduced (Crozier 1963).
- *Michael Lipsky*, an American political scientist, demonstrated that frontline employees in public sector service organizations rapidly became "street level bureaucrats" who utilized their professional discretion to favour (or disfavour) different types of clients, despite clear organizational rules regarding equal treatment of all eligible citizens (Lipsky 1981).
- *Geert Hofstede*, a Dutch anthropologist, concluded after years of study of a large private sector multinational corporation that efforts by management to modify the corporate culture to improve productivity would inexorably be "patiently smoothed" by the organization's workforce until the old cultural norms had been restored (Hofstede 1980).

Drawing on these (and other) analyses and observations, a wide range of researchers has found that large public and private sector organizations alike have been and remain broadly resistant to the periodic but sporadic efforts by policymakers and/or managers to adjust and/or re-structure existing organizational arrangements.

There is a plausible claim, therefore, that large modern-day hospitals—both publicly and privately operated—exhibit many of these same dysfunctional organizational characteristics. Hospital-focused studies have found that both clinical and support staff are broadly resistant to intentional outside intervention seeking to permanently re-configure day-to-day behaviour (Saltman and Young 1981; Saltman 1985, 1987). Moreover, even when substantial operational changes have in fact been implemented, they typically have a relatively short half-life, surviving intact only until the political and/or managerial impetus—or sometimes the managerial and/or political careers involved—move on.

Health Professional Dysfunction

A second major structural impediment to effective organizational change in hospitals is the role, authority and institutional prerogatives of health-care professionals, particularly physicians. Physicians have asymmetrical clinical knowledge, as well as patient trust, enabling them largely to control the rate and pace of their own workloads as well as much of the work-flow of the rest of the organization around them. Hospital managers—even senior executives whom current clinicians tartly view as "previously having been physicians" (Young and Saltman 1985)—find that they lack the ability to intervene effectively and/or consistently in the hospital's clinical production process. Mintzberg (1979) referred to this problem as "disconnected hierarchy", in which hospital managers lack the means to control the most important positive reinforcers for physicians (e.g. peer respect, publication in peer-reviewed journals), and therefore must rely upon less central and often less effective negative actions around the allocation of funding and—the most prized commodity in a tertiary care hospital—space (for an attending's patients, staff, and research). Mechanic (1968—"The Profession of Medicine") detailed the clash inside hospitals between physicians' standing and responsibilities as seen within the medical profession, and numerous organizational obstacles that interfered with efficient—sometimes with effective—delivery of medical services.

Built-in structural tensions, especially in large tertiary care hospitals, between physicians and nurses, between physician and nurse leadership, also between internists and surgeons have been observed by many academics and management consultants to hamper effective hospital management. Physician group strategies to maximize their intra-organizational standing and authority can be viewed as successfully reflecting their strategies to influence hospital decision-making, based on their ability to control the bases of organizational uncertainty: patient recruitment and the clinical production process (Saltman and Young 1981, op. cit.; Saltman and de Roo 1989; Saltman 1988).

In the current period, physician leverage over the pace of hospital development and its rate of change continues to be found across many standard inpatient and outpatient management practices in public hospitals. As one example, public hospitals in the English NHS as well as in Sweden and Finland for many years booked patient outpatient appointments to the clinic, not to a specific physician, and booked individual patients only to the half-day session (e.g. "afternoon session"), not to a specific time—both measures that maximized the flexibility of the outpatient clinic physicians at the cost of an entire afternoon to working patients (Saltman 1988, op. cit.). As one ophthalmologist in a large Finnish district hospital bluntly put it, "Coming to a public hospital is like being in the army. My patients are glad when I come". Such examples can be confirmed from other country cases.

Governance Induced and Political Dysfunction

Hospitals by their very nature are politically sensitive institutions. What services they provide, which patients they treat, where they are located, who they hire, who manages them, who supplies them, are all inherently interesting questions for the political class. When the (very large) funding of these institutions is generated from public (tax-based) and/or publicly sanctioned (social-health-insurance based) sources, the level of political interest becomes even greater. Viewed pragmatically in terms of the scale, scope, and societal importance of their inputs and outputs, it would in practice be surprising if policy and management decision-making for hospitals were *not* a highly politicized process.

The complex political texture that colours hospital-related activity affects all three key areas of institutional decision-making: (a) at the *macro*/policymaking level, (b) at the practical *macro/meso* implementation level, and (c) at the day-to-day *micro*-clinic managerial level (both *meso*/institutional and *micro*/clinic level are located within the hospital) (Duran et al. 2011).

At the *macro*/policymaking level, the explicitly political character of hospital-related policymaking necessarily influences management decision-making as well. Among the more regularly noted examples are the following:

1. Hospitals are often one of the largest employers in a city, and, in a smaller regional centre, may be the only large source of jobs and regular pay checks. Further, hospitals are central to industrial policy, particularly in more rural or less-populated areas: the presence of a

multi-specialty hospital is seen as an attractive factor in convincing new industry to locate (e.g. bringing in additional new jobs and income). Conversely, closing a hospital is seen politically not only as discouraging new industrial development, but putting at risk existing companies that may subsequently decide to leave. In countries where hospitals are part of the public sector directly, this link between publicly funded and/or operated hospitals and continued and/or future industrial development inevitably and inexorably skews policy decisions about available services, staffing levels, and size and quality of facilities. Ask any national or regional politician in large and geographically scattered countries like Sweden, Norway or Finland what they view as the hardest political decision to make, they will nearly always tell you, "closing a local hospital". This is also true in public systems in Spain and Italy. Issues of cost, efficiency, quality, and outcome inevitably pale in the face of political necessity. Moreover, existing institutions nearly always have submitted "business proposals" for expanding medical staff and service facilities based on "projections of future growth". The resulting outcome, not surprisingly, is that the close oversight and control of particularly public hospitals by political actors typically results in a set of less than technically or managerially optimal organizational or managerial outcomes.

2. Hospital staff in many European health systems are public sector civil servants (whether formally municipal, regional or national government), with legislatively protected jobs and pensions, strong politically connected unions, and thus little incentive to take risks or be innovative. Efforts to sanction or dismiss public employees are complex, elongated, expensive, and rarely pursued.
3. When political actors do give grants of semi-autonomous decision-making and/or management to publicly operated hospitals, those grants almost always are conditional upon "good behaviour" as seen by their political superiors. Institutions which make politically uncomfortable decisions tend to see their semi-autonomy clawed back in part or whole (Saltman et al. 2011, op. cit.). Indeed, sometimes writs of managerial autonomy to public hospitals are less than they seem on paper. As one example, in some instances of hospital semi-autonomy established in Spain in the late 1990s, the executive committee set up to manage the new institutional decision-making process was chaired (or significantly conditioned) by a representative of the regional minister of health (Duran et al. 2011, op. cit.).

A Closer Look at Three Compounding Contextual Dimensions

In addition to the complex effects of the three dysfunctional organizational dilemmas that constrain hospitals as just discussed, there also are three centrally important contextual dimensions of public hospitals that further complicate effective strategies for institutional and managerial reform:

1. *Complexity of organizing high-quality, effective healthcare*: High levels of technically sophisticated and financially onerous capital equipment, carefully configured physical space, and high levels of coordination and cooperation among different categories of medical and non-medical staff both within and beyond hospitals walls.
2. *Market failure in public hospitals:* Difficulty balancing between effective market pressure, political control, and maintaining core public healthcare obligations and responsibilities.
3. *Generalized and specific anxiety*:
   Patients often have high anxiety;
   Medical staff experience anxiety about outcomes;
   Managers have the anxiety that comes from limited control;
   Politicians are held accountable for outcomes they cannot affect.

Taken together, the combination of the three structurally fixed *dysfunctions*, occurring within the three difficult-to-reduce contextual dilemmas, establishes a managerial and decision-making environment around hospitals that is both malign and self-reinforcing. To be sure, privately owned and operated hospitals suffer from the first two organizational dysfunctions (size and professional priorities) and the first and third of the contextual dilemmas (complexity of modern care delivery and generalized and specific anxiety). In this important sense, all contemporary hospitals have innate structural and contextual dimensions that make them difficult to manage effectively. However, the public hospital additions of political organizational dysfunction and financial market failure suggest that it is publicly owned and operated hospitals—those hospitals which are officially owned by and operated only in the interests of their patients—that have in practice continued to have the most difficulty in delivering on their (non-politicized) care delivery operational promises (Saltman 2019; Stubbs 2016).

How to Break—Or At Least Palliate—The Stasis

The initial chapters in this volume suggested strongly that a more effective future for hospitals generally involves strengthening governance, and developing more robust and sustainable models of healthcare business. These would in turn draw their sustainability from the appropriateness of the models of care they employ; most importantly, all this would, and could only, take place within and be matched to each specific health system context.

This chapter has now suggested that efforts to resolve the two intertwined sources of public hospitals' managerial and service delivery dilemmas cannot be based simply on *clever* new policy proposals devised as single mechanisms at healthcare, economic, or political level. On the contrary: the operational dysfunctionalities exacerbated by complicated contexts will yield—and only in some modest degree—to a re-thinking of what hospitals consist of, how they operate, and how they fit into their wider system environment.

The image of the way to develop and run hospitals presented in this book offers a set of ideas which have the virtue of handling, or at least recognizing, the difficult contexts enumerated above in which hospitals operate—and doing so explicitly:

- Precepts of good governance will include contingencies to reduce the anxiety of patients (and the population as ultimate payers), managers, professional clinical staff, and politicians. Differing interests can be worked out better when there is better trust or social capital between players;
- A model of care can be as sophisticated as wished to cope with the technical complexity of real-life healthcare situations, limited only by the ability to conceptualize and model it;
- A model of business can be oriented to achieve adequate performance even in situations of market failure.

In addition, by its very nature, the vision developed here elicits information which will enable transparent discussion about the organizational dysfunctions mentioned above. While discussion by itself does not resolve problems, it does at the minimum help standardize a vocabulary which reveals the different agendas of the different stakeholders—within complex healthcare and hospital organizations, between clinical and management personnel, and between populations and their political decision-makers.

The "governance/business models/models of care" structure is flexible enough to accommodate a variety of value judgements about what the healthcare system should deliver, whilst imposing a discipline on expectations of how the logical implications of those judgements should play out. Also, it exposes the danger of wanting ends without willing the means, thus increasing realism.

It would be naïve to assume that words within a debate will mean the same to different parties, or that different groups will be able to agree on the objectives at which the system should aim simply by using the same words and concepts. The next chapter about "decision-making" draws together a number of themes about how the concepts we have proposed can (start to) be used in practice.

References

Balabanova, D., McKee, M., Pomerleau, J., Rose, R., & Haerpfer, C. (2004). Health Service Utilization in the Former Soviet Union: Evidence from Eight Countries. *Health Services Research, 39*(6), 1927–1950.

Barr, D. A., & Field, M. G. (1996). The Current State of Health Care in the Former Soviet Union: Implications for Health Care Policy and Reform. *American Journal of Public Health, 86*(3), 307–312.

Blom-Hansen, J. (2003). Is Private Delivery of Public Services Really Cheaper? Evidence from Public Road Maintenance in Denmark. *Public Choice, 115*(3/4), 419–438. https://doi.org/10.1023/A:1024274527502.

Bonilla-Chacin, M. E., Murrugarra, E., & Moukim Temourov, W. B. (2003). *Health Care During Transition and Health Systems Reform: Evidence from the Poorest CIS Countries* (Lucerne: CIS-7 Initiative) 2003 Conference of the CIS-7 Initiative, January 20–22. Retrieved from http://web.worldbank.org/archive/website00504/WEB/PDF/MURRUG-2.PDF.

Braithwaite, J., Westbrook, J., Coiera, E., Runciman, W. B., Day, R., Hillman, K., & Herkes, J. (2017). A Systems Science Perspective on the Capacity for Change in Public Hospitals. *Israel Journal Health Policy Research, 6*, 16. Retrieved from https://ijhpr.biomedcentral.com/articles/10.1186/s13584-017-0143-6.

Chanturidze, T., Ugulava, T., Duran, A., Ensor, T., & Richardson, E. (2009). Georgia: Health System Review. *Health Systems in Transition, 11*(8), 1–116. Retrieved from http://www.euro.who.int/__data/assets/pdf_file/0003/85530/E93714.pdf.

Crozier, M. (1963). *The Bureaucratic Phenomenon*. Chicago: University of Chicago Press.

Duran, A., Saltman, R. B., & Dubois, H. F. W. (2011). A Framework for Assessing Hospital Governance. In R. B. Saltman, A. Duran, & H. F. W. Dubois (Eds.), *Governing Public Hospitals, Reform Strategies and the Movement Towards Institutional Autonomy*. Brussels: European Observatory on Health Systems and Policies. Observatory Studies Series No. 25, 38.

Edwards, N., & Saltman, R. B. (2017). Re-thinking Barriers to Organizational Change in Public Hospitals. *Israel Journal Health Policy Research, 6*, 8. https://doi.org/10.1186/s13584-017-0133-8.

Fidler, A., Bredenkamp, C., & Schlippert, S. (2009). Innovations in Health Services Delivery from Transition Economies in Eastern Europe and Central Asia. *Health Affairs, 28*(4), 1011–1021.

Footman, K., & Richardson, E. (2014). Organization and Governance (Chapter 3). In B. Rechel, E. Richardson, & M. McKee (Eds.), *Trends in Health Systems in the Former Soviet Countries* (pp. 29–50). Copenhagen: WHO Regional Office for Europe. Retrieved from http://www.euro.who.int/__data/assets/pdf_file/0019/261271/Trends-in-health-systems-in-the-former-Soviet-countries.pdf.

Habicht, T., Habicht, J., & Jesse, M. (2011). Estonia. In R. B. Saltman, A. Duran, & H. F. W. Dubois (Eds.), *Governing Public Hospitals, Reform Strategies and the Movement Towards Institutional Autonomy*. Brussels: European Observatory on Health Systems and Policies, Observatory Studies Series No. 25, 141.

Habicht, T., Reinap, M., Kasekamp, K., Sikkut, R., Aaben, L., & Van Ginneken, E. (2018). Estonia: Health System Review. *Health Systems in Transition, 20*(1), 1–189. Retrieved from http://www.euro.who.int/__data/assets/pdf_file/0011/377417/hit-estonia-eng.pdf?ua=1.

Hofstede, G. (1980). *Culture's Consequences: International Differences in Work-Related Values*. Beverly Hills: Sage Publications.

Jeurissen, P., Duran, A., & Saltman, R. B. (2016). Uncomfortable Realities: The Challenge of Creating Real Change in Europe's Consolidating Hospital Sector. *BMC Health Services Research, 16*(Suppl 2), 168. Retrieved from https://bmchealthservres.biomedcentral.com/track/pdf/10.1186/s12913-016-1389-3.

Katsaga, A., Kulzhanov, M., Karanikolos, M., & Rechel, B. (2012). Kazakhstan Health System Review. *Health Systems in Transition, 14*(4), 1–154. Retrieved from http://www.euro.who.int/__data/assets/pdf_file/0007/161557/e96451.pdf.

Koupilova, I., Epstein, H., Holcik, J., Hajioff, S., & McKee, M. (2001). Health Needs of the Roma Population in the Czech and Slovak Republics. *Social Science & Medicine, 53*(9), 1191–1204.

Kujawska, J. (2017). The Efficiency of Post-Communist Countries' Health Systems. In *Advances in Health Management*. London: InTech. Retrieved from https://www.intechopen.com/books/advances-in-health-management/the-efficiency-of-post-communist-countries-health-systems.

Lawson, C., & Nemec, J. (2003). The Political Economy of Slovak and Czech Health Policy: 1989–2000. *International Political Science Review, 24*(2), 219–235.

Lindblom, C. E. (1959). The Science of "Muddling Through". *Public Administration Review, 19*(2, Spring), 79–88.

Lipsky, M. (1981). *Street Level Bureaucrats*. Washington: Russell Sage Foundation.

Marquez, P. V., & Bonch-Osmolovskiy, M. (2010). Action Needed: Spiraling Drug Prices Empty Russian Pockets. *Europe and Central Asia Knowledge Brief, 19*, 1–4.

Mathauer, I., & Wittenbecher, F. (2013). Hospital Payment Systems Based on Diagnosis-Related Groups: Experiences in Low- and Middle-Income Countries. *Bulleting of the World Health Organization, 91*, 746–756A. Geneva: World Health Organization. Retrieved from https://www.who.int/bulletin/volumes/91/10/12-115931.pdf. doi: https://www.who.int/bulletin/volumes/91/10/12-115931.pdf.

McKee, M., & Healy, J. (Eds.). (2002). *Hospitals in a Changing Europe*. Buckingham: Open University Press. European Observatory on Health Systems and Policies.

McKee, M., & Nolte, E. (2004). Health Sector Reforms in Central and Eastern Europe: How Well Are Health Services Responding to Changing Patterns of Health? *Demographic Research, 2*(7), 163–182.

Mechanic, D. (1968). *Medical Sociology: A Selective View*. New York: Free Press.

Mintzberg, H. (1979). Cited by G. Best in NHS Management Surfeit or Shortage. Health Director. *Journal of the National Association of Health Authorities and Trusts, 25*, 16–17.

NIHD – National Institute for Health Development. (2018). *Health Statistics Database*. Tallinn. Retrieved from http://pxweb.tai.ee/PXWeb2015/pxweb/en/04THressursid/04THressursid__01TTosutajad/TTO20.px/table/tableViewLayout2/?rxid=1787cb5e-1109-4f09-ab69-6bf13cf8d9cf.

OECD. (2017). *State of Health in the EU: Estonia Country Health Profile 2017*. Paris: OECD Publishing.

OECD. (2018). *OECD Data*. Retrieved from https://data.oecd.org.

Polluste, K., Kallikorm, R., Meiesaar, K., & Lember, M. (2012). Satisfaction with Access to Health Services: The Perspective of Estonian Patients with Rheumatoid Arthritis. *Scientific World Journal, 2012*, Article ID 257569. https://doi.org/10.1100/2012/257569.

Preker, A., & Harding, A. (Eds.). (2003). *Innovations in Health Service Delivery, The Corporatization of Public Hospitals*. Washington, DC: The World Bank.

Pressman, J. L., & Wildavsky, A. B. (1972). *Implementation: How Great Expectations in Washington Are Dashed in Oakland*. Berkeley: University of California Press.

Rahminov, R., Gedik, G., & Healty, J. (2000). *Health Care Systems in Transition: Tajikistan.* Copenhagen: WHO Regional Office for Europe. Retrieved from http://www.who.int/iris/handle/10665/108325.

Rechel, B., Mladovsky, P., Ingleby, D., Mackenbach, J. P., & McKee, M. (2013). Migration and Health in an Increasingly Diverse Europe. *Lancet, 381*(9673), 1235–1245.

Rechel, B., Richardson, E., & McKee, M. (2014). *Trends in Health Systems in the Former Soviet Countries.* Copenhagen: WHO Regional Office for Europe.

Richardson, E. (2013). Armenia Health System Review. *Health Systems in Transition, 15*(4), 1–99. Retrieved from http://www.euro.who.int/__data/assets/pdf_file/0008/234935/HiT-Armenia.pdf?ua=1.

Richardson, E., Sautenkova, N., & Bolokhovets, G. (2014). Pharmaceutical Care. In B. Rechel, E. Richardson, & M. McKee (Eds.), *Trends in Health Systems in the Former Soviet Countries* (Vol. 9, pp. 145–158). Copenhagen: WHO Regional Office for Europe. Retrieved from http://www.euro.who.int/__data/assets/pdf_file/0019/261271/Trends-in-health-systems-in-the-former-Soviet-countries.pdf.

Robertson, R., Sonola, L., Honeyman, M., Brooke, B., & Kothari, S. (2014). Specialists in Out-of-Hospital Settings Findings from Six Case Studies. In *Ideas that Change Health Care.* London: The King's Fund. Retrieved from https://www.kingsfund.org.uk/sites/files/kf/field/field_publication_file/specialists-in-out-of-hospital-settings-kingsfund-oct14.pdf.

Roubal, T., & Hrobon, P. (2011). Czech Republic. In R. B. Saltman, A. Duran, & H. F. W. Dubois (Eds.), *Governing Public Hospitals, Reform Strategies and the Movement Towards Institutional Autonomy.* Brussels: European Observatory on Health Systems and Policies. Observatory Studies Series No. 25, 38.

Saltman, R. B. (1985). The Capital Decision-Making Process in Regionalized Public Health Systems: Some Evidence from Sweden and Denmark. *Health Policy, 4,* 99–112.

Saltman, R. B. (1987). Management Control in a Publicly Planned Health System: A Case Study from Finland. *Health Policy, 8,* 283–298.

Saltman, R. B. (1988). National Planning for Locally Controlled Health Systems: The Finnish Experience. *Journal of Health Politics Policy and Law, 13,* 27–51.

Saltman, R. B. (2003). Melting Public-Private Boundaries in European Health Systems. *European Journal of Public Health, 13,* 24–29. https://doi.org/10.1093/eurpub/13.1.24.

Saltman, R. B. (2018). The Impact of Slow Economic Growth on Health Sector Reforms: A Cross-National Perspective. *Health Economics Policy and Law, 13,* 1–24. https://doi.org/10.1017/S1744133117000445.

Saltman, R. B. (2019). Structural Effects of the Information Revolution on Tax Funded European Health Systems and Some Potential Policy Responses. *Israel Journal Health Policy Research, 8,* 8.

Saltman, R. B., & Bankauskaite, V. (2006). Conceptualizing Decentralization in European Health Systems: A Functional Perspective. *Health Economics, Policy, and Law, 1*(Pt 2), 127–147. https://doi.org/10.1017/S1744133105001209.
Saltman, R. B., & de Roo, A. A. (1989). Hospital Policy in The Netherlands: The Parameters of Structural Stalemate. *Journal of Health Politics Policy and Law, 14*, 773–795.
Saltman, R. B., & Young, D. W. (1981). The Hospital Power Equilibrium: An Alternative View of the Cost Containment Dilemma. *The Journal of Health Politics, Policy and Law, 6*, 391–418.
Saltman, R. B., Duran, A., & Dubois, H. F. W. (Eds.). (2011). *Governing Public Hospitals, Reform Strategies and the Movement Towards Institutional Autonomy.* Brussels: European Observatory on Health Systems and Policies. Observatory Studies Series No. 25.
Simon, H. (1947). *Administrative Behavior.* New York City: Macmillan.
Sparkes, S., Durán, A., & Kutzin, J. (2017). *A System-Wide Approach to Analysing Efficiency Across Health Programmes.* Geneva: World Health Organization. Health Financing Diagnostics and Guidance No 2.
Statista. (2019). Retrieved January 29, 2019, from https://www.statista.com/statistics/556798/hospitals-in-estonia/.
Stubbs, H. (Ed.). (2016). *The Health of the Nation: Averting the Demise of Universal Healthcare.* London: Civitas.
Summers, L., & Yamey, G. (2015). The Astonishing Returns of Investing in Global Health R&D. *Innovation Countdown 2030.* Retrieved from http://ic2030.org/2015/07/investing-rd/.
Transparency International. (2012). *Transparency International: Georgia 51st in 2012 Corruption Perceptions Index.* Tbilisi: Transparency International Georgia. Retrieved from https://www.transparency.org/news/pressrelease/20121205_transparency_international_georgia_51st_in_2012_corruption_percept.
Turcanu, G., Domente, S., Buga, M., & Richardson, E. (2012). Republic of Moldova Health System Review. *Health Systems in Transition, 14*(7), 1–151. Retrieved from http://www.euro.who.int/__data/assets/pdf_file/0006/178053/HiT-Moldova.pdf.
Tynkkynen, L. K., & Vrangbæk, K. (2018). Comparing Public and Private Providers: A Scoping Review of Hospital Services in Europe. *BMC Health Services Research, 18*, 141. https://doi.org/10.1186/s12913-018-2953-9.
Wagstaff, A., & Moreno-Serra, R. (2009). Europe and Central Asia's Great Post-Communist Social Health Insurance Experiment: Aggregate Impacts on Health Sector Outcomes. *Journal of Health Economics, 28*(2), 322–340.
Weber, M. (1947). *The Theory of Social and Economic Organization.* Parsons, T. (Ed.). Free Press.
Young, D. W., & Saltman, R. B. (1985). *The Hospital Power Equilibrium: Physician Behavior and Cost Control.* Baltimore: Johns Hopkins University Press.

CHAPTER 9

Decision Analysis

Stephen Wright and Antonio Durán

Introduction

Before reaching the next chapter of conclusions, it is important to note explicitly that all of the reasoning in this book ought necessarily to feed into *decisions* related to hospitals. These are made by decision-makers, not analysts. The reasoning in this pre-final chapter is that *models* should be used to support *decision analysis*. The two are intrinsically linked, meaning that they can be addressed together. The book deals with some technocratic issues and a political context; indeed, the discussion in this book on governance as a central concept puts politics central to our thinking about hospitals. It should be recognised that such an idea is in fact well known in the health sector, and that there is more to it than getting the technocratic elements right; we accept that, at their heart, all decisions dealing with public goods like healthcare are political. What then is the value added of this chapter?

S. Wright (✉)
Independent Consultant, Ingleton, UK
e-mail: steve.wright@echaa.eu

A. Durán
ALLDMHEALTH, Seville, Spain
e-mail: aduran@alldmh.com

A. Durán, S. Wright (eds.), *Understanding Hospitals in Changing Health Systems*, https://doi.org/10.1007/978-3-030-28172-4_9

There are a number of themes developed throughout this book:

- Firstly, we emphasised the characteristics of hospitals as sites for delivery of healthcare which, relative to all other settings, are particularly highly physical capital, human capital and technology intensive. A hospital does have unique production profiles derived from these characteristics, but it always remains just a part of a wider system, and can only be understood accordingly. Decisions about hospitals were made in a rather isolated manner until the classical work of the World Health Organization (WHO) in the World Health Report 2000 (WHO 2000) prescribed the need to articulate other elements in the field of health promotion and disease prevention, diagnostics, treatment, rehabilitation and care: that is, the *health system*. This is defined in as "the ensemble of persons, resources and institutions whose primary intention is producing 'health actions'—that is, any effort, whether in personal health care, public health services or through inter-sectoral initiatives, whose *primary purpose* is to improve—promote, restore or maintain—health" (Chap. 1).
- Secondly, these features are best explored through the lenses of "governance" (Chap. 2) and "business models" (Chap. 4), with the latter incorporating "models of care" (Chap. 3).
- Chapters 5 and 6 address issues such as ownership of hospitals and payment methods, and these all have a bearing on interpreting the role of hospitals in the framework proposed in this book.
- Chapters 7 and 8 deal with practical aspects of the situation of hospitals around the world today; a main intention there (despite recognised limitations of coverage of certain geographical areas) is to show how hospitals are being affected by changes, and that this is not only in developed countries.

The interrelationship of these themes, and the onwards link to real-world decision-making, is illustrated in Fig. 9.1.

All the above chapters include valuable lessons related to decision-making at all levels. We develop further the decision-making issues here, then finally move to sum up in the conclusions and recommendations of Chap. 10.

The true point in writing this chapter is not thus to state as a "discovery" that society should use decision analysis for hospitals, with accompanying quantified decision models—that is obviously happening now, and

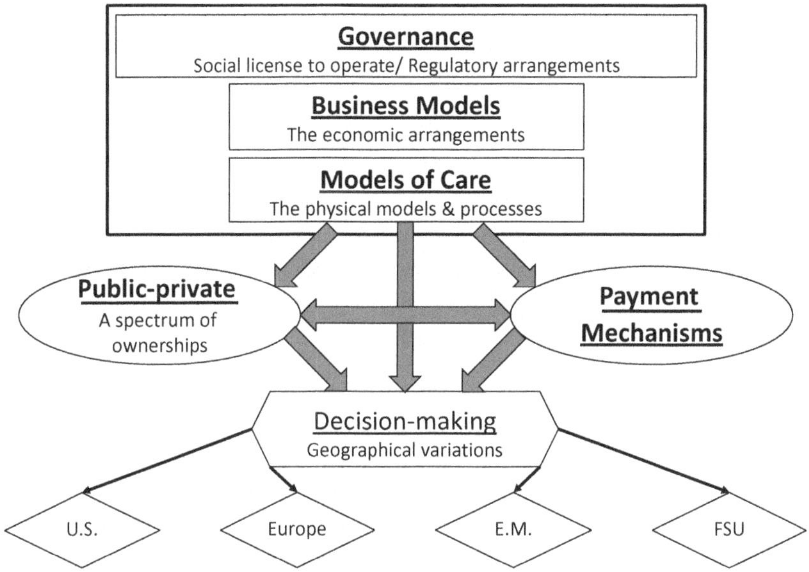

Fig. 9.1 Decision-making in (our) context

is true irrespective of the proposals in this or any other book on the sector. Rather, the suggestion here lays out the decision analysis and modelling approaches *that build specifically on the themes of this book*. This chapter will try to show that decision analysis and modelling methods can be envisaged that are *consistent with the above approaches* (in particular, *what should be key elements in hospital investment decision-making*?). Some aspects are more straightforward than others, and indeed there are issues the shape of which we can barely guess at this stage. In doing so, we hope to demonstrate a potentially useful perspective on what needs to happen in the real healthcare world, and/or for which the aspiration is at least to join the many authors that are addressing these complex topics elsewhere.

Current Decision Analysis in Health Systems and Hospitals: Is It Good Enough?

Decisions about hospitals and, still more, health systems cover a vast range of issues—certainly beyond what we can sensibly address here, and that applies equally to the analysis and models that we can identify. A useful way of thinking about this is that decisions and analysis are done for various purposes and over different time horizons; it is worth noting that these two dimensions often mean similar things.

For our purposes, we can narrow down the problem, and categorise decision analysis models as including four relevant "classes" or types (there are doubtless many others) which capture at some level key features requiring social and economic decisions. The classes below are simplified, used descriptively, and have grey areas between them; they cover analysis of financial status, comparative systems, service redesign, and investment appraisal (the last-named is further developed, in the section on "Capacity and Economic Analysis" of this chapter).

Accounting Financial Analysis

The "examination of financial information to reach business decisions" usually focuses on the current financial year, or potentially a little longer, through notions such as solvency, stability, liquidity, profitability and so on. This level of analysis delivers management support for the everyday operations of the institution or system (Ehrhardt and Brigham 2008). Another classic purpose would be annual reporting to shareholders, whether the state or the private sector. Financial models of this kind use dedicated and often highly sophisticated profit-and-loss/balance sheet accounting software, or adapted general-purpose spreadsheets. They could, just, be also used for longer term projections. However, such models broadly take the existing assets (physical and human) and pattern of service processes and outputs as *givens*, and rely on relatively known market or administered prices for inputs and outputs.

When projected into the future, embedded assumptions within such models would drift out of sync with reality quite quickly. The focus of this book, however, is on much longer timeframes than this; they therefore have little to offer in this regard, and we will not discuss this sort of analysis further.

Comparative System and Hospital Analysis

One of the key concerns of any decision-maker in health policy is efficiency, in fact on moral as well as economic grounds (though we mostly focus on the latter here). Health systems deliver outputs and outcomes, and they consume input resources to do so. The balance between these, defined in various ways and allowing for quality considerations, concerns the efficiency of the system (Cylus et al. 2017). It is a commonplace in health policy that markets in healthcare are extremely dysfunctional and that, although a health facility is carrying out among other things an economic activity, it is difficult to assess the efficiency with which inputs are converted to outputs. Absolute measures of efficiency are non-existent or unreliable. One route out of this is to compare the population, or a significant sample, of health systems or hospitals against each other, and make judgements from that. Some will be relatively more efficient than others. The best systems or units become the benchmark against which others are judged, and those at the efficiency "frontier" are as good as it gets (whatever that means each time). Correspondingly, if a given hospital ranks worse than others, it ought to be improved towards the performance of the better or the best.

Modelling like this of health system and hospital costs is often carried out using statistical and econometric methods. Such methods provide suggestive evidence of potential improvement, but *they do not embody any theory as to how a system or facility works.* Joumard et al. (2010) provide much insight here, suggesting that three main cross-country efficiency analyses can be done: at sub-sector, disease-based, and system levels.

- The sub-sector level has ambiguities relating to the way that care is delivered by different sub-sectors in different countries, and because it is difficult to disentangle impact on any one sub-sector from another (additionally, there are also data problems);
- Disease-level analysis looks at health gain from specific treatments, but data are often lacking particularly for comparable definitions of outcome by disease and cost incurred in different regions or countries;
- Finally, system-level analyses make a stab at resolving the problem that sub-sector and disease-based approaches might show local efficiency where the overall system is, however, globally inefficient; amenable mortality studies are a notable way to begin to tackle this issue.

Some studies use panel data regressions, where unexplained differences in health status indicators across countries are assumed to reflect *only* efficiency differences in the use of inputs. Using this method, Joumard et al. (2010, op. cit.) suggest that "health care spending is the single most important factor explaining differences in health status across countries, though other factors also play important roles".

A more advanced methodology than regression for cross-country analysis is data envelopment analysis (DEA)—and evidence is that this correlates well with panel regressions, giving extra confidence. The DEA econometric technique is non-parametric (i.e. it does not assume that output is created a certain way, and this is less demanding of data), deterministic, and generates a snapshot using at most a few years of data to help determine if a system or hospital is at the "efficiency frontier"—in other words, it could generate more output for the given inputs or the same output for less input.

Joumard et al. show that the measured impact within a system is stronger using as the output measure a sophisticated index such as amenable mortality rather than simpler health quality metrics. Interestingly, they point out that "correlations between overall system (outcome-based efficiency estimates) and (output-based) efficiency indicators often used for hospitals (e.g. average lengths of stays and occupancy rate for hospital acute care beds) are very low. This suggests that medical outputs can be produced very efficiently in one sub-sector but still have only a limited impact on the population health status, or that high performance in the in-patient care sector is offset by inefficiencies in other sub-sectors of the health care system or that coordination problems exist across sub-sectors". The finding points very clearly to the value of the whole-system approach promoted by this book: looking at hospitals in isolation is not a successful tactic.

These various methods will typically show that population health status could be improved significantly by moving towards what is achieved by better performers. Joumard et al. (2010, op. cit.) compare the gain in life expectancy at birth that can be achieved through efficiency, rather than through additional spending. In their analysis, life expectancy at birth could be raised through efficiency gains by more than two years across OECD countries, while a 10% increase in healthcare spending per capita would increase life expectancy by only 3–4 months.

Stochastic cost frontier analysis (SFA/SCF) has similarities to DEA, but with a specific parametric form. It is stochastic, and can generate estimates for both errors and inefficiency and, while complex because of the need to devise a "production function", for example, it can be used as a sensitivity check on DEA (Medeiros and Schwierz 2015).

Apart from this system-level analysis, DEA and so on have been applied to cross-country hospital comparisons. Adam et al. (2003) is a study largely directed at developing countries, and finds reasonable estimation results but notes that the unit costs within a particular country can differ by as much as an order of magnitude. Also at hospital level, Erlandsen (2008) reviews differences in the unit costs of typical interventions, differences in aggregate hospital efficiency between pairs of countries and differences in the within-country dispersion of individual hospital efficiency. On average, costs could be reduced by between 5–48%, or there is input-saving potential of 6–36%; even across the specific geography of the Nordics, cost-saving potentials are high at 23–44%. But he suggests "analysing the ***determinants*** of the observed cross-country differences in hospital performance is beyond the scope of this study ... The ultimate objective would be to link measures of hospital performance to factors describing the institutional setting under which hospitals operate" (our emphasis): in other words, studies like this reiterate the importance of the wider setting, and of considerations of governance.

Work has also been carried out on this topic for Valencia, Spain (Caballer-Tarazona et al. 2010). This used DEA (though the study found that simpler discriminant analysis indicators performed about as well). The research had the additional advantage that there was a variety of organisational forms including novel PPP concessions in the region to enhance comparisons.[1] One of their interesting results is that it is not useful to study the overall efficiency of a whole hospital, because of differences in performance between services within the hospital; that is, the hospital in its own right is a system, not a unit.

Some work dissents from the power of these conclusions on econometric methods. Jacobs 2000 for the UK uses DEA and SCF, suggests that precise model specifications do matter but that, however, there "appears to be a large amount of random 'noise' in the study which suggests that there are not truly large efficiency differences between Trusts, and savings from bringing up poorer performers would in fact be very modest".

On balance, most of this work, allowing for uncertainty concerning, for example, data quality, finds that there are large—and often extremely large—differences between the efficiency of different national health systems, and their respective hospitals. But DEA or comparable analyses can-

[1] As a curiosity, the levels of efficiency of the services analysed for the PPP hospitals were above the mean (cf. Chap. 5).

not show *why these differences occur*, nor give much of a hint concerning *what to do about it* ("approach the efficiency of the best" is not much of a guide to action; in what respect and how?). The suggestion that analysis of hospitals should be disaggregated is almost certainly right, but also poses difficulties, because it is unlikely that adequate datasets will be available at present to do this.

In the current state of play with comparative analyses, it is scarcely possible:

- to show more than indicatively the differences in efficiency between hospitals;
- nor to work out where within the hospital the problems lie;
- nor how any differences relate to the wider system; and
- *nor what to do about differentials when they are found.*

The conclusion on this class of analysis then is that it addresses a very serious issue, and one which is central to the book, *but is not establishing at all clearly what to do.*

Service (Re)design and/or Addition of Specific Equipment

This area of decision-making deals with rather common purposes, notably including redesign of services and models of care, and the planning of acquisition of pieces of capital stock (but not usually whole facilities). The mirror image of the size of the changes concerned means that this level is concerned with more extended timelines, up to a few years, than the operational and financial planning discussed in the section above on Accounting Financial Analysis.

Key decision-support techniques employed here are derived from operational research (OR) methods—mathematical representations of operational processes and systems. At its heart, this is flow modelling, particularly of patients through the facility concerned but potentially of materials and supplies also. These are classic simulation models. They are often very micro in format, and data heavy, but can be helpful when a problem cannot be "solved" analytically. OR-based simulation modelling uses a group of techniques, for which there is a vast literature (Pitt et al. 2016; Health Services Research Network 2014; de Silva 2013; Montgomery and Davis 2013; Gunal 2012; Proudlove et al. 2007). The techniques are dominated by the following:

- Discrete event simulation (DES). The most common methodology, based on mathematical representation over continuous time, with a strong queueing structure. The activities covered are generally of individual patients, but could be materials or information and so on. There is an operational-level focus, and the technique is stochastic;
- System dynamics (SD). This deals with stocks, and the flows between them. It uses as the basic element cohorts, not individuals, so is much less data heavy. It uses feedback loops representing causal deterministic relationships. SD is best at strategy-level questions;
- Agent-based simulation (ABS). A dynamic, adaptive and autonomous technique. It incorporates the behaviour of self-deciding agents. There are relatively few examples of ABS applied to the health sector.

Gunal (op. cit.) shows that these different methodologies presuppose *different frames of thinking*. The concern ranges from the hospital as black box (simple input-output) to detailed departmental breakdowns. In hospital analysis—though not necessarily other sectors—using these methods, cost and value elements are neither prominent nor well-integrated, so as such this type of work is not always truly normative (i.e. in balancing what we want to do against the cost of doing so). There is, however, clear evidence from this research tradition that methods to improve patient flow can reduce waiting time and length of stay (de Silva, op. cit.) and these are clearly very important targets for health systems, which typically run hot.

The key driver for simulation modelling is often the functioning of the emergency department (ED), because the ED is both critical to the operation of many other hospital departments (paediatrics, pathology, imaging, orthopaedics etc.), and because flow problems invariably manifest themselves here both quickly and with great severity. Again, the literature is considerable (Mohiuddin et al. 2017; Karakusevic 2016; Vargas-Palacios 2015; Clissold et al. 2015; Mackay et al. 2013; Fletcher and Worthington 2009; Brailsford et al. 2004).

Simulation modelling incorporates *stocks* (defined as "the accumulation of something, which can include short-term 'buffers'") and *flows* (the "rate at which individual entities such as patients move through the system"). In healthcare, there are typically non-linearities, feedback loops, and a large number of variables evolving dynamically over time. Simulation modelling deals with these complexities well but, for hospital modelling, simulation raises implicitly the question of the meaning of the capital stock of the facility. It should be remembered that quite simply, *we do not meaningfully know how to measure the true capacity of a hospital*. One of the obvious metrics is the bed stock, and this is often a target for modelling, even of simulation, which may mainly be dealing with other equipment areas. In this context, it is clear that if a hospital or its ED is not functioning efficiently, one response is to bring extra beds into use—at the minimum, patients can be stored in them (so beds act as a short-term buffer rather than a true stock solution to a long-term functional problem). Simulation modelling allows a more sophisticated treatment of capacity than many other model types but can still struggle with this over more than quite short-term horizons. The issue is dealt with in the section below "What Should Be Key Elements in Hospital Investment Decision-Making?" of this chapter, and then further developed in the section "The Authors' Proposition 1".

We can observe that these types of decision settings, and the modelling techniques which seem to correspond with them, rarely combine in explicit terms *both physical and economic processes*. Hospitals are by any judgement very complex processing institutions, with non-linearities and feedback loops. Part of this complexity is because there is a need for both clinical and managerial efficiency. The former is very much the decision-making prerogative of clinicians in order to provide high quality medical services depending on the complexity and severity of each patient's situation. The latter is the responsibility of non-clinical managers (who may originally have been clinicians), who are responsible for the overall operation of the hospital: especially its use of resources. In this book as a whole, we explicitly aim at balancing these two domains, via the concept of *business models* which incorporate and depend on *models of care* (see also below).

Further, with the simulation approaches listed above, any coupling of hospitals to the wider health system will be rudimentary, and often static. As said, for the authors of this book, the hospital is conceived as only one unit of many, within any particular health system and the given governance environment.

The conclusion on simulation modelling is that it could provide useful modules for inclusion in wider decision-support efforts, but it:

- does not constitute a stable, long-term description;
- rarely has a proper articulation to the wider healthcare system; and
- does not incorporate value assumptions satisfactorily.

Capacity and Economic Analysis

The final domain of decision-making, analysis, and modelling that we will discuss is investment appraisal. This is carried out most visibly for hospitals, since investment appraisal is designed to evaluate the worth of a capital investment, and hospitals are by some way the biggest physical capital assets of any healthcare system.

The meaning of "capacity", as discussed above, is a key point: it is very difficult—not to say impossible—traditionally to define the capacity of a hospital. As indicated, what is usually done at present for investment appraisal (and for some other purposes too) is to calculate bed numbers—typically using, as a proxy for the whole-unit ability to do work, calculations based on more or less sophisticated "Hill-Burton"[2] formulae (US Department of Health, Education and Welfare 1974). This methodology centres on forecasting *activity*, based on population and other demographic and epidemiological features. It allocates beds to the activity, usually conditioned by clinical disease or organ categories, and the bed numbers so derived are the key expression of hospital *capacity*. There is often a similar analysis for operating theatre activity and capacity. Other clinical zones, such as outpatient space, are either related to beds by rules of thumb or, at best, are also tied somehow to the demand activity forecasts. The routine with non-clinical areas (offices, utilities, carpark, corridors, walls etc.) is usually to uplift them from the square meters of the clinical areas by a coefficient or—better—by links of some kind to patient numbers. Many healthcare/hospital administrations use this style of analysis. One of the more documented versions is that employed in the UK (see Box 9.1).

[2] An early example of this calculation was the so-called Hill-Burton model, developed from the eponymous act of 1946 in the US. It was developed to justify augmenting hospital capacity in the South and in areas of deprivation and implicitly with a high black population; it worked. Hill-Burton originally proposed a target bed number per state based on 4.5 beds per 1000 population, but this caused issues in that the national average was anyway only 3.4. From 1963, the calculation was amended to look at population forecasts over five years, "use rate" in terms of patient days per 1000 population, and an occupancy factor. See DEHW (1974 op. cit., p. 4). It is the essentials of this analysis which is widely replicated today in hospital planning everywhere.

Box 9.1 Public Investment Appraisal in the UK and Its Application to Hospitals

Cross-sectoral

There is a disciplined central government investment appraisal methodology used in the United Kingdom for several decades. Key elements originate in the Treasury "Green Book" (HM Treasury 2018), which sets out an economic—wider than financial—appraisal methodology for use in many economic sectors (i.e. not by any means just health) where public expenditure, sale or use of existing assets, structural change, taxation and so on are involved. It therefore also covers investment policies, programmes and projects. It is designed to tease out the effects, trade-offs, and overall impact of options.

A starting point of the process is the generation of a long list of options in order to ensure that a full range of possibilities is considered. This is informed by stakeholder engagement, international best practice and the wider evidence base. There is explicit consideration of distributional impacts. The long list is filtered down to a viable short list, determined by issues like strategic fit to policy objectives, value for money, affordability and achievability.

It is at this stage that the method turns to explicit consideration of the trade-off between costs and benefits, using a social cost-benefit analysis (CBA) or a social cost-effectiveness analysis (CEA). The methods work on a "with-and-without" basis: impacts are assessed relative to the counterfactual of what would have taken place in the absence of intervention ("business as usual", but also a "do-minimum" which meets merely the core requirements). There is an attempt to value costs and benefits even when these are non-marketed (using "shadow prices"—that is, opportunity costs). This picks up a number of issues such as public goods, imperfect information, moral hazard, externalities and market power. The definition of "benefits" is a complex area, encompassing cash-releasing benefits, monetisable and non-monetisable (but quantified) benefits, and qualitative benefits. A rule of thumb is that benefits are more difficult to arrive at than costs—and this is certainly true in the health sector and hospitals.

All this analysis is done in constant, non-inflating values. Calculation is carried out over the lifetime of the intervention or asset—up to 60 years. There is allowance for "optimism bias", and procedures for risk and sensitivity analysis. Because of the CBA/

CEA framework, costs and benefits in money values—both capital and operating—are discounted, which assumes a rate of time preference. The total value of discounted benefits less costs provides the net present social value (NPSV) and benefit/cost ratio.

To put an analysis into context, it is treated as forming a "business case". This is assembled from a variety of dimensions: strategic (the fit to wider policy), economic (the analytical heart of the process, constituting the NPSV proper), commercial (particularly to the extent that there is engagement with the private sector), financial (public sector budget impact) and management (is the delivery plan robust against risk, and monitoring and evaluation steps planned).

Hospital or Other Healthcare

There is of course much that is specific to a hospital investment appraisal analysis. Here, the origin of the UK hospital business case process can be seen clearly as lying in the Hill-Burton tradition, albeit much ornamented. The graphic below this paragraph is from a published UK outline business case for a hospital development, in the early 2000s, during its project approval phase. Although it is not always expressed this way, the activity forecasts are very much a function of the expected *model of care* within the hospital, because they are based on physical modelling of patient demand in terms of projected admission frequencies by clinical treatment area together with the average length of stay per disease area. Allowance for "admission avoidance", where changes are expected in the surrounding health economy, brings in the impact of the *model of care* of the wider healthcare system. The main focus of the calculation is the required bed stock, with similar analysis for operating theatre capacity and outpatient rooms.

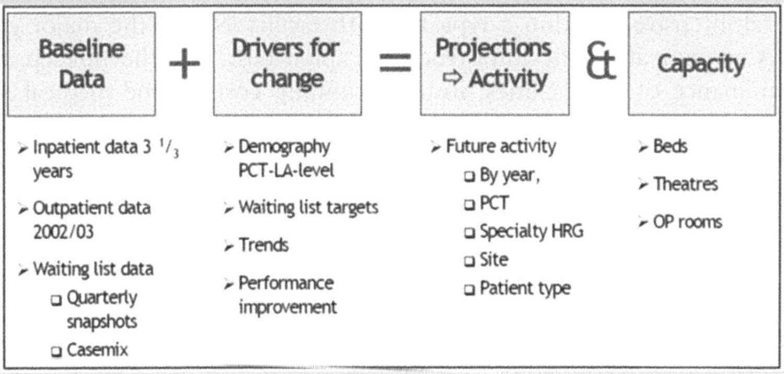

The capital expenditures for the required number of beds, theatres and operating rooms are costed, at early stages of the process, via cost/M2 coefficients; cost estimation becomes, of course, very much more sophisticated, or at least more complex, the further into the planning approval and construction procurement that the process goes, and will eventually have relatively solid facility and equipment purchase data. Operational costs, dominated by staff salaries but including the other ongoing expenditures such as drugs, utilities and so on, are often related to the bed numbers; or maybe directly to the activity levels. The capital and operating costs can then all be summed over time, and discounted to give the lifetime cost of the facility. The business case will involve computation of the net present value for the cost of the various build options considered ("do nothing", "do minimum", plus "two or three viable refurbishments or new builds").

Qualitative benefits will usually be taken into account externally to the main model as weighting scores qualifying the main net present value (NPSV) of costs.

All the above should be understood in the governance context and tradition of an Anglo-Saxon society. Although the Hill-Burton framework is used extremely widely—indeed, almost universally—other societal environments would require adjustments of different types to the model structure, to be determined in each case.

It is worth recording as a matter of perspective that, although hospitals are capital-intensive relative to the rest of the system, they are also highly service-intensive (that is, labour-intensive or, otherwise put, human capital-intensive). Within a typical health facility NPSV, the major cash flows are not at all the infrastructure capital cost, nor the upkeep and maintenance of the facilities; instead, running costs of the medical services—even though many are incurred far into the future and are therefore heavily discounted in today's terms—are utterly predominant. Without going quite so far as to say that the capital cost is unimportant (because what is built partly determines how the facility will operate and what it will produce), what matters is these medical running costs, and any ability to extract productivity changes over time in them. Figure 9.2 shows this feature by means of a so-called spider chart for a hospital project investment,

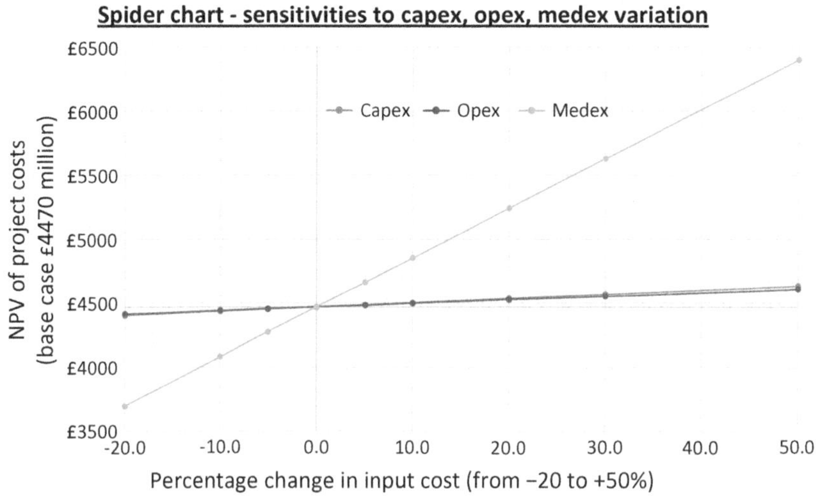

Fig. 9.2 Spider chart of project sensitivities in hospital investment appraisal (NPV, GBP million) (Authors' calculations, based on a PPP "outline business case" for a mid-size English hospital)

showing the sensitivity of whole-life NPV against variation in capital cost, facility management cost, and medical expenditures (staff, drugs etc.). To repeat, this is for an English case—which of course would be different from the particular governance environment, business model and model of care of other societies.

What is visible in this example is that a hospital with a modest turnover and a capital investment of GBP260 million will still represent a cost of many billion GBP (the currency in this case) across its lifetime: a sum which might seem surprising to some observers. That is—as many stakeholders have learnt only through experience—building a hospital is an expensive habit, because of the fact that running one is. Furthermore, the effect on the viability of an investment in such a hospital is that variation in capital or facilities management cost is always absolutely dwarfed by the expenditures on ongoing medical activity.

None of this is to say that current investment appraisals are necessarily ill-disciplined or without a clear target outcome. For example, the UK—aside from the business case procedure outlined above—also around the same time fostered the creation of new capacity with the explicit aim of reducing waiting lists and queues for elective surgery. These were the so-called independent sector treatment centres, of which nearly 35 were built by the private sector but intended for National Health Service patients (that is, a form of PPP). It is not sure in the outturn that the ISTCs have had a big effect on waiting times, working methods or the role of competing private suppliers, but their strategic intent was very specific and clear (Naylor and Gregory 2009). Similarly, the Coxa Hospital in Finland was developed with the explicit aim to increase quality in orthopaedic joint replacement work (reduced revision surgeries and infection rates) and reduce waiting times and lists (Kivisaari et al. 2004).

However, while state-of-the-art, these types of appraisal methodology suffer from two serious and related flaws:

- Firstly, there is little or only primitive modelling of the processing paths of patients through the facility (at least, not much more than: "they arrive into a bed, into a theatre, back into bed, depart out of a bed"). In other words, the internal hospital model of care is not well specified, at least in terms of its through-life cost implications.
- Secondly, there is only a tenuous connection—to say the least—to what happens in the surrounding health environment and economy. The quoted UK example (there are numerous other published cases available) makes use of an assertion concerning what is anticipated in very broad terms in the wider health economy, but there is no route to ensure an integrated policy outside the hospital, or frankly much expectation that the hypothesised changes will actually occur. This is tantamount to saying that the whole-system model of care is not well specified in such analyses.

The text above has drawn heavily on UK cases. In our experience, the process—while often using similar elements (i.e. modified and sophisticated Hill-Burton)—is much more haphazard in most other country jurisdictions.

This approach therefore raises some problems. Bluntly put, beyond the point made above about the model of care inside/outside the hospital, if "capacity" cannot be defined within an economic appraisal in a fashion which is more sophisticated than this concentration on bed numbers, how reliable will decisions be on what sort or size of hospital to add, or what to close? And more so, how to drive different stages of a complex process? The reality is that honest or even moderately comprehensive investment or disinvestment appraisal within the hospital sector can simply not be carried out today without much better analysis and information than normally used. It is not that the decision process followed everywhere is political (which of course it is); it is that *it is usually not sufficiently good* in the sense that it lacks both solid intellectual support and robust empirical evidence.

What Should Be Key Elements in Hospital Investment Decision-Making?

From the beginning, this book has noted that, at their core, hospitals live immersed in a paradox:

- On the one hand, they are evidently key settings for health services delivery, perhaps the major symbol of the urban fabric to citizens and often the biggest single employer and energy consumer in a city. Irrespective of whether or not they are tertiary institutions, hospitals house much of the knowledge activities, teaching, and research occurring in their areas, and their contribution is mightily appreciated by most of the population. All this sounds like an impressive, highly valued set of assets;
- On the other hand, big sections of the health policy community in both developed and developing countries do not universally regard hospitals with much sympathy. They are (possibly because of the symbolic intent) rather in favour of diverting the resources currently used by hospitals towards public health provision and primary care. In short, the sentiment is usually expressed that the top priority is taking resources away from hospitals (although it is not implausible to believe that all of these sub-sectors require more resources). At the minimum, it can safely be said that these considerations imply that the role of hospitals is not well understood.

Are there *means of reconciling these rather opposite judgements*? Elements for a shift of mental model have been suggested in this book, in order to structure thinking about hospitals as critically important institutions; in hospital analysis, there should be something better than what we do at the moment. But indeed, a mere change in mindset is one thing; somebody actually doing something different as a result is more important. Doing something different requires converting the new mindset into routes to make *decisions*, about both hospitals and the health systems and economies in which they are embedded. Can different decision analysis/modelling methods be envisaged, based on thinking in the current book, *which would add extra value, and invite different decision-making actions?*

The core of the proposal in this chapter is that *unless it is modelled quantitatively, in principle, a business "model" for a hospital will just be a descriptive notion.* Within this book (see Chap. 4), business models for hospitals are characterised to fall into one of three types: (1) solution shops, or (2) value-added processes, or (3) facilitated networks.[3] In all these three cases (and any other conceivable formulation of a business model), it necessarily will constitute a physical process model—the model of care—around which is wrapped an economic arrangement—with the whole framework subject to considerations of governance. All this would state the need to develop analytical methods which show whether or not one business model (with its embedded model of care and in its particular governance environment) generates a better social outcome across the system than another; as a result, the alternative business model would be worth supporting.

Our intention in concluding this chapter is encapsulated in two propositions and a reflection, presented below.

The Authors' Proposition 1

We suggest that the business *model* for a hospital should be expressed as a business *case for investment*, not as an abstract concept. Further, along the lines developed above, this business case should be evaluated thoroughly at system—not unit or facility—level. This means in plain words that an investment in or even the continued support for a hospital should always be considered together with its repercussions and consequences on other parts of the health system—that is, other hospitals and specialised facilities, health centres, primary care and health promotion units and so on.

The main point is that proper "whole system" (economic, or even clinical + economic) analysis on capital investments in healthcare is rarely or never done. That may not be too important, *perhaps*, for modest investments, but it is a big oversight when considering major investments. And hospitals are always major, in their respective health systems. That is the point: hospitals are (by definition) capital intensive—which applies both to

[3] Such a three-part characterisation of business models, taken from Christiansen, may well be insufficient in many senses, but serves for the moment as an initial thought experiment.

the fixed capital (the infrastructure and equipment) and to the human capital (many highly skilled clinical staff and technicians).

More specifically, the suggested approach requires therefore thinking about the following:

1. *Purpose.* What domain would business case procedures look at? Such a domain will not be "annual financial management", which is outside the scope of health policy proper because it is purely short term, (and existing tools anyway do a good job there for the purpose). Also, it will not be "comparative hospital studies" either, because existing models (DEA etc.) delineate well the narrow purpose of discovering relative under-performance. It can be envisaged that business case analysis, however, should be applied to service redesign, but incorporating more of an economic capability to the questions asked and using methods which are less micro and data heavy. It seems to us in general that *investment appraisal* is systematically an area where business case analysis should be applied and improved;
2. *Time frame/stickiness of the capital stock.* This is in large part a reinterpretation of the previous point. In the short term (one year or so), both physical and human capital stock are fixed, so the key questions are only operational. Clearly, in the medium term (say 5–10 years), some of the physical capital, and much of the human capital, can be altered. The shape of the healthcare system as a whole can be dramatically altered in the long term (up to 50–60 years), with an extensive amount of investment and, probably more to the point, disinvestment. This is therefore likely to be where the most interesting heath policy, and hospital policy, questions reside today (for completeness, there might be a very long-term time horizon which is equivalent to a blank slate, but this is too abstract to spend significant time on);
3. *Model computation.* Whatever the sector, there are three broad decision model types developed for long-term economic modelling, including of investment rationales—simulation, computerised general equilibrium models (CGEM) and optimisation:

    - *Simulation* has been discussed above, and rejected as data heavy and short term (and with ambiguous meaning with respect to decisions);

- *CGE models* use a "production function" (the processes linking inputs to outputs), "transaction values"[4] (the numerical values attributed to the process mechanism), "elasticities" for behavioural responses, and some exogenous inputs. CGEM assumes that the system being modelled moves to an equilibrium. These models use a prodigious number of assumptions and of data, which probably make CGEM unviable for a domain as poorly structured and measured as healthcare and hospitals.

The Authors' Proposition 2: *Develop Optimisation Models for Health*

The authors believe that analyses which are simply facility-based are inadequate. To our knowledge, whole-system *optimisation* models have not been extensively used in healthcare or hospital analysis. The general idea is to optimise an objective function (e.g. minimise costs), subject to a number of constraints, equalities and inequalities, in how the system works—for example, that service capacity must equal or exceed demand—and with the use of a mathematical technique to seek the optimum. These models are typically prescriptive, and employ the mindset of "a social planner with perfect foresight" (albeit that the prudent use of sensitivity analysis and so on implies that actually the planner isn't sure). Many process industries use such optimisation models—particularly in the energy sector (oil, power) but also chemicals, water resource planning and finance. These models are regarded as absolutely essential to sensible decision-making, partly for current or medium-term issues (analogous to the service redesign discussed in section "Service (Re)design and/or Addition of Specific Equipment") but certainly for long-term planning and particularly investment appraisal (section "Capacity and Economic Analysis"). The sort of models used here include linear and non-linear programming, with the latter evidently covering cases where the underlying problem is not linear, at the cost of more complexity and intrinsically far greater difficulty mathematically to find the solution.

The idea of linear programming is not so very different from the data envelopment analysis discussed above, in that it searches for an efficiency

[4] The earliest use of this idea was in the "input-output tables" developed from the 1940s (Leontief 1986).

frontier. And indeed, linear programming has been marginally used in health, among others, for example, to optimise performance in surgery (Mulholland et al. 2005), for nurse scheduling (Trilling et al. 2006), preventive services (Wang et al. 1999), ongoing resource allocation (Cromwell et al. 1998) and so on. However, it is presently limited to such scheduling-type problems. There have been tentative efforts at more ambitious approaches, but little coherent thinking here (Epstein et al. 2005). It seems plausible that rather more could, and should, be done; and linear programming could be one approach to explore in this area.

A Further Reflection: How Other Process Industries Do It

The discussion above has reviewed briefly the classes of decision analysis presently carried out for investments in health systems and hospitals, and has pointed out the key flaws in current practices. It has correspondingly *suggested the need to do better analysis, linking business models (incorporating the respective models of care) to evaluation of long-term business cases, accepting the need for reflection on the prevailing and desired governance environment; and has asserted that relevant analysis can only sensibly be done at system, not facility, level.*

The chapter authors contemplated displacing a proposal for future decision modelling protocols to an appendix/epilogue, yet decided, after debate, that it should be treated within this chapter. Note that the ownership and payment mechanism issues developed in the book also need to be reflected in the new "healthcare/hospital system economics" methodology sketched in this chapter.

As suggested in the previous section, an analogy could be used with the economic analysis carried out in other process industries, such as the energy sector. An area where optimisation models are greatly used is in electricity system planning (also, differently but with some of the same optimisation principles, in hydrocarbon refining). Adding a new power station of whatever type (technology, fuel, size etc.) will invariably have an impact on the way other stations in the power system operate, so the net effects of one new station ripple through to the operations of others throughout the plant's lifetime. There is *no* such thing as the economics in isolation of a single power station; just as there is no such thing as the economics, or functioning, in isolation of a single hospital. Experience shows that even if the system "needs" new capacity, it is not at all evident that the response should be to add a new plant of the size which intuitively appears to be lacking. The obvious reason why this is so is that other facilities can be worked harder, or for that matter less hard, with the addition of a new plant.

Furthermore, pursuing the power system analogy, adding some high-capital cost nuclear capacity would introduce the possibility of generating power at very low marginal cost, and thus a nuclear plant will always be called to produce at maximum when technically available.[5,6] In some circumstances, the total "net present cost" (discounted through its life; cf. the NPSV discussion in Box 9.1) of such a station might be low (high capital cost offset by low running cost). However, this may in the actual outturn not be a good idea economically, if for example there is too much "base-load" capacity already existing on the system (the new station will just kick some other slightly older but still low marginal cost capacity to a lower operating utilisation rate on the system).

In any event, there will have been a capital expenditure, and some reduced operation cost, but whether this constitutes a good balance is not certain. In fact, and this is the point, in strictly economic terms, it is not possible to say at all what the result will be of inserting a new station without modelling the *full* system. The broad process of such system modelling is to project the output and costs of the total power system forward *without* the new plant (i.e. as-is), and calculate the discounted lifetime net present cost of doing that (system NPC1). Then the parameters for the new station, with its respective capital costs and operating costs, are added to the model and it is projected forward again *with* the new plant, yielding

[5] Of course, it could be pointed out that a power system produces just one output: kilowatt hours (kWh). However, this is not quite true, since a kWh at 03.00 on a weekend in summer is worth a great deal less than one at 17.00 on a winter weekday. The relevant models at least take this sort of timing and quality issue into account. Hospitals have hundreds—perhaps thousands—of outputs, and this would need gross simplification to be calculable (a traditional hospital NPSV analysis already uses a comparable degree of simplification, but without the connection to the wider healthcare system).

[6] The discussion in this section "A Further Reflection: How Other Process Industries Do It" is not intended to be more than outline-illustrative on power system economics, and particularly not in an age of renewable energy such as wind and solar. These raise special problems, because they are high capital cost/zero marginal cost, but cannot be "called" as required; they work when the sun shines or the wind blows, which may not be when the system most needs the power.

a different lifetime (system NPC2). If NPC2 < NPC1, the investment is worth making.

This discussion does not intend a linear or direct comparison with the production of electricity. There are in fact already examples of similar thinking in the health system, which is rather familiar with the unexpected consequences of measures which in isolation sounded perfectly rational. When the need for a health system response to cost pressures became high a number of years back, hospitals were considered the crucial node, given that they are the biggest point sources of spending in the sector. The rationale for years had been for action on a number of variables (first and foremost, reduction in the number of hospital beds), which was not universally successful in cutting costs without repercussions on performance. As presented before, a study in Canada of 20 hospitals in a ten-year period showed that bed reductions in hospitals were accompanied by increases in the number of times the emergency services became congested, as measured by their inability to accept ambulance-led emergency admissions (Schull et al. 2001). In reaction, an arguable defence of "efficiency" became popular under the slogan of "sweating resources": new technologies and models of care were introduced based on high utilisation and occupation rates. The unexpected outcome was again, however, often more problems than the measures solved: frequent bottlenecks (between operating theatres and wards, and between emergency and regular/elective care). Additionally, from time to time increases in nosocomial infections were observed.

A related approach but with less dramatic consequences was that hospital admissions became a support instrument in the relationships between hospital specialists and patients; such an approach could be used whenever necessary and implemented quickly. The proposed solution was hospital admission avoidance by domiciliary (hospital) care, as a scheme under which a healthcare professional actively treats a patient who otherwise would need to go to a hospital. A study in the United Kingdom (Shepperd et al. 2009), discussed in Chap. 4 above, showed that for some particular patient groups, this type of domiciliary services—'Hospital at Home Programme', HaHP—produces results comparable to those that would be obtained with an inpatient stay, with similar or even reduced costs. Outpatient departments also shifted their preferred objective from being a follow up of previously admitted patients to a pivotal element around which a given specialty's activities get structured.

All the above taken into account, the conclusion is that a better analysis of the *mechanisms* through which hospitals have changed and are likely to change (process flow versus craft, isolated solutions versus chains or networks approaches etc.) is indispensable in order to propose adequate solutions. For example, the term *intermediate care* (Steiner 2001) now describes those services related with patients in their transition from hospital to home, as well as from medical and social dependence to functional independence, in an attempt to prevent the risk of new hospital admissions. These services play the bridging role between social and primary as well as specialised care.

The analogous idea to the industrial sector planning discussed above for a healthcare system would treat all settings as places which produce a portfolio of different types of care, at a given cost. To do this, it uses a variety of types of capital stock: beds (yes) but also operating rooms, imaging and diagnostics, outpatient facilities, and associated utilities such as energy, storage, car parking and office space and so on. And, most important, human capital in the form of medical and other staff. The facility can only be properly modelled if all of these, and their interactions with the wider system, are taken into account. Any hospital produces a lot of care, since it is by definition big, compared with other facilities. Adding a new hospital to the system would incur some capital cost (say ~€100–1000 million in today's circumstances) and *presumably* reduced operational cost relative to the existing settings of care because there is greater efficiency, or because the model of care absorbs fewer resources to achieve the same ends.[7] Having a new facility causes ripple effects on most of the other facilities in existence. The costs of running the health system as a whole can be projected for the lifetime of the new unit, on a without-and-with basis, and then comparisons can be made (NPC2 – NPC1!). If it is cheaper to run the healthcare ensemble *with* the new hospital, it should be built, but otherwise it should not.

The sort of optimisation model suggested here also provides an implicit answer to defining the capacity of a hospital per se—something presently almost impossible, as already explained (if the more-than-basic, daft metric of bed numbers is ignored). The capacity would be calculated from the ability of the facility to produce work, that is, to carry out activity, in the

[7] There is *of course* a quality angle which needs careful thought. That is, if the new hospital produces better outcomes than other settings, that ought to be taken into account. We acknowledge that, at present, just as a thought experiment, that is being ignored here.

context of the system within which it sits, including other service production units. The number of beds, or theatres, or outpatient rooms are merely the instruments which enable activity to be carried out.

This all may look rather like an almost outlandish idea, but the point is that at present *no* healthcare system looks "systematically", as it were, at *system* cost when deciding on investments. In a similar vein, it is rather sweeping for health policy thinkers to talk about it being cheaper to provide care in a community versus a secondary environment, but without paying attention at the same time to *the total activity carried out and the repercussions on one part of the system of doing things differently in another, or indeed all others.*

References

Adam, T., Evans, D. B., & Murray, C. J. L. (2003). Econometric Estimation of Country-Specific Hospital Costs. *Cost Effectiveness and Resource Allocation, 1*, 3. Retrieved December 19, 2018, from http://www.resource-allocation.com/content/1/1/3.

Brailsford, S. C., Lattimer, V. A., Tarnaras, P., & Turnbull, J. C. (2004). Emergency and On-Demand Health Care: Modelling a Large Complex System. *Journal of the Operational Research Society, 55*(1), 34–42.

Caballer-Tarazona, M., Moya-Clemente, I., Vivas-Consuelo, D., & Barrachina-Martínez, I. (2010). A Model to Measure the Efficiency of Hospital Performance. *Mathematical and Computer Modelling, 52*, 1095–1102. Retrieved from https://ac.els-cdn.com/S089571771000124X/1-s2.0-S089571771000124X-main.pdf?_tid=76f432ae-c61c-4add-ac37-da815453cfb7&acdnat=1552640153_44ac12bc173625e179c7eefb9a0566b5.

Clissold, A., Filar, J., Mackay, M., Qin, S., & Ward, D. (2015). Simulating Hospital Patient Flow for Insight and Improvement (Sidney: Health Informatics and Knowledge Management). In A. Maeder & J. Warren (Eds.), *Health Informatics and Knowledge Management 2015 (HIKM 2015)*. Conferences in Research and Practice in Information Technology (CRPIT), Vol. 164. Retrieved from https://50years.acs.org.au/content/dam/acs/50-years/journals/crpit/Vol164.pdf.

Cromwell, D. A., Viney, R., Hassall, J., & Hindle, D. (1998). Linking Measures of Health Gain to Explicit Priority Setting by an Area Health Service in Australia. *Social Science & Medicine, 47*(12), 2067–2074.

Cylus, J., Papanicolas, I., & Smith, P. (2017). *How to Make Sense of Health System Efficiency Comparisons?* Brussels: European Observatory on Health Systems and Policies, Policy Brief.

Ehrhardt, M., & Brigham, E. (2008). *Corporate Finance: A Focused Approach* (3rd ed.). p. 131. ISBN 978-0-324-65568-1.
Epstein, D., Chalabi, Z., Claxton, K., & Sculper, M. J. (2005). *Mathematical Programming for the Optimal Allocation of Health Care Resources*. York: Centre for Health Economics, University of York, Published Online. Retrieved January 10, 2019, from https://www.york.ac.uk/che/pdf/mathprog.pdf.
Erlandsen, E. (2008). *Improving the Efficiency of Health Care Spending: What Can Be Learnt from Partial and Selected Analyses of Hospital Performance?* (Paris: OECD Publishing). *OECD Journal: Economic Studies, 2008*(1), 1–33.
Fletcher, A., & Worthington, D. (2009). What Is a 'Generic' Hospital Model?—A Comparison of 'Generic' and 'Specific' Hospital Models of Emergency Patient Flows. *Health Care Management Science, 12*, 374–391. https://doi.org/10.1007/s10729-009-9108-9.
Gunal, M. M. (2012). A Guide for Building Hospital Simulation Models. *Health Systems, 1*, 17–25.
Health Services Research Network. (2014). *Change by Design: Systems Modelling and Simulation in Healthcare* (Published Online) June 2014, Version 1. Retrieved December 28, 2018, from https://mashnet.info/wp-content/files/2016/09/Change-By-Design-Booklet.pdf.
HM Treasury. (2018). *The Green Book: Central Government Guidance on Appraisal and Evaluation*. London: Her Majesty's Treasury. Retrieved from https://assets.publishing.service.gov.uk/government/uploads/system/uploads/attachment_data/file/685903/The_Green_Book.pdf.
Jacobs, R. (2000). *Alternative Methods to Examine Hospital Efficiency: Data Envelopment Analysis and Stochastic Frontier Analysis*. York: Centre for Health Economics, University of York, Discussion Paper 177, February 2000.
Joumard, I., André, C., & Nicq, C. H. (2010). *Health Care Systems: Efficiency and Institutions*. Paris: OECD, Economics Department Working Papers, No. 769, ECO/WKP(2010)25.
Karakusevic, S. (2016). *Understanding Patient Flow in Hospitals*. London: Nuffield Trust. Retrieved from https://www.nuffieldtrust.org.uk/files/2017-01/understanding-patient-flow-in-hospitals-web-final.pdf.
Kivisaari, S., Saranummi, N., & Väyrynen, E. (2004). *Knowledge-Intensive Service Activities in Health Care Innovation. Case Pirkana*. Tampere: VTT Technology Studies, VTT Research Notes 2267, 2004. Retrieved from https://www.vtt.fi/inf/pdf/tiedotteet/2004/T2267.pdf.
Leontief, W. (1986). *Input-Output Economics*. New York: Oxford University Press.
Mackay, M., Qin, S., Clissold, A., Hakendorf, P., Ben-Tovim, D., & McDonnell, G. (2013). *Patient Flow Simulation Modelling – An Approach Conducive to Multi-Disciplinary Collaboration Towards Hospital Capacity Management*. Adelaida: 20th International Congress on Modelling and Simulation, 1–6 December 2013. Retrieved from http://www.mssanz.org.au/modsim2013/A1/mackay.pdf.

Medeiros, J., & Schwierz, C. (2015). Efficiency Estimates of Health Care Systems. *European Economy Economic Papers* 549, June 2015.

Mohiuddin, S., Busby, J., Savovic, J., Richards, A., Northstone, K., Donovan, J. L., & Vasilakis, C. (2017). Patient Flow Within UK Emergency Departments: A Systematic Review of the Use of Computer Simulation Modelling Methods. *BMJ Open, 7*(5), e015007. https://doi.org/10.1136/bmjopen-2016-015007.

Montgomery, J. B., & Davis, K. (2013). *The Hospital Patient Flow Model: A Simulation Decision Support Tool.* New Orleans: Society for Health Systems, 2013 Healthcare Systems Process Improvement Conference Proceedings. Retrieved from https://www.promodel.com/pdf/7.%20Montgomery%20SHS%20Conf%20Paper%20(IEE).pdf.

Mulholland, M. W., Abrahamse, P., & Bahl, V. (2005). Linear Programming to Optimize Performance in a Department of Surgery. *Journal of the American College of Surgeons, 200*(6), 861–868.

Naylor, C., & Gregory, S. (2009). *Briefing: The Independent Sector Treatment Centres.* London: The King's Fund, October 2009. Retrieved from https://www.kingsfund.org.uk/sites/default/files/Briefing-Independent-sector-treatment-centres-ISTC-Chris-Naylor-Sarah-Gregory-Kings-Fund-October-2009.pdf.

Pitt, M., Monks, T., Crowe, S., & Vasilakis, C. (2016). Systems Modelling and Simulation in Health Service Design, Delivery and Decision Making. *BMJ Quality and Safety, 25*(1), 38–45. https://doi.org/10.1136/bmjqs-2015-004430.

Proudlove, N. C., Black, S., & Fletcher, A. (2007). OR and the Challenge to Improve the NHS: Modelling for Insight and Improvement in In-Patient Flows. *Journal of the Operational Research Society, 58*, 145–158.

Schull, M. J., Szalai, J. P., Schwartz, B., & Redelmeier, D. A. (2001). Emergency Department Overcrowding Following Systematic Hospital Restructuring: Trends at Twenty Hospitals over Ten Years. *Academic Emergency Medicine, 8*(11), 1037–1043.

Shepperd, S., Doll, H., Angus, R. M., Clarke, M. J., Iliffe, S., Kalra, L., Ricauda, N. A., Tibaldi, V., & Wilson, A. D. (2009). Avoiding Hospital Admission Through Provision of Hospital Care at Home: A Systematic Review and Meta-Analysis of Individual Patient Data. *Canadian Medical Association Journal, 180*(2), 175–182.

de Silva, D. (2013). *Improving Patient Flow Across Organisations and Pathways.* London: The Health Foundation, Evidence Scan No.19.

Steiner, A. (2001). Intermediate Care – A Good Thing? *Age and Ageing, 30*(S3), 33–39.

Trilling, L., Guinet, A., & Le Magny, D. (2006). Nurse Scheduling Using Integer Linear Programming and Constraint Programming. *IFAC Proceedings Volumes, 39*(3), 671–676. Retrieved January 10, 2019, from https://ac.els-cdn.com/S1474667015360602/1-s2.0-S1474667015360602-main.pdf?_

tid=f57341b5-3bf3-4dad-b602-016443298d50&acdnat=1547163583_34df586882268d16d88cffd5e2cdfc5d.

US Department of Health, Education and Welfare. (1974). *Report to the Health Sub-Committee, Committee on Labor and Public Welfare United States Senate by the Comptroller General of the United States.* Retrieved January 4, 2019, from https://www.gao.gov/assets/120/113233.pdf.

Vargas-Palacios, A. 2015. *Economic Evaluation of Complex Intervention Using Simulation Modelling Techniques.* Leeds Institute of Health Sciences, *Mimeo.*

Wang, L. Y., Haddix, A. C., Teutsch, S. M., & Caldwell, B. (1999). The Role of Resource Allocation Models in Selecting Clinical Preventive Services. *The American Journal of Managed Care, 5*(4), 445–454.

WHO – World Health Organization. (2000). *World Health Report 2000. Health System Improving Performance.* Geneva: World Health Organization.

CHAPTER 10

Conclusions

Antonio Durán, Stephen Wright, Paolo Belli, Tata Chanturidze, Patrick Jeurissen, and Richard B. Saltman

A. Durán (✉)
ALLDMHEALTH, Seville, Spain
e-mail: aduran@alldmh.com

S. Wright
Independent Consultant, Ingleton, UK
e-mail: steve.wright@echaa.eu

P. Belli
The World Bank, Nairobi, Kenya
e-mail: pbelli1@worldbank.org

T. Chanturidze
Oxford Policy Management, Oxford, UK
e-mail: Tata.Chanturidze@opml.co.uk

P. Jeurissen
Radboud University Medical School, Nijmegen, Netherlands

Ministry of Health, Welfare and Sports, Hague, Netherlands
e-mail: Patrick.Jeurissen@radboudumc.nl

R. B. Saltman
Department of Health Policy and Management, Rollins School of Public Health, Emory University, Atlanta, GA, USA
e-mail: rsaltma@emory.edu

A. Durán, S. Wright (eds.), *Understanding Hospitals in Changing Health Systems*, https://doi.org/10.1007/978-3-030-28172-4_10

Introduction

In this book, we have proposed a framework for understanding the institutions and facilities that are called "hospitals". Hospitals concentrate combinations of qualified staff and asset-specific technology investments in order to take care (especially at diagnosis and treatment level) of the more severe groups of patients. They are a core element of each country's response to health needs, with involvement of the public and private sectors, the medical and nursing professions, political decision-makers, academic analysts and so on. Finally, they deliver a sizeable share of the education and training of health sector staff, including those in public health, and participate in, carry out or support the majority of the research which underlies medical progress: in all cases, much more than any other setting.

Hospitals are dominant points of expenditure and of complex service delivery, but confront serious paradoxes and dilemmas. We hope that the discussions in this book will contribute to future debate about the direction of the hospital sector. The label "hospital" is used worldwide, but the entities which are being described vary so dramatically (from place to place, from system to system and from time to time) that common sense would say that a common term is almost untenable. However, on the basis that observers all know what an elephant is even if they cannot describe it well, the effort of discarding the label is probably not worth it. We therefore retain the name here, with our understanding of it linked to it being the most important collection of physical capital stock, technology and human capital stock in the health system.

This concluding chapter does not aspire to be comprehensive, but rather to offer some reflections on the implications of our reasoning. As authors from different professions, and as individuals coming from different countries and regions, we are very aware that the underlying circumstances of health systems vary. We believe, however, that the paradigm here can be used to shed some light—and enough for vision—on a variety of geographical and institutional settings. This includes Europe, the US, Japan, other developed, ex-Semashko and LMIC (some of these groupings overlap).

The framework we have proposed to explain what—accepting the above—makes a "good" hospital in its context builds on two main concepts. Firstly, hospitals can be understood by reference to the way that they are *governed*, within the wider society and particularly the health system concerned. Secondly, hospitals deploy resources to generate outputs (with the understanding that these outputs become outcomes if the governance arrangements are suitably robust). This deployment of resources to a given end is the domain of the relevant *business model*, which needs to be consistent with how the rest of the system operates, and it is applied in relation to health irrespective of whether the system concerned is private or dominated by the state and, to a certain extent, irrespective of how the organization is paid. Any business model must contain a physical process—the model of care—selected or evolved to be consistent with it. In the case of hospitals, this applies both within the walls and between the institution and the wider health system.

Somebody has to own the capital stock used in the hospital production system. The US is said to be a system of private healthcare, but in reality not far off half of the total provision of care is delivered by public entities of one kind or another (Veteran's Administration, city hospitals etc.), and evidently a lot of the funding (Medicare, Medicaid). Ownership in the US, and in other countries, of hospitals themselves and notably of the services provided to them is a patchwork of for-profit, not-for-profit, PPP and public.

Hospitals, as with other parts of health systems, are paid for the economic resources they use in a variety of ways. It is often implied that the price mechanism can be used to incentivize hospitals to do just what the stakeholders wish, and this book has explored (Chap. 6) the extent to which this is true—it turns out, only in part. Hospital payment mechanisms at least in public sectors have migrated from block payments or fee-for-service, through various types of pay-for-performance (P4P) to—very rarely—capitation. The DRG system was intended to be a P4P, and to incentivize provision at high efficiency and low cost. However, in reality, once institutions learn to game the system, DRGs turn out to be closer to FFS in not optimizing care using the latest processes and not sharing care across other parts of the health system. Put simply, too much weight has been placed on care prices of one kind or another, as though health could be regarded as a conventional market, clearing at certain prices. On balance, the payment mechanism should certainly be consistent with the aims and purposes of the hospital as a constituent part along with others, but cannot steer it alone.

A Recognition That the Issues Are Complicated…

In this book, we put forward what perhaps looks like a deceptively simple set of suggestions for rethinking what hospitals are and should be. It is worth stating, however, that we do not believe that answers are obvious.

We in fact show (Chap. 7) that there is a very messy reality out there, in all of developed country, developing country and ex-Soviet systems. Indeed, we document innumerable efforts at hospital reform which have been characterized by variety, but also by lack of success.

We therefore maintain that we are not proposing easy solutions. For context, Chap. 8 describes in more detail recent reform efforts, two perpetual favourites of which are repeated cycles of centralization and decentralization, and attempts to create pseudo-markets with price incentives for the latest desired institutional behaviour. We go so far as to say that stasis in the sector has been almost the norm. Further, there are powerful reasons for the stasis and why the inevitable reform efforts go astray—profound obstacles exist across a range of dimensions which make hospitals, and perhaps particularly public ones, resistant to change. There is a general level of dysfunction in all complex organizations, and hospitals in fact have more than their share of specific ones too. A major complication additionally is the mismatch between professional management of the overall resources, but control of the main work processes in the hands of the medical professions which operate to a different rhythm and drivers.

This book has reinterpreted the past, using a particular paradigm. Governance, historically, has been certainly confused, if not weak, in the health sector. After decades of Weberian models by which hospitals had to be run by modern bureaucracies, a variety of institutional forms for hospitals have been recently tried, along the spectrums of autonomy and regulation, without dominating examples of success. In our terminology, some of this lack of clarity arises because of the lack of robust linkage to the business model being employed or developed.

The business models of hospitals have very often, indeed almost universally, been unclear. Tertiary hospitals always rely heavily on their knowledge-based, high-skilled and high-tech nature to offer complex diagnoses and treatments—but the measurement of the efficiency of this is incomplete. There has been the development of "process factories"—such as perhaps most prominently the Hospital for Specialist Surgery group in the US, and Coxa in Finland; both focus on orthopaedics and joint replacement. Similar outfits offer eye care or in some cases cardiac treatment, in countries like India. But, in a sense, the overall picture has been very messy, with institutions trying to be "all things to all men"; it can be argued that most hospitals have not adequately differentiated their offer, or at least have not understood the degree to which they should do so.

The physical processes by which hospitals deliver care, in their context, has changed out of all recognition over the centuries. Initially "alms houses" or "poor old people's homes", they were places to go to die. With the development of anaesthesia, surgery became more frequent and invasive but, if anything, more hazardous—because surgeons could do more, with the result that infection then carried off more patients, typically around a half (Fitzharris 2018). Only gradually as antiseptic processes were generalized, building on the scientific understanding of Pasteur and Koch, did surgery become very much safer. Similarly, other key scientific advances included diagnostic and imaging systems. Over time, what had been essentially structured as associations of senior physicians consolidated intermediate-care and outpatient consultation units around emergency departments, operating rooms and specialized equipment (and soon with intensive [ICU] and critical care [UCC] units and beds).

Variations reflected different origins and structures, including the process of learning to manage hospitals professionally. Seeing their impact reflected in health outcomes took decades, ***unknown because the issue had not then been fully studied***. Since around the second quarter of the twentieth century, hospitals have become immensely more complex institutions, inserted in more complex societies. In a foreseeable future, the handling of big amounts of data, remote-monitoring technologies, high-speed internet, robotics and mobile phones and so on will force major realignments; "***managing hospitals well***" is no longer sufficient.

Public Hospitals' Changes and the Deepening of Governance Arrangements

The implications of ***burden of disease-related*** service needs, the unstoppable escalation of costs, the movement towards patient choice and co-production of health, the changing modalities of acute and scheduled clinical care, the demands for comprehensive care for chronic and elderly persons, and the insistence upon voice and choice by the patient, all call for a thorough reform of the way hospitals are run (***governed***). Better delineated, more efficient business models, clearer schemes including stronger technical and managerial capacities at facility level, increased accountability by all involved and more refined high-level leadership are needed.

Public hospitals in particular are expected to continue having a major role in the delivery of specialized care to people in countries all over the world. But in many countries many facilities produce virtually all and any types of services, as the distinctions between levels and types of hospitals have almost become meaningless. Evidence suggests that such a structure is not likely to be economically viable, unless the processes concerned are strictly separable and can therefore be managed appropriately inside the institution. Case mixes need to be re-assigned to each public hospital in a more systematic manner while responding to the expansion of primary care, and the governance of hospitals needs dramatic reinforcement. The reassignment should be done by responding to health needs in a more efficient manner through innovation, after proper trial and error, using mechanisms and tools for building up coherent business models with their advantages and disadvantages.

Prior to the 2008 Global Financial Crisis, there was some theoretical consensus about hospital autonomy in many forums, but the delegated authority for public hospitals to allow rationalization of specialized care was not homogeneously understood and practiced. The entitlements and accountability relationships varied too much, and so did the checks and balances, reporting mechanisms and so on. Directly related to the delegation of authority is the issue of performance incentives that public hospitals would be allowed to offer. Finally, there is an extreme paucity of evaluation in the amounts and types of economic and non-economic stimuli that public hospitals have been offering to their professionals and other stakeholders in recent years, and of the consequences of doing so.

Thus, public hospitals need to re-define their niche (economic relationships with the funders, functional profiles and linkages, sizes, staffing patterns etc.) in a wide process of implementing innovative and varying business models. In other words, lines of urgent action are the reconfiguration of outpatient and less-intensive modalities of care, and the setting up of adequate inter-hospital boundaries coupled with the choosing of legal *vehicles*. It is essential to select the services to be shared between hospitals. Reconfiguring any group of hospitals must take properly into account the context and the *precise* reasons for change. Before acting, the inefficiencies must be well understood and the best suited structural and governance models to solve them identified.

The theory of governance will certainly affect hospitals, especially public ones, yet how resources should be allocated and how conflicts should be solved in applying the "hospital governance" concept remain at rather an embryonic stage. The changing modalities of clinical care, the demands for comprehensive care for chronically ill and elderly patients, and the bigger demand by the patient all call for a thorough reform of the way hospitals are run, paid and governed. The voice of professional groups (the main one being clinical: doctors, nurses etc.) should be heard in a specific way for the reasons explained. Failing to properly serve *current* social needs questions the very relevance of hospitals. Under the new governance umbrella, hospital planning should respond to these and related changes with more refined tools (e.g. "clinical pathways" dealing with the entire patient needs).

Policy formulations of what governments "should do" (often behind the word *stewardship* as defined by the World Health Organization's (WHO) World Health Report 2000) go way beyond the capacities of current average ministries of health. Population coverage criteria, distances and other geographical and sociological aspects should be much better articulated. Transforming nominal coverage into efficient and satisfactory utilization within a resource-use framework requires replacing capacity planning with its traditional population ratios and numbers of beds by proper analysis of separate flows of patients, staff and assets.

Hospitals should be governed with as close a match as possible to their way of operating. This will require a greater involvement of professionals, and accountability protocols. The process of re-aligning professional and administrative staff to fit the required new capacities will be essential to their success. In the long run, (public) hospitals will remain socially relevant figures in the institutional realities of countries, but will have to adapt to the new constellation of actors and institutions. It is not clear, however, when, how and to what extent the current pressures will impact the behaviour of professionals (doctors and nurses) as they are manifested today. The relationships between hospitals, local governments and other owners, including ministries of health, will for sure be reshaped. Nursing and primary care, less dependent on super-specialized clinical knowledge, will adapt their position by managing innovative technologies as other foci of improvement.

Exploring Future Sustainable Hospital Business Models

Mergers, integrations and functional convergences might be related to the modifications of the hospital business model(s)—looking for economies of scale and scope, less duplication of resources, more effective training, greater market influence and more efficient service provision. The performance of inter-hospital groups seems to depend on the nature of the relevant cooperative agreement. Experience indicates that single-entity-owned/

managed groups or systems tend to be more successful (in terms of efficiency gaining and quality improving) than hospital networks formed through strategic alliance or by simple contractual agreement (Fulop et al. 2005).

Some hospitals will remain super-specialty, multipurpose operating centres mostly handling high cost, high variation, and low frequency care. Hospitals with this business model will remain *centres of reference* for the treatment of complex pathologies and *high capacity* for serious emergencies. These hospitals will continue specializing in complex processes and non-standardized approaches to solve diagnostic and therapeutic puzzles, focused on complex treatments—such as certain types of cancer, neurosurgery, neonatology and so on. They will continue providing top-notch examples of medical practice and will maintain their influence through that line of activity, irrespective of whether the hospital concerned is public or private. It could be envisaged that the case mix of sophisticated hospitals like this will continue to intensify.

There is a balance between trends which reduce Average Length of Stay (day-case surgery, laparoscopic and other less intrusive procedures) and to increase it (sicker patients with more technologically-intensive interventions). In the past, the average trend has been a reducing net ALoS, but it is conceivable that this could even reverse, for these hospitals, in the future. Additionally, the role of tertiary institutions in scientific research and development will also remain extremely strong, and they will continue to be the main focus of health workforce training (combined, R&D and training are and will continue to be more, and in some cases much more, than 10% of their turnover).

Many other hospitals will become concentrated on relatively low-cost treatments, "value-added processes" for high-frequency, low-variation conditions (e.g. with arthroscopies, cholecystectomies, herniorrhaphies, prostate cancer, cataract surgery and other scheduled ["elective"] surgeries as their core emphasis). A select range of products and services will optimize results through centres for repetitive standardized processes and production chains. Facilities with more operating rooms and emergency units, perhaps smaller than current giants, will be linked by information technologies, surrounded by large-scale outsourced services (e.g. early discharge, medi-hotel, home care, pathology and clinical labs, catering, laundry, archives etc.). Public hospitals may face greater obstacles to change—by, for example, segmenting customers and the like—than private ones, but they will most likely adapt by regulation. The extent to which care will be codified and systematized in this way will no doubt continue to enlarge.

Finally, other hospitals will be involved in networks and chains with service providers to facilitate patient follow up and care (as opposed to their diagnosis and treatment), maximizing contact with each other and the sharing of experiences. Providing "non-traditional" healthcare in networks around chronic (strictly speaking, "incurable") diseases would often conflict with other traditional activities of the hospital; such activity would often conflict also with the needs, aspirations and educational level of many patients who by now will be well aware of their illnesses (patients may learn not only from professionals, but from online or from each other's experiences). It is likely that this business model too will also significantly increase over time. In fact, the distinction between hospitals like this and local clinics will decrease, and the rise of the "hospital-at-home" will further augment the role of networked community hospitals (Christensen 2009).

One challenge is whether these three business models can, or should, be separated and carried out in different institutions or not. A tendency to cluster the models in differentiated hospital *complexes* certainly exists, but now often coincides with some grouping under the same governance umbrella around compact and homogeneous business models.

Can the value propositions for new business models in hospitals be articulated in our environment? That this is difficult even to think through makes it unsurprising that health service leaders and managers are not convinced when trying to implement change.

In this regard, the relationship to changing models of care is critical. The evolving model of care sketched above, and in Chap. 3, is not by any means the only driver of change in health systems and hospitals. However, it is an obvious point of entry to see change in the delivery of care, since all systems, irrespective of whether they are at the cutting edge of management, can see the direction in which medical science and technology are going and want to participate; most doctors are motivated to try out new equipment and procedures.

Healthcare of comparable quality to that of hospitals can now be provided in non-traditional physical settings, because many technologies are transportable. Less invasive surgical techniques and more efficient organizational schemes (e.g. laparoscopic procedures, insulin pump, devices for continuous measurement of blood glucose, and treatment of certain cancers with chemotherapy) are increasingly carried out in other settings, replacing hospital inpatient work.

Day centres, and even the patient's home, outside the hospital walls, now allow the withdrawal of *traditional* workloads from within the hospital. Linking the outpatient and day-care sector to patient needs means removing processes from the hospital building, and this may trigger decentralizing decisions within the hospital, substituting other forms of care for traditional care, re-engineering hospital processes with clinical protocols and multidisciplinary care teams and so on, with the precondition or addition of certain minor design and redesign of the physical environment.

At a macro level, chronicity and consumerism linked to demographic and epidemiological trends will also have an impact on resource allocation, probably withdrawing resources, reallocating them away from hospitals. Many conditions are now usually amenable to behavioural change strategies, and rarely should be treated in only one place (and indeed, not necessarily only in just one site). The focus on population-based social determinants of health as precursors to individual illness will require decisions about how to re-allocate constrained public resources between upstream preventive measures (requiring many years to reduce patient load levels) and resourcing increasingly hard-pressed acute care hospitals. More emphasis on non-linear complexities ("*experimentalist governance*"?) will probably be required.

The Importance of Ownership and Payment Methods

For ownership, we find that it matters, but only if governance is poor will it become a decisive factor. Public sector systems can be inefficient, and run for the convenience of their professional staff (management and clinicians). Private systems can in turn be abusive and rent-seeking. Importantly, they can also operate as silos (with the appropriate degree of information-sharing implied) which do not respect the need for integration of care at primary, community, rehabilitation, long-term, palliative and social care levels. But neither of these public versus private adverse contingencies is inevitable as such.

In some countries, the boundaries between the public and private sector hospitals are blurred—with the exception of university clinics—and the distinction between the political, managerial and administrative spheres is becoming diluted. With appropriate governance mechanisms, the business model involved—at either end of the public-private spectrum, or in the middle (PPP)—can usually be made to work. This may require reinterpreting the conventional models—for example, many PPP models like the UK's Private Finance Initiative (an estate-only structure) are clearly inappropriate, given that the main physical business asset is then managed separately from the main business line. But there are public-private relationships in healthcare which work much better than this.

The image of *payment mechanisms* as a way of creating markets where none currently exist is beguiling but much over-simplified. The key in the future will be to orient payment mechanisms not to a single attribute of hospital functioning (such as acute care) or even to a disease focus (e.g. disease management programmes) but specifically to support the relevant business model. When an institution has a single business model—such as what Chistensen calls "solution shops"—this can be difficult enough, but where a single institution is trying to be a solution shop for some of its activities but a value-adding processor for others, the difficulty will be compounded. Should capitation be the principal revenue stream for all hospital types? In that case, there would need to be the usual add-ons to remove incentives for under-treatment, and the quality top-ups mentioned in Chap. 6. The complexities of the current "bundled payments" anticipate such issues.

The Impact on Other Areas (e.g. Architecture, Academic Centres etc.)

Different non-hospital institutions will also be affected. There is in general a body of evidence about current approaches to resolve hospital problems which are related to the environment in which hospitals work:

- Aligning architecture with the new realities is a must. Multifunctional buildings and "acuity-adaptable" rooms—capable of accommodating at one end of the spectrum relatively intensive care and at the other rehabilitation, which by avoiding moving the patient from the room lessen medical errors—are increasingly available in Europe. The central question in a competition for architects in the Netherlands (Netherlands Board for Health Care Institutions 2005) was: "What functions should absolutely be in the central building of the hospital and what others may be located in different places?", hypothesizing that hospitals include four components (hot floor, hotel, offices and utilities) of different costs and usable life. Some hospitals now merge the operating theatres and surgical admission beds of various specialties (German private group Helios Kliniken, Coxa Hospital in Tampere, Finland [a PPP, but publicly owned] and the New Martini Hospital in Groningen and Erasmus MC in Rotterdam), whereas others do not separate the medical, surgical or diagnostic departments, but rather split the hot (emergency assistance) and cold (programmed) activity flows, transferring to others centres—with or without beds—consultations for short, diagnostic and therapeutic stays;

- A growing trend is to change the legal status of institutions in order to give them legal and operational capacity to defend their own interests in a changing environment. The degree of autonomy public hospitals should enjoy—to convert them into (semi) autonomous or corporatized entities—is a moving target, but many public centres already have a supervisory board capable of signing (short-term) personnel contracts under private law, encouraging staff financially according to performance (up to a ceiling), keeping for the following year any operating surplus and/or borrowing capital (up to a limit), massively outsourcing support services when organizing the operations of the units and so on. Some hospitals can open (or close) clinical services at their convenience. These changes in any case remain a highly political issue, as they are often (mistakenly) equated with privatization;
- New operating and technical capacities need to be developed. A common framework is needed to assess performance, plus the control systems, arbitration schemes and institutions to implement them, the design and operation of the management information systems to make them possible and so on. Operational excellence and skills related to information technologies may sometimes be even more important than those linked to routine medical procedures in the consultation room per se. In practice, the pressures favouring organizational models different from those already known will continue to increase, and better network integration schemes and processes with more added value will emerge. Yet most countries lack active buyers of care with sufficient capacity to make effective value-based refined contractual arrangements with service providers. Only when (and if) the healthcare purchasing function is reinforced will hospital change patterns show more identifiable trends;

- The selection of hospital managers continues to rely sensu stricto upon a variety of sources not necessarily related to proficiency in hospital care but often based on intuitive rules, and influenced by local circumstance and tradition (Dorgan et al. 2010). More importantly, the training of those professionals lacks an empirically applicable reference, which questions its very pertinence. A long-ranging realistic picture of the human resources needed and available for public hospital reconfiguration in the post-austerity era is essential. Reviewing how professional help to citizens—specifically, in public hospitals—should be re-organized will become essential.

Summary

It has been asserted that "[p]reserving the current hospital structure is not a sustainable strategy to offer value" (Dalton Review, NHS Confederation 2014) and, similarly, that "[i]f the same trends are maintained, the current 'hospital model' is 'non-sustainable'" (The Joint Commission 2008). A few decades after their transition to centre-stage in the healthcare scene, hospitals—as the dominant points of expenditure and service delivery in every health system—confront major functional, economic and political *pressures for change*.

Many such pressures faced by hospitals have specific technological, epidemiological and sociological foundations. Others are related to the organization and running of facilities, in the context of their health systems. While improvements in health are being pursued in a context of *globalization*, the (valid) emphasis on collective population-based social determinants of health and their link to individual illness experience coincide with challenges faced by contemporary society.

Our main contribution, despite all the above, is an optimistic statement that "the hospital" isn't, and shouldn't, go away, for very good reasons—but we need to have a clearer view of what should be within the walls, and how to govern that in a responsible way. Embedded in a comparative international technological, epidemiological and political economy perspective, signals abound that hospitals as institutions will continue occupying a central role in health systems, for solid reasons:

1. Inpatient admissions are increasingly focused on less intensive treatments and frail elderly (if only because of the volumes of aged patients—with the rest of patients' case mix, the intensity of treat-

ment is rising significantly). There are no clear alternatives at the moment to hospital stays. At least in theory, hospitals can be more responsive to changing healthcare needs than most other provision types;

2. Furthermore, with regards to care coordination, hospitals can bring in more strengths and all kinds of specialist expertise in treating multi-morbidity efficiently (community hospitals will have to transform their care model in this direction);
3. By their sheer existence, hospitals protect access for vulnerable populations (e.g. indigents, immigrants etc.). Hospitals are open 24/7 and generally cannot and do not turn patients away in the way that many physician practices can do;
4. High technology care is on the rise; ICU beds, for example, are growing almost everywhere. The hospital will be paramount since it is probably the most natural coordinator for networks of care for specific patients;
5. Training of professionals, scaling up good practices and sharing patients are all important for sustainable health systems and not doable without hospitals;
6. Supply-induced demand might actually be a bigger problem for those services carved out of the hospital (including value-added processes, ITC-related etc.) than for core hospital care.

The discussion in this book has dwelt on the scarce level of agreement about the definitions and the measurement of hospital performance. Emphasis has been put on frequent methodological and practical problems of *misaligned* relationships between governance, business models and models of care.

Crucially, a balanced way is needed to explain what society really thinks and expects of its hospitals, and the external context of legal structures and values provided in the governance sphere. Hospitals confront a number of paradoxes. On the one hand, there is a central contradiction between hospitals facing policy abandonment, for want of a better word, while at the same time a multiplicity of *strong innovations* can be detected all over the field.

Also, in official statements in most countries and in international health policy dialogues, *hospitals do not always seem to receive adequate policy attention*, yet paradoxically they continue receiving what could be interpreted as the lion's share of healthcare funding. As this volume has explained, the argument that hospitals take an undue proportion of overall health sector resources shows only arguable empirical validity in several senses and contexts. In most developed countries, hospitals now account for around a historically low one third or so of total health system expenditure and, in fact, when a detailed analysis is performed, a continuing inadequacy of public revenues to support and re-configure the existing hospital sector is often revealed. But even if hospitals are "expensive" to run, whether this is too expensive is much more a moot point. And anyway, removing resources from hospitals in favour of public/population health and primary care ought to be an empirical rather than an emotional judgement—to be decided along the lines of the intellectual arguments of Chap. 9.

This book has explained that there are pressures to address inefficiencies, overlaps and duplications in the balance of care between hospitals, primary care and other settings, as well as in the distribution of the respective roles assigned to the public and the private sectors. It has also addressed—albeit tangentially—new payment methods and ownership modalities, issues which will continue to evolve even if such tools seem rather unable to "solve" the big issues in this book only by themselves.

The Danish physicist Neils Bohr (among others[1]) is reported to have humorously said in these regards that "Predicting is very difficult—especially about the future" (The Economist 2007). Less ironically but more practically, "predicting is not a respectable human activity beyond a minimum time-term (we need to plan precisely because we cannot predict)" (Drucker 1993). More to the point, it is increasingly clear that prediction in uncertain fields like hospital development will most probably over-represent the best scenarios, *for those doing the prediction* (Kahneman 2011).

With these caveats regarding content, a joint effort is needed to reach an *evidence-based diagnosis* to trigger the necessary *political will* and mobilize an adequate *drive for change.*

Leadership for an objective technical review of the situation is clearly critical. Three central questions are worth exploring in terms of process:

1. The viable *metrics* of the effort to reform hospitals and the health systems that host them, in line with global health needs, technologi-

[1] The baseball legend Yogi Berra, for example, as quoted by Edward Luce in "The Retreat of Western Liberalism", Little, Brown, 2017, p. 57.

cal opportunities and affordability considerations (World Economic Forum 2011);

2. Assuming the perspective of short-term and long-term developments, the *trial-and-error* process to be run, able to provide lessons while avoiding disproportionate risks, as per—for example—the lessons from the handling of *adverse events* in the US (Weinberg et al. 2005);
3. The identification of leaders with *the legitimacy and prestige* to direct a global hospital re-thinking process, when in recent decades new stakeholders have emerged in the field of health, some of them public and others private (Ottersen et al. 2014).

Hospitals are not necessarily comparable institutions, and between them they do focus on different competencies and specializations. Furthermore, hospital institutions reflect different historical and political backgrounds, even though groups of countries may face relatively similar challenges. Observations in this text therefore have methodological limitations in terms of extrapolation; what has been analysed here must be passed through the sieve of institutional approaches, social norms and political decision-making in each national and sub-national environment.

One of the innovations of this book has been the emphasis on the need to test hospitals against the wide perspective of the system in which they sit—and particularly any commitment to invest capital in them. Chapter 9 fleshes out this proposition of "with-and-without" system-wide economic modelling. Although the assumptions to carry out such modelling would no doubt be heroic, it is categorically even more heroic to operate our healthcare systems, and especially the cost-intensive entities called hospitals, without such quantitative testing. It is not done today, and it should be.

Of course, any debate on hospitals is likely to become explicitly and quickly political. Probably too little attention is given also to the fact that cost containment is not an objective shared by all parties involved, nor by all professional groups—in other words, many hospitals themselves will certainly oppose many (if not all) forms of strict cost control, whoever raises them (see Chap. 8). The prospect of an explicit over-politicization of the hospital debate should not be ruled out. It seems inevitable that in the medium and long run, society will have to introduce changes in the production of quality medical care inside and outside hospitals. In this perspective, the key goal for politicians, policymakers and managers is to facilitate these changes without causing major distortions in institutions or destroying the necessary hospital capacity with its so far achieved ability to produce quality assistance.

Summing up, in our opinion hospitals will continue to dominate health-care resource use and high-end provision, mainly by becoming either, on the one hand, more complex or, on the other, more process-driven. In all cases, hospitals will be more networked into hospital hierarchies and community health structures (including hospital-at-home), such that some facilities still called "hospitals" will be indistinguishable from community clinics. There should always be a quantitative examination of the role, and any expansion, of hospitals within their health system contexts. But in any event, more and better research is needed in order to decide what should be within the institutional and facility walls, and how to govern that, as well as what would be best done outside those walls.

References

Christensen, C. (2009). *The Innovator's Prescription a Disruptive Solution for Healthcare*. New York: McGraw Hill.

Dorgan, S., Layton, D., Bloom, N., Homkes, R., Sadun, R., & Van Reenen, J. (2010). *Management in Healthcare: Why Good Practice Really Matters*. London: The London School of Economics and Political Sciences, LSE and McKinsey & Comp. Retrieved from http://cep.lse.ac.uk/textonly/_new/research/productivity/management/PDF/Management_in_Healthcare_Report.pdf.

Drucker, P. (1993). *Management: Task, Responsibilities, Practices* (pp. 123–126). New York: Harper Business.

Fitzharris, L. (2018). *The Butchering Art: Joseph Lister's Quest to Transform the Grisly World of Victorian Medicine*. London: Penguin.

Fulop, N., Protopsaltis, G., King, A., Allen, P., Hutchings, A., & Normand, C. (2005). Changing Organisations: A Study of the Context and Processes of Mergers of Health Care Providers in England. *Social Science & Medicine, 60*, 119–130.

Joint Commission. (2008). *Health Care at the Crossroads: Guiding Principles for the Development of the Hospital of the Future*. Retrieved from http://www.jointcommission.org/assets/1/18/hosptal_future.pdf.

Kahneman, D. (2011). *Thinking, Fast and Slow* (p. 250). London: Allen Lane.

Netherlands Board for Health Care Institutions. (2005). *Future Hospitals: Competitive and Healing. Competition Report*. Utrecht: Netherlands Board for Health Care Institutions, quoted in Rechel, B., Wright, S., Edwards, N., Dowdeswell, B., & Mckee, M. (2009b). *Investing in Hospitals of the future*

(European Observatory on Health Systems and Policies). Observatory Studies Series No. 16. Retrieved April 13, 2010, from http://www.bouwcollege.nl/smartsite.shtml?id=2065.

NHS Confederation. (2014). *Examining New Options and Opportunities for Providers of NHS Care*. Retrieved from https://www.nhsconfed.org/resources/2014/12/the-dalton-review-slide-pack-for-members.

Ottersen, O. P., Dasgupta, J., Blouin, C., Buss, P., Chongsuvivatwong, V., Frenk, J., et al. (2014). The Political Origins of Health Inequity: Prospects for Change. *Lancet, 383*, 630–667. Retrieved March 8, 2019, from https://www.thelancet.com/action/showPdf?pii=S0140-6736%2813%2962407-1.

The Economist. (2007, July 15). *The Perils of Prediction*. Retrieved from https://www.economist.com/letters-to-the-editor-the-inbox/2007/07/15/the-perils-of-prediction-june-2nd.

Weinberg, J., Hilborne, L. H., & Nguyen, Q. T. (2005). Regulation of Health Policy: Patient Safety and the States. In K. Henriksen, J. B. Battles, E. S. Marks, et al. (Eds.), *Advances in Patient Safety: From Research to Implementation (Volume 1: Research Findings)*. Rockville, MD: Agency for Healthcare Research and Quality. Retrieved from https://www.ncbi.nlm.nih.gov/books/NBK20479/.

World Economic Forum. (2011). *Global Health Data Charter*. Retrieved from http://www3.weforum.org/docs/WEF_HE_GlobalHealthData_Charter_2011.pdf.

Index[1]

A
Ability to do work, 6, 63, 203, 216
Accountability, 13, 30, 31, 34–36, 43, 77, 117, 124, 136, 173, 225–227
Alms houses, v, 60, 124, 167, 225
Anxiety, 180, 186, 187
Attributes, 6, 9, 10, 41, 62, 181–183, 231

B
Bailout, 117
Bed numbers, 203, 203n2, 206, 208, 216
Biochemistry, v, 58
Business cases, 205–207, 210, 211, 213
Business models, vi, 17, 25, 52, 55, 68, 75–97, 103, 110, 112, 117, 121, 122, 134, 135, 151, 167, 170, 178, 188, 194, 202, 207, 210, 210n3, 213, 223–231, 234

C
Capacity, 6, 20, 21, 31, 33–37, 41, 42, 62–64, 77, 78, 91, 96, 133, 134, 140, 145, 147, 148, 151, 152, 170, 202–209, 212, 214, 216, 227, 232, 237
Capitation, 21, 127, 132, 132n4, 135, 179, 223, 231
Christensen, Clayton, 9, 26, 60, 79, 80, 82, 88, 92–96, 122, 135, 229
Comparable system analysis, 196–200
Complexity, 9, 34, 64, 78, 79, 130, 147, 160, 180, 186, 187, 202, 212, 230, 231
Contractability, 116, 117

D
Data envelopment analysis (DEA), 53, 198, 199, 211, 212
Decision analysis, 53, 213
Demography, 33, 54

[1] Note: Page numbers followed by 'n' refer to notes.

A. Durán, S. Wright (eds.), *Understanding Hospitals in Changing Health Systems*, https://doi.org/10.1007/978-3-030-28172-4

Determinants of health, 15, 49, 67, 168, 230, 233
Developing countries, 4, 7, 49, 61, 125, 141–144, 169, 180, 199, 209, 224
Diagnostic-Related Groups (DRG), 18, 84n4, 130, 130n2, 135, 141, 157, 158, 178, 223
Disruptive innovation, 9, 84, 95

E
Efficiency, 51n4, 53, 68, 77, 78, 83, 86, 87, 94, 96–97, 104, 105, 107, 109–112, 115, 117, 124, 131, 134, 136, 137, 147, 148, 152, 153, 155, 159, 168, 170, 173, 175, 185, 196–200, 199n1, 202, 212, 215, 216, 223, 224, 228
Emergency care, 5, 144
Empirical medicine, 60
Epidemiology, 11, 33, 54
Evidence-based medicine, 148, 149
Ex-Communist, 3
Expectations, 3, 5, 11, 12, 42, 45, 51, 54, 55, 84, 86, 107, 112, 188, 208

F
Facilitated networks, 82, 91, 92, 122, 134, 135, 210
Factors of production, 10, 11, 14–17, 52–56, 59, 63, 68, 80
Fee-for-service (FFS), 124, 128, 130, 132, 135, 137, 223
Financial analysis, 196
Flows, 19, 20, 79, 88–92, 96, 97, 123, 156, 157, 200, 201, 206, 216, 227, 232
Frugal innovation, 144
Functions
  of health system, 2
  of hospitals, v, vi, 2, 19, 59, 136, 231

G
Global budgets, 129, 130, 136, 155
Governance, vi, 4, 10–19, 25–45, 55, 68, 92, 96, 103, 105, 107, 111–116, 122, 124, 128, 134–136, 139, 141, 145, 150–153, 155, 168, 170, 171, 173–176, 178, 180, 184–185, 187, 188, 193, 194, 199, 202, 206, 207, 210, 213, 223–227, 229, 230, 234
Government, 2, 7, 13, 17, 27, 30–33, 44, 45, 60, 61, 78, 103, 104, 107, 112, 115, 117, 128–130, 134, 140, 141, 148, 152–155, 158, 159, 172–175, 185, 204, 227

H
Health status, 3, 10, 11, 15, 16, 49–51, 50n3, 53, 54, 63, 83, 96, 197, 198
Human capital, 10, 14, 15, 52, 53, 59, 63, 66, 80, 82, 134, 194, 211, 216, 222

I
Imaging, v, 15, 15n3, 58, 59, 62, 84, 201, 216, 225
Incentives, 13, 18, 34–36, 43, 55, 64, 68n7, 77, 105, 110, 111, 122–125, 128–132, 136, 137, 148, 151, 152, 156, 168, 171, 185, 224, 226, 231
Intuitive medicine, 60

L

Line-item budgets, 125, 129, 130, 136

M

Macro, 26, 32, 154, 184, 230
Management, 2, 13, 15, 25, 28, 30–33, 35n3, 36, 37, 40–45, 53, 55, 58, 67, 79, 83, 91, 105, 107–109, 135, 137, 141, 150, 153–156, 160, 168, 172, 174, 182–185, 196, 205, 207, 224, 229–232
Managerial capacity, 35, 36, 41, 225
Market, 10n1, 16, 18, 27, 54, 55, 61, 67, 78, 80, 93, 94, 96, 104–106, 109, 113–118, 123, 128, 142, 171–173, 186, 196, 197, 204, 223, 227, 231
Market failure, 180, 186, 187
Meso, 26, 32, 42, 154, 184
Metrics, 93, 143, 198, 202, 216, 235
Micro, 25, 32, 84, 154, 168, 184, 200, 211
Modelling, 6, 19, 63, 92, 195, 197, 200–203, 205, 208, 210, 211, 213, 214, 236
Models of care, 13–16, 19, 25, 45, 49–68, 78, 79, 86, 116, 136, 137, 139, 167, 170, 178, 187, 188, 194, 200, 202, 213, 215, 229, 234

N

New public management (NPM), 30, 104, 107, 153, 154

O

Operating theatres, 59, 86, 91, 203, 205, 215, 232
Operational research (OR), 77, 200
Optimisation, 211–213, 216
Organisational dysfunction, 186, 187
Outcomes, 3, 5, 8, 9, 18, 19, 30, 36, 36n4, 37, 42, 50, 51, 54, 54n6, 59, 66, 68, 106, 110, 113, 123, 130, 135, 140, 151–154, 156, 157, 168, 171, 173, 178–181, 185, 186, 196, 197, 207, 210, 215, 216n7, 223, 225
Outputs, v, 10–12, 14, 16–18, 33, 35, 51–55, 53n5, 63, 68, 110, 123, 129, 135, 151, 168, 184, 196–198, 212, 214, 214n5, 222, 223
Ownership, vi, 3, 16, 17, 26, 30, 45, 60, 68n7, 79, 103, 105–111, 113, 114, 116–118, 133, 134, 136, 140, 144, 168, 169, 172, 174, 181, 194, 213, 223, 230–231, 235

P

Pay-for-performance (P4P), 127, 130, 223
Payment mechanisms, 16, 18, 55, 93, 124, 130, 133, 136, 174, 213, 223, 231
Per diem, 157
Physical capital, 10, 15, 19, 53, 80, 97, 134, 194, 203, 211, 222
Political dysfunction, 180, 184–185
Precision medicine, 60
Private, vi, 7, 27, 50, 77, 104, 126–127, 140, 167, 170, 196, 222
Process industries, 212–217
Producer surplus, 80n3
Product, 9, 11, 41, 58, 80, 82, 89, 96, 107, 228
Production frontier, 16, 53, 53n5, 60
Professional dysfunction, 180, 183–184
Profit formula, 79, 80, 86, 93
Prospective, payment system (PS), 124, 131–137

Pseudo-markets, 129
Public, vi, 27, 50, 77, 104, 125, 140, 167, 193, 222
Public health, v, 2, 4, 20, 44, 50, 107, 146, 154, 194, 209, 222
Public-private partnership (PPP), 7, 18, 33, 104, 107, 107n1, 108, 111, 133, 134, 144, 179, 199, 199n1, 207, 208, 223, 231, 232
Purchaser-provider split, 112

Q

Quality, 2, 9, 14, 16, 31, 32, 34, 37, 51, 53, 54n6, 55, 59, 77, 78, 86–89, 94, 95, 106, 107, 109, 110, 117, 123, 129–134, 131n3, 136, 137, 144–146, 150, 153, 156, 158, 169–173, 175, 185, 197–199, 202, 214n5, 216n7, 228, 229, 236, 237

R

Regulations, 4, 30, 32, 35, 42, 51, 85, 104, 107, 111, 113, 114, 116, 129, 173, 175, 224, 228
Resources, vi, 4, 7, 9–12, 14–17, 19–21, 31, 35, 42, 43, 45, 50–52, 51n4, 55–59, 63, 65, 67, 68, 75–80, 82, 83, 86, 87, 90, 94, 104, 106, 109, 110, 117, 123–125, 123n1, 129, 142, 143, 145, 148, 150–152, 157, 169, 174–176, 178, 194, 196, 202, 209, 212, 213, 216, 222–224, 226, 227, 230, 233, 235, 237
Responsiveness, 12, 14, 32, 34, 63, 142
Retrospective, payment systems (PS), 80, 124, 125, 133–135, 137
Risk selection, 131

S

Semashko, 145, 148, 175, 178
Separability, 94
Service production, 4, 51, 77, 168, 217
Simulation, 19, 92, 200–202, 211
Social health insurance (SHI), 7, 159, 169, 176, 184
Solution shops, 82, 83, 88, 89, 92, 94, 122, 134, 135, 210, 231
Stocks, 10, 14, 15, 19, 42, 52, 76, 134, 200–202, 205, 211, 216, 222, 223

T

Technical capacity, 34, 36, 41, 64, 232
Technology, 9–13, 16, 26, 27, 33, 34, 50, 52, 54, 59, 60, 62–64, 66, 77, 84–87, 90, 91, 93–96, 104, 115, 124, 142, 146, 150, 159, 167, 168, 171, 194, 213, 215, 222, 225, 227–229, 232, 234
Time dependence, 151

U

Universal access, 117, 145

V

Value-added processes, 82–84, 89, 92–95, 117, 210, 228, 234
Value proposition, 79, 80, 83, 86, 93, 94, 96, 122, 134, 135, 229
Variation, 9, 16, 34, 55, 64, 67, 76, 77, 110, 168, 169, 207, 225, 228

W

Whole-system modelling, 208

The manufacturer's authorised representative in the EU is Springer Nature Customer Service Centre GmbH, Europaplatz 3, 69115 Heidelberg, Germany. If you have any concerns regarding our products, please contact ProductSafety@springernature.com

Printed and bound by CPI Group (UK) Ltd, Croydon, CR0 4YY
30/09/2026
02225656-0009